Understanding Science 2

Teachers' Resource Book

Understanding Science 2

Teachers' Resource Book

Joe Boyd

Head of Chemistry, Beeslack High School, Penicuik

and

Walter Whitelaw

Assistant Science Adviser, Lothian

JOHN MURRAY

Advisory panel
Peter Leckstein: *Inspector for Living Science, London Borough of Wandsworth*
Lesley Campbell: *Health Education Adviser*
Terry Allsop: *Lecturer in Education Studies, Oxford University*

First published 1990
by John Murray (Publishers) Ltd
50 Albemarle Street, London W1X 4BD

Reprinted 1990

Designed by Impress International, 33540 France
Typeset by Blackpool Typesetting Services Ltd, Blackpool
Printed by Edmundsbury Press, Bury St Edmunds

British Library Cataloguing in Publication Data
Boyd, Joe
Understanding science book 2.
Teachers' bk
1. Science
I. Title II. Whitelaw, Walter
500

ISBN 0-7195-4624-9 Teachers' resource book
ISBN 0-7195-4623-0 Pupils' book

Contents

Acknowledgements

LINE DRAWINGS: RDL Artset; CARTOONS: Ainslie MacLeod;
NATURAL HISTORY ARTWORK: Nancy Sutcliffe;
COVER PHOTO: Kay Chernush/The Image Bank

Thanks are due to copyright holders who have allowed the following extracts from, or reproductions of, their material to be used

p.131–2 Professor Sir Francis Graham-Smith FRS, from *The Guardian* 26 August 1989;
p.132 James Erlichman, from *The Guardian* 26 August 1989;
p.145 Oxford University Press, from *The Oxford Senior Dictionary* (Oxford University Press 1982);
p.147 *top* Transworld Publishers Ltd, from back-cover blurb of *Hospital Station* by James White (Corgi Books 1972);
p.147 *bottom* Century Hutchinson Publishing Group Limited, from *2001: A Space Odyssey* by Arthur C. Clarke (Hutchinson 1973);
p.154 Postage stamps reproduced by permission of Royal Mail Letters – a part of the Post Office;
p.155 *top* Hodder & Stoughton Publishers, from *Supernature* by Lyall Watson (Hodder & Stoughton 1973);
p.155 *bottom* Guardian News Service Ltd, from *The Guardian* 9 August 1989;
p.156 *top* William Collins Sons & Co. Ltd, from *Food For Free* by Richard Mabey (Collins 1972);
p.156 *bottom* Prue Leith, from *The Guardian* 9 August 1989;
p.157 Abner Stein (Authors' Agents), from (*How We Found Out About*) *Outer Space* by Isaac Asimov (Longman 1982);
p.160 Extracts taken from *The Hobbit* by J. R. R. Tolkien (Allen & Unwin 1966) reproduced by kind permission of Unwin Hyman Limited. © George Allen & Unwin 1966;
p.167 William Collins Sons & Co. Ltd, from *The Living Planet* by David Attenborough (BBC/Collins 1984);
p.168 Ed Victor Ltd Literary Agency, from *The Hitch Hiker's Guide To The Galaxy* (Pan Books 1979), © Douglas Adams 1979;
p.175 *New Scientist* 24/31 December 1987; this passage was taken with permission from New Scientist magazine London, the weekly review of science and technology;
p.179 William Collins Sons & Co. Ltd, from *Food For Free* by Richard Mabey (Collins 1972);
p.182 Wayland (Publishers) Ltd, from *Famous Names in Medicine* by G. De Stevens (Wayland 1979);
p.184–5 BBC Enterprises Limited and Curtis Brown Ltd (Literary Agents), from *Discovering Hedgerows* by David Streeter and Rosamund Richardson (BBC 1982);
p.189 Random Century Group Limited, from *The Joy of Computers* by Peter Laurie (Hutchinson 1983);
p.191 Wayland (Publishers) Ltd, from *Famous Names in Science* by P. Clark (Wayland 1979);
p.192 Paul Morrison for the saltmarsh passage from *Bird Habitats of Great Britain and Ireland* by Paul Morrison (Michael Joseph 1989), quoted from *The Guardian* 18 August 1989;
p.197 from the former Ladybird title *How it works – The Camera* by David Carey (Ladybird 1970) with the permission of the publishers Ladybird Books Ltd, Loughborough, England.

Every effort has been made to contact copyright holders and obtain permissions: the Publishers will be grateful for notification of any omissions for correction in subsequent printings.

Introduction

Using this course

Understanding Science has been written to support modern science education. Learning in science is an active process and the pupil is therefore encouraged to be involved in different types of activity, within a carefully structured and organised course. The approach is flexible and can be adapted to suit most teachers' methods while providing the hard scientific input which will be needed later in assessed and certificated work.

This course can be taught in any type of classroom, although it will work best in a science laboratory equipped with gas, water and electricity services. The wall space of the classroom should be used to display pupils' work, particularly the results of the Unit Problems and Talkabouts.

If possible, keep all the practical equipment for the current unit in the room. This alleviates much of the need for technician and other auxiliary back-up. It is helpful to have much of the unit apparatus in a labelled tray, with one tray for each topic in the unit.

Practical activities occur throughout the course. Pupils usually work best with a partner or in a group of three. A basic set of laboratory equipment for each pupil group is:

safety glasses for *each* pupil
bunsen burner
heatproof mat
tripod stand and gauze
test-tube rack
boiling tubes
test tubes
6 beakers of various sizes (plastic and glass)
$100\ cm^3$ measuring cylinder
test-tube holder
gas lighter
coloured pencils
rulers

Written work has a key role in the course. Pupils write their own notes, mainly to express their ideas and to show the quality of their understanding. In addition, each pupil learns to present ideas, observations and descriptions in a form that other people can understand and react to positively. Each pupil will need a notebook or file and access, if possible, to a junior dictionary.

Organisation of the Pupils' Book

Within Book 2 there are six units, each broken down into topics. Each topic has three levels: core, reinforcement and extension.

- **Core work** (labelled **A**) provides work essential to all pupils.
- **Reinforcement** material (labelled **B**) consolidates the core work and is appropriate for pupils who find the core fairly demanding or difficult.
- **Extensions** are considerably more demanding and best suited to those pupils who find the core work straightforward. They may also be beneficial to highly motivated children. The extensions are grouped together at the end of the pupils' book.

Within a topic, pupils are guided to various activities.

Reading: Information is given at the beginning of a topic. Pupils should read this, and all instructions, before starting an activity. There may be instances when the teacher wishes the pupils to copy this information.

Doing (surrounded by red boxes)**:** In these activity sections, pupils do the activity as well as they can, sometimes after guidance or a demonstration. The equipment required is listed in the yellow panels. It should be returned when the activity is finished.

Answering : The questions and written activities should be answered in a notebook or file. Pupils' writing skills will develop gradually. Points for the teacher to insist on are that:

- the notes make sense to the pupil
- the written work expresses the pupil's idea
- the heading is copied and the work dated
- all the questions are answered
- answers are (where appropriate) in sentences
- all written work is read through slowly by the pupil before bringing it forward for marking at a Checkpoint.

Checkpoints : These are informal assessment points. The intention is that work is marked as soon as possible by the teacher and discussed where necessary. Initially, the quality of the written work will probably be a major teaching point, but in later units teachers are likely to be more concerned with the quality of the scientific thinking.

Each checkpoint requires a routing decision from the teacher. What does the pupil do next? There are several possibilities because the material lends itself to a flexible response. Obviously the routing decisions will become more obvious as the teacher gets to know the pupils better.

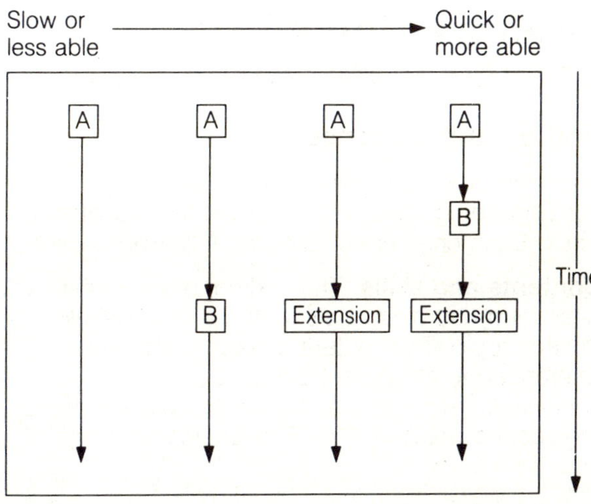

Discussion: There are many opportunities for pupils to discuss work with their partner(s), particularly when investigating problems or developing concepts.

Problem pages

The open-ended problems in each unit can be tackled in a number of ways and could be used as assessment exercises. The earlier problems need to be fully presented to the class before the pupils discuss them. Pupils are then encouraged by the text to consider possible solutions in groups. It is the group, not the teacher, who should then solve the problem.

Talkabouts

Talkabouts encourage pupils to express and develop their ideas about open-ended subjects. Discussion work is very difficult to initiate and organise. However, some points to consider for **group** discussions are:

- stress the focus of the discussion before the pupils begin and exemplify it with photographs or video material, if available
- self-selected groups of four work well
- give pupils a time limit
- arrange the seating so that each group is in a ring
- require that some modest report-back or summary activity be completed after the discussion.

For **whole class** discussion:

- take an active role in keeping order, but not an active role in discussing
- arrange the class as nearly as possible in a circle
- encourage debate between pupils
- encourage listening

Readabouts

A Readabout is included as a longer passage of unbroken text. These passages introduce pupils to the applications and social implications of science and encourage the development of reading and library skills.

Organisation of the Teachers' Resource Book

Unit by unit guidance

For each unit in the Pupils' book there is a corresponding chapter in the Teachers' resource book. Each chapter contains the following sections.

Contents and skills: The content of the unit is described and a list is given of the skills developed in each topic. The content of each topic is cross-referenced to attainment targets 2–17 of the National Curriculum. For example, topic 2.7 meets the second point, at level 5, of attainment target 2, and this is indicated by *AT 2-5b*. Attainment target 1 is covered throughout the course.

Equipment: Detailed equipment lists are given for each topic as well as helpful hints on setting up and running the experiments.

Assessment: There is a short photocopiable assessment test for the unit and answers.

True/false statements: These are to be completed by the pupils. They cover all the attainment targets introduced in the unit.

Summary: Photocopiable summary sheets cover the main points of the unit. They require pupils to fill in missing words in simple statements.

Resources: The photocopiable resources include extra instruction sheets, worksheets, diagrams etc. Their use is indicated in the equipment lists, and each is numbered; for example, R2.4 would be a resource sheet for unit 2, topic 4.

Skills Sheets

The Skills Sheets provide an extra tier of extension material (or homeworks). They build on the Skills Sheets in book 1. They cover the skills of:

- reading
- writing
- number
- revision
- experimental design

within a scientific context. The activities are suitable for all pupils and each one should take about 10–15 minutes. They are arranged roughly in order of difficulty of skill.

It is suggested that all 45 Skills Sheets are photocopied and added to the Skills Sheets for book 1. Pupils then work, in order, through the sheets, either when asked, or when they have a few spare minutes at the end of a lesson. The activities are answered in the back of their notebooks or files and each one is self-corrected from the teacher's master set as soon as it is completed.

Pupils will complete a widely varying number of skills sheets, depending on their ability. Less able pupils could be encouraged to concentrate on selected sheets.

Meeting the demands of the National Curriculum

This analysis of the Statutory Orders for science and the pupils' textbooks and the assessment material in **Understanding Science, Books 1** and **2** has been prepared with help from teachers who are using the course. Attainment Target 1 is covered throughout.

Understanding Science Book 1

The list shows the statements of attainment which are covered in the individual topics of **Understanding Science 1**. The coverage is divided between the core activities and the extension activities. Some topics do not relate to specific statements but are used to prepare students for later topics or to cover the Exploration of Science. The letters *a, b, c* etc. denote the statement within a given level.

Topic	Core and reinforcement	Extensions
1.5	*AT 17—5a, b*	—
1.6	*AT 17—4a*	—
2.1	*AT 2—3a; b*	*AT 2—3a, b*
2.2	*AT 2—3a; AT 3—3a*	—
2.3	*AT 2—4a; AT 3—3a*	*AT 2—3a*
2.4	*AT 2—3b; 4a*	*AT 2—4a*
2.5	*AT 2—6a; AT 3—3a; AT 4—4a*	—
2.6	*AT 2—4a, 5b*	*AT 2—4a*
2.7	*AT 2—5b*	*AT 2—5b*
2.9	*AT 17—5a, b*	—
2.10	*AT 17—4a*	—
3.1	*AT 6—4d; AT 9—5c; AT 13—4e*	*AT 6—4d*
3.2	*AT 8—4a*	—
3.3	*AT 8—4a*	—
3.4	*AT 6—5c*	—
3.5	*AT 6—4d, 5c*	*AT 6—4d, 5c*
3.6	*AT 6—5c*	—
3.7	*AT 17—5a, b*	—
3.8	*AT 17—4a*	—
4.1	*AT 13—4a*	*AT 13—4c*
4.2	*AT 13—4c*	*AT 13—4c*
4.3	*AT 13—3a, c*	—
4.4	*AT 13—3b, 4a, b, d*	*AT 13—6d*
4.5	*AT 13—5a, b*	—
4.6	*AT 17—4a*	—
5.1	*AT 6—4c; AT 13—3b, 4d*	—
5.2	*AT 4—4a*	—
5.3	*AT 4—4a*	*AT 13—3b, 4d*
5.5	*AT 17—5a, b*	—
5.6	*AT 17—4a*	—
6.1	*AT 11—3b, 4a, 5a*	*AT 11—3b, 5a*
6.2	*AT 11—3a, 4a, 5a*	—
6.3	*AT 11—4a, 5a, b*	*AT 11—5a*
6.4	*AT 11—4a, 5a*	—
6.5	—	*AT 11—5b, 6a*
6.6	*AT 11—6b*	—
6.7	*AT 11—5a*	—
6.9	*AT 17—4a*	—
7.2	*At 3—5a*	*AT 3—5a*
7.3	*AT 3—5a*	*AT 4—5a*
7.4	*AT 3—4c*	*AT 3—3b, 4c, 6f*
7.5	*AT 3—4d*	*AT 3—4d*
7.7	*AT 17—5a, b*	—
7.8	*AT 17—4a*	—

The following shows where specific statements of attainment are covered in **Book 1**.

AT 2	*3a*	2.1, 2.1E, 2.2, 2.3E
	b	2.1, 2.1E, 2.4
	4a	2.3, 2.4, 2.4E, 2.6, 2.6E
	5b	2.6, 2.7
	6a	2.5
AT 3	*3a*	2.2, 2.3, 2.5
	b	7.4E
	4c	7.4, 7.4E
	d	7.5, 7.5E
	5a	7.2, 7.2E, 7.3
	6f	7.4E
AT 4	*4a*	2.5, 5.2, 5.3
	5a	7.3E
AT 6	*4c*	5.1
	d	3.1, 3.1E, 3.5, 3.5E
	5c	3.4, 3.5, 3.5E, 3.6
AT 8	*4a*	3.2, 3.3
AT 9	*5c*	3.1
AT 11	*3a*	6.2
	b	6.1, 6.1E
	4a	6.1, 6.2, 6.3, 6.4
	5a	6.1, 6.1E, 6.2, 6.3, 6.3E, 6.4, 6.7
	b	6.3, 6.5E
	6a	6.5E
	b	6.6
AT 13	*3a*	4.3
	b	4.4, 5.1, 5.3E
	c	4.3
	4a	4.1, 4.4
	b	4.4
	c	4.1E, 4.2, 4.2E
	d	4.4, 5.1, 5.3E
	e	3.1
	5a	4.5
	b	4.5
	6d	4.4E
AT 17	*4a*	1.6, 2.10, 3.8, 4.6, 5.6, 6.9, 7.8
	5a	1.5, 2.9, 3.7, 5.5, 7.7
	b	1.5, 2.9, 3.7, 5.5, 7.7

Assessment in Book 1

The following indicates which attainment targets are assessed in the end-of-unit tests and problem-solving activities. Application or Communication refer to the sections detailed at the beginning of the Programme of Study for Key Stage 3. *AT 1* has been included in this analysis but assessment is dependent on the teaching methods employed.

Test 1

1 *AT 1—3i*	4 *AT 1—4f*
2 *AT 1—3i*	5 *AT 1—4f*
3 *AT 1—4f*	6 *AT 1—4f*

7 *AT 1—2d*	11 *AT 1—3f*
8 *AT 1—2*	12 *AT 1—3h*
9 *AT 1—4g*	13 *AT 1—3i*
10 *AT 1—2f*	14 *AT 1—4i*

1.5 Problem (and R1.5): *Communication*

Test 2

1 *AT 2—3b*	8 *AT 2—4a*	15 *AT 2—5b*
2 *AT 1—2d*	9 *AT 3—3a*	16 *AT 2—5b*
3 *AT 1—2d*	10 *AT 3—3a*	17 *AT 2—5b*
4 *AT 1—2b*	11 *AT 2—6a*	18 *AT 2—5b*
5 *AT 2—3a*	12 *AT 2—6a*	19 *AT 2—3b*
6 *AT 2—3b*	13 *AT 2—4a*	20 *AT 3—3a*
7 *AT 2—4a*	14 *AT 2—5b*	21 *AT 2—4a*
		22 *AT 2—5b*

2.8 Problem (and R2.8) *AT 1—3b, d, f, h, i. Communication*

Test 3

1 *AT 6—4d*	9 *AT 6—5c*
2 *AT 6—4d (Application)*	10 *AT 6—4d*
3 *AT 8—4a*	11 *AT 6—5c*
4 *AT 8—4a (Application)*	12 *AT 8—4a*
5 *AT 8—4a*	13 *AT 8—4a*
6 *AT 6—5c*	14 *AT 8—4a; AT 1—4f*
7 *AT 8—4a*	15 *AT 8—4a*
8 *AT 6—5c*	16 *AT 6—5c*

3.6 Problem (and R3.6): *AT 1—4f, j. Communication*

Test 4

1 *AT 13—4a*	7 *AT 13—3a*
2 *AT 13—4a*	8 *AT 13—4a*
3 *AT 13—4a*	9 *AT 13—4c*
4 *AT 13—4c*	10 *AT 13—6d*
5 *AT 13—4c*	11 *AT 13—3a (Application)*
6 *AT 13—3a*	12 *AT 13—4b*

4.5 Writeabout (and R4.5): *AT 13—5a, b; AT 1—4j, 5d. Communication, Application*

Test 5

1 *AT 1—3d*	6 *AT 1—4h*
2 *AT 13—3b*	7 *AT 1—4i*
3 *AT 1—3d*	8 *AT 1—4e*
4 *AT 1—4h*	10 *AT 1—4i*
5 *AT 1—4i*	

5.4 Problem (and R5.4): *AT 1—4a, f, g, h. Communication*

Test 6

1 *AT 11—5a*	9 *AT 1—4j*
2 *AT 11—3b*	10 *AT 11—5a*
3 *AT 11—3a*	11 *AT 11—5b*
4 *AT 11—5a, b*	12 *AT 11—5a*
5 *AT 11—4a, 5a*	13 *AT 11—5b*
6 *AT 11—5a*	14 *AT 11—6a*
7 *Application*	15 *Application*
8 *AT 11—6b*	

6.7 Problem: *AT 1—5a, b. Application*

Test 7

1 *AT 1—5c*	6 *AT 3—4c*	11 *AT 1—5c*
2 *AT 1—5c*	7 *AT 3—4c*	12 *AT 1—5c*
3 *AT 1—5a*	8 *AT 3—4d*	13 *AT 1—4i, AT 3—5a*
4 *AT 3—5a*	9 *AT 3—4d*	14 *AT 4—5a*
5 *AT 3—5a*	10 *AT 3—4d*	15 *AT 3—4d*

7.6 Problem: *AT 1—3c, 4i, j, 5a, b. Communication, Application*

The following shows which question from the end-of-unit tests or problem-solving activities can be used to test specific Attainment Targets. We have only included items which are part of the formal assessment and teachers may wish to add marks from the many other activities throughout the course. 5—1 is used to indicate Test 5, Question 1 and 2—Prob indicates the problem-solving activity in Unit 2.

AT 1	*3b*	2—Prob
	c	7—Prob
	d	2—Prob, 5—1, 5—2
	f	1—11, 2—Prob
	h	1—12, 2—Prob
	i	1—1, 1—2, 1—13, 2—Prob
	4a	5—Prob
	c	5—8
	f	1—3, 1—4, 1—5, 1—6, 3—14, 3—Prob, 5—Prob
	g	1—9, 5—Prob
	h	5—4, 5—6, 5—Prob
	i	1—14, 5—5, 5—7, 7—13, 7—Prob
	j	3—Prob, 4—Write, 5—10, 6—9, 7—Prob
	5a	6—Prob, 7—Prob
	b	6—Prob, 7—Prob
	c	7—1, 7—2, 7—11, 7—12
	d	4—Write
AT 2	*3a*	2—5
	b	2—1, 2—6, 2—19
	4a	2—7, 2—8, 2—13, 2—21
	5b	2—14, 2—15, 2—16, 2—17, 2—18, 2—22
	6a	2—11, 2—12
AT 3	*3a*	2—9, 2—10, 2—20
	4c	7—6, 7—7
	d	7—8, 7—9, 7—10, 7—15
	5a	7—3, 7—4, 7—5, 7—13
AT 4	*5a*	7—14
AT 6	*4d*	3—1, 3—2, 3—10
	5c	3—6, 3—8, 3—9, 3—11, 3—16
AT 8	*4a*	3—3, 3—4, 3—5, 3—7, 3—12, 3—13, 3—14, 3—15
AT 11	*3a*	6—3
	b	6—2
	4a	6—5
	5a	6—1, 6—4, 6—5, 6—6, 6—10, 6—12
	b	6—4, 6—11, 6—13
	6a	6—14
	b	6—8
AT 13	*3a*	4—6, 4—7, 4—11
	b	5—2
	4a	4—1, 4—2, 4—3, 4—8

b	4—12
c	4—4, 4—5, 4—9
5a	4—Write
b	4—Write
6d	4—10

Understanding Science Book 2

The list shows the statements of attainment which are covered in the individual topics of **Understanding Science 2**. The coverage is divided between the core activities and extension activities. Some topics do not relate to specific statements but are used to prepare students for later topics or to cover the Exploration of Science. The letters *a, b, c* etc. denote the statements within a given level.

Topic	Core and reinforcement	Extensions
1.1	*AT 2—5a; AT 5—3a*	*AT 2—4c*
1.2	*AT 2—5a; AT 9—4a*	*AT 9—3d*
1.3	*AT 2—3c, 5a; AT 9—3e, 4a, b*	*AT 9—3d, 6c*
1.4	*AT 4—3a*	—
1.5	*AT 2—5d*	*AT 3—4a, 6b*
1.6	*AT 5—3a; 5a*	*AT 5—5a*
1.7	*AT 5—3a, b*	—
1.8	*AT 5—5c*	—
1.9	*AT 2—5c; AT 9—3a, c, 5a, b*	—
2.1	—	*AT 3—6a*
2.2	*AT 6—3b, 4b*	—
2.3	—	*AT 6—3b*
2.4	*AT 8—6c*	—
2.5	—	*AT 7—5c*
2.6	*AT 6—5b*	*AT 6—5b*
2.7	*AT 7—4a, 6c*	*AT 7—4a, 6c*
2.10	*AT 6—3a; AT 7—4b, 5a*	—
3.1	*AT 3—4a, 5e*	*AT 3—5e, 6a*
3.2	*AT 3—4b, 5b*	*AT 3—4b, 5b*
3.3	*AT 3—4b*	*AT 3—4b*
3.4	*AT 3—5c*	*AT 3—5c; AT 8—6c*
3.5	*AT 3—5b, e*	*AT 3—4b, 5d, 6e*
3.6	*AT 3—5b*	*AT 3—5b*
3.7	*AT 3—4b, 6e*	*AT 3—4b, 6e*
3.8	*AT 3—5e*	*AT 3—5e*
3.9	*AT 3—4b, 5b*	—
3.10	*AT 3—4b, 5d, 6e*	—
3.11	*AT 3—4b, 5d*	—
4.1	*AT 10—3a*	*AT 10—4d, 5c*
4.2	*AT 10—4c*	*AT 10—4a; AT 11—6c*
4.3	*AT 10—4a, 5a, d*	*AT 10—4b, 5d*
4.4	*AT 10—3b, 4a*	*AT 10—4a, 5c, 6c*
4.5	*AT 10—4a*	*AT 10—4a*
4.6	*AT 6—4a; AT 10—5b*	*AT 6—4b*
4.7	*AT 6—4a, b; AT 10—5b*	—
4.8	*AT 10—3a*	—
4.9	*AT 6—4b; AT 10—3a*	—
5.1	*AT 16—3b; AT 17—5a, b*	—
5.3	*AT 8—4a*	*AT 17—5a*
5.4	*AT 8—4a; AT 17—5a, b*	*AT 8—5a*
5.5	*AT 8—4a; AT 17—5a*	*AT 8—4a*
5.6	*AT 8—4a*	*AT 8—4a*
5.7	*AT 16—4a*	*AT 16—4b*
5.8	*AT 8—6a; AT 17—6a*	*AT 6—4e*
5.9	*AT 6—4d; AT 8—6a, b; AT 17—6a*	*AT 6—4d; AT 8—6b; AT 17—6a*
5.11	*AT 17—5a*	—
5.12	*AT 17—4a, 6a, 7a*	—
6.2	*AT 12—3a, b, c, 4a, b, 5a*	*AT 12—5b, 6a*
6.3	*AT 12—3b, c, 4a, 6b*	—
6.4	*AT 7—5b; AT 8—6c*	—
6.5	*AT 7—5b*	—
6.6	*AT 6—3a, b, 4a, b; AT 7—4b*	*AT 5—4a, 5b*
6.7	*AT 7—5c; AT 13—4b, 5a, b*	—

The following shows where specific statements of attainment are covered in **Book 2.**

AT 2	3c	1.3
	4c	1.1E
	5a	1.1, 1.2, 1.3
	c	1.9
	d	1.5
AT 3	4a	1.5E, 3.1
	b	3.2, 3.2E, 3.3, 3.3E, 3.5E, 3.7, 3.7E, 3.9, 3.10, 3.11
	5b	3.2, 3.2E, 3.5, 3.6, 3.6E, 3.9
	c	3.4, 3.4E
	d	3.5E, 3.10, 3.11
	e	3.1, 3.1E, 3.5, 3.8, 3.8E
	6a	2.1E, 3.1E
	b	1.5E
	e	3.5E, 3.7, 3.7E, 3.10
AT 4	3a	1.4
AT 5	3a	1.1, 1.6, 1.7
	b	1.7
	4a	6.6E
	5a	1.6, 1.6E
	b	6.6E
	c	1.8
AT 6	3a	2.10, 6.6
	b	2.2, 2.3E, 6.6
	4a	4.6, 4.7, 6.6
	b	2.2, 4.6E, 4.7, 4.9, 6.6
	d	5.9, 5.9E
	e	5.8E
	5b	2.6, 2.6E
AT 7	4a	2.7, 2.7E
	b	2.10, 6.6
	5a	2.10
	b	6.4, 6.5

	c	2.5, 6.7
	6c	2.7, 2.7E
AT 8	*4a*	5.3, 5.4, 5.5, 5.5E, 5.6, 5.6E
	5a	5.4E
	6a	5.8, 5.9
	b	5.9, 5.9E
	c	2.4, 3.4E, 6.4
AT 9	*3a*	1.9
	c	1.9
	d	1.2E, 1.3E
	e	1.3
	4a	1.2, 1.3
	b	1.3
	5a	1.9
	b	1.9
AT 10	*3a*	4.1, 4.8, 4.9
	b	4.4
	4a	4.2E, 4.3, 4.4, 4.4E, 4.5, 4.5E
	b	4.3E
	c	4.2
	d	4.1E
	5a	4.3
	b	4.6, 4.7
	c	4.1E, 4.4E
	d	4.3, 4.3E
	6c	4.4E
AT 11	*6c*	4.2E
AT 12	*3a*	6.2
	b	6.2, 6.3
	c	6.2, 6.3
	4a	6.2, 6.3
	b	6.2
	5a	6.2
	b	6.2E
	6a	6.2E
	b	6.3
AT 13	*4b*	6.7
	5a	6.7
	b	6.7
AT 16	*3b*	5.1
	4a	5.7
	b	5.7E
AT 17	*4a*	5.12
	5a	5.1, 5.3E, 5.4, 5.5, 5.11
	b	5.1, 5.4
	6a	5.8, 5.9, 5.9E, 5.12
	7a	5.12

Assessment in Book 2

The following indicates which Attainment Targets are assessed in the end-of-unit tests and problem-solving activities. *AT 1* has been included in this analysis but is dependent on the teaching methods employed.

Test 1

1 *AT 1—4e; AT 2—5a*
2 *AT 2—5a*
3 *AT 2—3c; AT 2—5a; AT 9—3e*
4 *AT 4—3a*
5 *AT 2—5c, 5d*
6 *AT 5—3a, 5a*
7 *AT 9—3c, 5a, 5b*
8 *AT 2—4c*
9 *AT 9—3d*
10 *AT 9—4a*
11 —
12 *AT 1—5b; AT 3—6b*
13 *AT 1—4i*

1.7 Problem: *AT 5—3b*

Test 2

1 *AT 1—4j*
2 —
3 —
4 *AT 6—3a, 4b*
5 *AT 6—4b*
6 *AT 6—7c*
7 *AT 8—6c*
8 *AT 8—6c*
9 —
10 *AT 7—7d*
11 *AT 6—5b*
12 *AT 6—5b*
13 *AT 7—4a, 6c*
14 —
15 *AT 1—4j; AT 7—5c*
16 *AT 3—6a; AT 7—5c*
17 *AT 1—3c, 4c, d, j*
18 —
19 *AT 7—4a, 5c*
20 *AT 7—4a*
21 *AT 6—3b*
22 *AT 7—4b, 5a*

Test 3

1 *AT 3—4a*
2 *AT 3—4b, 5b*
3 *AT 3—4b*
4 *AT 3—5c*
5 *AT 3—5b, e*
6 *AT 3—4b, 6e*
7 *AT 3—5e*
8 *AT 3—5e, 6a*
9 —
10 —
11 *AT 3—4b*
12 *AT 3—5c; AT 8—6c*
13 *AT 3—5d, e*
14 *AT 3—5b*
15 *AT 3—5e*

Test 4

1 *AT 10—3a*
2 *AT 1—3h, 4i; AT 10—4c*
3 *AT 10—5d*
4 *AT 10—3b, 4a, 5a*
5 *AT 10—4a*
6 *AT 1—3c, 4c; AT 6—4a; AT 10—3a*
7 *AT 1—3e; AT 10—4d*
8 *AT 1—3h, 4i; AT 11—6c*
9 *AT 1—3g, 4i; AT 10—4b, 5d*
10 *AT 10—4a, d, 6c*
11 *AT 1—3h, 4i*
12 *AT 1—3i, 4d, j; AT 6—4b*

4.7 Problem: *AT10—5b*

Test 5

1 *AT 8—4a*
2 *AT 8—4a*
3 *AT 17—5a, b*
4 *AT 1—3a*
5 *AT 1—3h*
6 *AT 1—3i; AT 8—4a*
7 *AT 8—4a*
8 *AT 8—4a*
9 *AT 1—3i*
10 *AT 16—4a*
11 *AT 1—3a*
12 *AT 1—3a*
13 *AT 8—6a*
14 *AT 8—6b*
15 *AT 8—6b*
16 *AT 17—4a, 6a, 7a*
17 *AT 1—4j*
18 *AT 8—6a*
19 *AT 1—4i; AT 17—5a*
20 *AT 1—4i*
21 *AT 8—5a, 7c*
22 *AT 8—4a*
23 *AT 16—4b*
24 *AT 8—6a*
25 *AT 6—4e; AT 8—6a*
26 *AT 6—4d*
27 *AT 16—3b*

Test 6

1 —
2 —
3 *AT 12—4a, b*
4 —
5 *AT 12—4a*
6 *AT 12—6b*

7 *AT 12—3b, c*
8 *AT 7—5b*
9 *AT 6—3a*
10 *AT 6—4b*
11 *AT 6—2b*
12 *AT 6—4b*
13 *AT 6—4b*
14 *AT 6—4b*
15 —
16 *AT 1—4c; AT 6—4a*
17 *AT 7—5c*
18 *AT 7—5c*
19 *AT 13—4b*
20 —
21 *AT 12—6a*
22 *AT 12—5b*
23 *AT 1—4c; AT 7—5b*
24 *AT 1—3g; AT 5—4a, 5b*
25 *AT 6—4b*
26 *AT 7—4b*
27 —
28 —
29 *AT 13—5a, b*
30 *AT 6—3b*

The following shows which question from the end-of-unit tests or problem-solving activities can be used to test specific Attainment Targets. We have only included items which are part of the formal assessment and teachers may wish to add marks from the many other activities throughout the course. 5—1 is used to indicate Test 5, Question 1 and 2—Prob indicates the problem-solving activity in Unit 2.

AT 1	*3a*	5—4, 5—11, 5—12
	c	2—17, 4—6
	e	4—7
	g	4—9, 6—24
	h	4—2, 4—8, 4—11, 5—5
	i	4—12, 5—6, 5—9
	4c	2—17, 4—6, 6—16, 6—23
	d	2—17, 4—12
	e	1—1
	i	1—13, 4—2, 4—8, 4—9, 4—11, 5—19, 5—20
	j	2—1, 2—15, 2—17, 4—12, 5—17
	5b	1—12
AT 2	*3c*	1—3
	4c	1—8
	5a	1—1, 1—2, 1—3
	c	1—5
	d	1—5
AT 3	*4a*	3—1
	b	3—2, 3—3, 3—6, 3—11
	5b	3—2, 3—5, 3—14
	c	3—4, 3—12
	d	3—13
	e	3—5, 3—7, 3—8, 3—13, 3—15
	6a	2—16, 3—8
	b	1—12
	e	3—6
AT 4	*3a*	1—4
AT 5	*3a*	1—6
	b	1—Prob
	4a	6—24
	5a	1—6
	b	6—24
AT 6	*3a*	2—4, 6—9
	b	2—21, 6—30
	4a	4—6, 6—16
	b	2—4, 2—5, 6—10, 6—12, 6—13, 6—14, 6—25
	d	5—26
	e	5—25
	5b	2—11, 2—12
	7c	2—6
AT 7	*4a*	2—13, 2—19, 2—20
	b	2—22, 6—26
	5a	2—22
	b	6—8, 6—23
	c	2—15, 2—16, 2—19, 6—17, 6—18
	6c	2—13
	7d	2—10
AT 8	*4a*	5—1, 5—2, 5—7, 5—8, 5—22
	5a	5—21
	6a	5—13, 5—18, 5—24, 5—25
	b	5—14, 5—15
	c	2—7, 2—8, 3—12
	7c	5—21
AT 9	*3c*	1—7
	d	1—9
	e	1—3
	4a	1—10
	b	1—3
	5a	1—7
	b	1—7
AT 10	*3a*	4—1, 4—6
	b	4—4
	4a	4—4, 4—5, 4—10
	b	4—9
	c	4—2
	d	4—7, 4—10
	5a	4—4
	d	4—3, 4—9
	6c	4—10
AT 11	*6c*	4—8
AT 12	*3b*	6—7
	c	6—7
	4a	6—3, 6—5
	b	6—3
	5b	6—22
	6a	6—21
	b	6—6
AT 13	*4b*	6—19
	5a	6—29
	b	6—30
AT 16	*3b*	5—27
	4a	5—10
	b	5—23
AT 17	*4a*	5—16
	5a	5—3, 5—19
	b	5—3
	6a	5—16
	7a	5—16

Record sheet KEY STAGE THREE

PUPIL NAME..

Exploration of science

Variety of life

Processes of life

Genetics and evolution

Human influences on earth

Types and uses of materials

Making new materials

Explaining how materials behave

Earth and atmosphere

Forces

Electricity & magnetism

IT inc. micro-electronics

Energy

Sound & music

Light & electro-mag. radiation

Earth in space

Nature of science

Unit 1 Lively places

Exploring environments

The first six topics make use of the skills developed in *Understanding Science 1* to study some aspects of the pupils' surroundings. The processes of observation, measurement and reporting are prominent. Some basic knowledge of types of British environments, weather, geological processes, food chains and examples of pollution and conservation is presented. Various techniques for describing the environment are employed including sampling methods and map reading. The final three topics comprise an open-ended project on conservation, a discussion and a short reading exercise. The content covers learning outcomes across several of the National Curriculum Attainment Targets (AT 2, AT 5, AT 9). In addition to meeting the general demands of Attainment Target 1 this unit deals specifically with the development of AT 1, levels 4e, 4f, 4g, 4h, 4i, 4j.

Core and Reinforcement	Extension
1.1 Describing places *AT 2–5a; AT 5–3a*	*AT 2–4c*
Observe a small area of school grounds and describe the environment. Describe three familiar environments given pictures. *page 8*	Read a passage on how fossils form and answer questions. Make and interpret fossil moulds. *page 128*
Communicate scientific observations in writing. Observe and record systematically.	Extract relevant information from text. Examine evidence and make decisions.
1.2 Measuring the environment *AT 2–5a; AT 9–4a*	*AT 9–3d*
Make measurements of some parameters of a small environment. Use a map to describe some parameters of an environment. *page 10*	Study the appearance, acidity and drainage of a soil. *page 129*
Select and use measuring devices accurately. Extract data from a given source (map). Recognise that measurement practices are subject to limitations.	Observe, measure and record accurately. Communicate observations in written form.
1.3 Looking at weather *AT 2–3c, 5a; AT 9–3e, 4a,b*	*AT 9—3d, 6c*
Describe weather conditions from given weather maps. Make measurements of some parameters of weather. *page 12*	Read a passage on weather forecasting and answer questions on it. *page 130*
Devise experiments for a stated purpose. Observe, measure and record systematically. Recognise that measurement practices are subject to limitations.	Extract relevant information from text and diagrams. Recognise a pattern in data.
1.4 Counting living things *AT 4–3a*	
Use sampling techniques to estimate number of 'fish' in a model pond. Apply the sampling technique to a real plant population. *page 14*	Build and use invertebrate animal traps. *page 131*
Calculate the average of three numbers. Observe, measure, record systematically. Recognise that sampling techniques are subject to limitations.	Build apparatus from a diagram. Record accurately.

Core and Reinforcement

1.5 Feeding living things *AT 2-5d*

Play a food chain game. *page 16*

Follow instructions accurately.
Recognise specific examples of the concept of a food chain.
Recognise a pattern in scientific observations.

1.6 Helping and harming the environment *AT 5-3a, 5a*

Identify examples of pollution and conservation from photographs. Detect signs of pollution in the local environment using indicators. *page 18*

Recognise specific examples of the concepts of pollution and conservation.
Observe systematically.

1.7 Problem—Winning an award *AT 5-3a,b*

Take part in a conservation award scheme by completing a number of conservation tasks. *page 20*

Relate scientific principles to everyday situations, and explain and evaluate social and environmental implications.

1.8 Talkabout—Making an impact *AT 5-5c*

Discuss the possible environmental impact on a given site of three proposed developments. *page 22*

Relate scientific principles to everyday situations, and explain and evaluate social and environmental implications.

1.9 Readabout—Forming the environment *AT 2-5c; AT 9-3a,c, 5a,b*

Read a passage on how landforms are created by geological processes. Answer questions on the passage. *page 23*

Extract relevant information from a passage.
Communicate scientific ideas in written and diagrammatic form.

Extension

AT 3-4a, 6b

Design and carry out an experiment to test whether or not the rate of photosynthesis changes as light intensity varies. *page 132*

Devise and carry out an experiment to test a hypothesis.
Draw conclusions from experimental observations and data.

AT 5-5a

Carry out an experiment to find the relationship between temperature and oxygen levels in water. *page 133*

Use experimental data to deduce a relationship.
Draw conclusions from experimental observations and data.

Video material will provide useful support throughout this unit.

Equipment

required for each pupil

1.1—Describing places

- Tape measure or metre rule
- Poster paper
- Coloured pencils
- Camera (if available)

Notes

Some preparation in identifying suitable places for pupils to visit is required. Areas should be small and diverse; e.g. corner of a wall, large boulder, tree, edge of path, bottom of stairway (inside or outside), any area where water might drip down wall or onto ground, drain in path/pavement.

Extension

- Plasticine
- Box of objects e.g. shell, pen, leaf, bone, tree bark
- Books/resources on fossils

The idea is to make pupils aware of the difficulty in identifying and interpreting fossils, as well as showing one method of formation

1.2—Measuring the environment

- Thermometer
- Light meter
- Metre rule
- Compass
- Spirit level
- Gardener's soil pH probe
- Soil water probe
- Anemometer or wind chart **(R1.3A)**
- Local Ordnance Survey map

A range of measuring instruments should be made available. Each pupil group can select/ask for/design the instruments they need.
Soil pH probes are easy to use, and don't require any understanding of pH, which is covered in Unit 2.

The wind chart from Topic 1.3 can be used as an alternative to the anemometer.

Extension

- Soil identification flow diagram **(RE1.2)**
- Soil sample
- Ceramic wool
- Plastic filter funnel
- Timer
- Measuring cylinder (100 cm^3)
- Retort and clamp
- Beaker (100 cm^3)
- Test tube
- Test-tube rack
- Blue and red litmus paper

The flow diagram will allow pupils to identify main soil types easily. If possible provide a 'home made' clay, sandy or loam soil. The diagrams provide pupils with an outline of the experimental procedure only. Some interpretation is required.

1.3—Looking at weather

- Coloured pencils
- Compass
- Flag/strips of material
- Anemometer
- Wind chart **(R1.3A)**
- Weather chart **(R1.3B)**
- Thermometer
- Light meter
- Books/pamphlets on weather

Wind speed and direction can be difficult to measure.
The wind chart shows how observations of the environment can indicate wind speed.
Pupils should be encouraged to design their own way of measuring wind direction.
Most decide to use a flag/strip of paper as an indicator.

Equipment

required for each pupil

Notes

Extension

- Books/pamphlets on weather

The geography dept may be able to lend some material.

1.4—Counting living things

- Tray or box with base covered by a layer of sawdust
- Small bar magnet (fishing rod)
- Cardboard quadrat (square frame cut from cardboard)
- Quadrat ($\frac{1}{4}$ m^2)
- Panel pins (either 50 or 100 depending on the area of the tray)

The tray/box should be at least A4 size.
The area of the quadrat is more critical. It should be 1/10th of the area of the tray to make the estimate of population easier.
The limitations of sampling as a guide to population size can be introduced.
Pupils fish for the panel-pin fish inside the quadrat to estimate population size.

Extension

- 10–15 cm diameter plastic flower pot
- 15 cm length of garden cane or dowling
- Sheet of newspaper
- Yogurt carton
- Garden trowel
- Sample tray
- Hand lens
- Soil organisms identification chart **(RE1.4)**

The flower pot trap is held in place by pushing the stick into the ground. It attracts slugs, ants, beetles, spiders.
The pitfall trap should be covered by a flat stone or plastic top. It will collect a wide range of invertebrates.

1.5—Feeding living things

- 1 die
- Red and green coloured pencils
- Food-chain game **(R1.5)**

Energy flow in a food chain is a very important ecological concept.

Extension

- Boiling tube
- Beaker (250 cm^3)
- Bottle of 0.1% solution sodium bicarbonate
- Bench lamp
- Metre rule
- Timer
- *Elodea* (Canadian pond weed)
- Paper clip

The diagram gives some idea of how the apparatus should be assembled but pupils will have to devise the actual experiment.
Elodea is available from pet shops but also grows in ponds. Fresh young shoots about 5 cm long should be cut from the main stem with a scalpel and kept in a well illuminated beaker of water.
Sodium bicarbonate provides a supply of CO_2.
Pupils should sink the stem with the cut end uppermost. Bubbles of oxygen are released here.
Pupils should be encouraged to look at the structure of other plants and consider where photosynthesis takes place.

1.6—Helping and harming the environment

- Local or national newspaper cuttings

Look out for pollution/conservation issues in the local and national press. Collect these in advance.
Weather and local environment permitting, pupils can be allowed to carry out a local survey of the pollution indicators shown.
The bushier/shrubbier the lichen species are, the cleaner the air.
The darker the body of the two-spot ladybird, the more polluted the air.
Black spot fungus can only grow in very clean air, on sycamore and rose leaves in particular.

Equipment

required for each pupil

Extension

- 50 cm³ burette
- Beaker (250 cm³)
- Measuring cylinder (100 cm³)
- Glass stirring rod
- Glass filter funnel
- Bottle ferrous sulphate solution (2.48 g/litre) labelled A
- Bottle Fehling's B solution (77 g sodium hydroxide, 175 g sodium potassium tartrate, 500 cm³ water) labelled B
- Dropping bottle of phenosaffranin (1% solution, 1 g/100 cm³) labelled red dye

Notes

Pupils will require some help in reading the burette scale to begin with.
The warmer the water the lower the oxygen concentration.
At the end point of the titration the red dye goes clear. Beyond this the solution becomes green.
The mayfly larvae gills will beat faster in warmer water.

1.7—Problem—Winning an award

- Paper
- Envelopes
- Telephone directories
- Local newspapers
- Award application form **(R1.7A)**
- Award certificate **(R1.7B)**

The resources required for this project are determined by the degree of involvement staff and pupils want to undertake.
The bronze award can be easily achieved by carrying out exercises in a single period. These will still raise awareness of local and global issues.
There is scope for intra- and inter-class competition.
The exercises could be used in a year-long project or as homework.
Whatever the approach the activities will generate a lot of interesting display material.

1.8—Talkabout—Making an impact

No equipment required (local material could be included)

This can be used as a homework exercise.

1.9—Readabout—Forming the environment

No equipment required

Assessment 1

The questions are designed to assess the skills and knowledge developed in the unit, as shown in the table. A selection of questions would be appropriate for a unit test.

Topic	*Core*	*Extension*
1.1	1	8
1.2	2	9
1.3	3	10
1.4	4	11
1.5	5	12
1.6	6	13
1.9	7	—

Answers

1 a **(i)** (Type of) place; **(ii)** 1—light meter, 2—thermometer, 3—meter tape/rule, 4—timer/stopwatch; **(iii)** rate of flow of water/how fast the water is flowing; **(iv)** fewer errors/avoid errors/more reliable result.

b Vicuna: cold mountain—thick wool and small ears minimise heat losses.
Elephant seal: Antarctic water—blubber minimises heat losses.
Holly: desert—leaves will minimise water losses, long roots enable water to be taken up from a wide area.
Mudskipper: seashore—fins/arms enable it to move on land and in water, eyes enable it to see what is happening above it.

2 a North east to south west
b A—steep slope, B—marshy ground, C—conifer forest.
3 a **(i)** Wind from the north, cold/2°C, foggy, cloudy sky with bright intervals; **(ii)** winter, because of the temperature.
b **(i)** fairly even throughout the year, slight increase between October and March; **(ii)** place A, as there is plenty of rain in March; **(iii)** August and September; **(iv)** 16 mm; **(v)** high winds *or* very high or low temperature.
c **(i)** A, D, F; **(ii)** B, C, E.
4 a Use a sampling square/quadrat, throw it down at random, take several samples, work out the average per sample, scale the average up to estimate the total.
b It would take too long *or* it would be too difficult to do *or* likely to have lots of mistakes.
c There could soon be no living blue whales.
5 a Green plants *make food* using *light energy* from the sun.
b B, E.
c **(i)** fox; **(ii)** rabbit; **(iii)** decomposers *or* cause decay *or* return essential minerals to the soil.
d Advantages: large crop, faster growth (*any one*). Disadvantages: expensive, causes pollution, soil depleted (*any one*).
6 a A—2, 3, 4, 6, 7, 8; B—1, 6; C—2, 8; D—5, 6.
b Answer should state source of pollution and indicate at least one way the environment is harmed.
c Helping the environment/preventing damage to the environment or the living things in it. Any sensible example.
7 a B, A, D, C
b A shows the rock being broken down/weathered and the bird decaying. D shows the rock cracked and the bird almost fully decayed
c Suitable description of any two mechanisms. Earthquakes: movement and cracks on earth surface, making ridges, crevices etc. Volcanoes: new landforms from volume of lava, destruction of existing landforms etc. Earth's crust: under surface of earth plates, push against each other. Over a long time produce new mountains.
8 a Replacement, impression, actual remains.
b Replacement—minerals replace hard parts such as bone *or* impression—mark left in mud becomes fossilised *or* actual remains—actual parts present in rock or amber.
9 a Measuring cylinder—to add same volume of water to each sample; beaker—to collect and measure water draining through sample; timer—to allow same time for the water to drain through.
b Same volume of soil at the start, same degree of dryness at the start.
c Plants are sensitive to acidity of soil *or* some plants cannot grow in acid/alkaline soil.
10 a air; air pressure; north; higher; low.
b **(i)** B; **(ii)** the *closer* the lines the *faster* the windspeed.
11 a Take more samples, put the pitfall traps at random.
b Put the pitfall traps in the woods, place them at random.
12 a A—oxygen, B—light, C—carbon dioxide.
b Increase
c Keep the light source at the same distance/intensity, alter the temperature of the water.
13 a Sample A.
b Sample B, the less oxygen there is the faster the mayfly is likely to have to beat its gills.

True/false 1

Each statement is marked as either true or false by the pupil. This gives a rapid assessment of a pupil's grasp of the Attainment Targets covered in the unit. The following list gives the Attainment Targets covered by each set of statements.

1 AT 2–3c
2 AT 2–5a
3 AT 2–5c
4 AT 2–5d
5 AT 4–3a
6 AT 5–3a
7 AT 5–3b
8 AT 5–5a
9 AT 5–5c
10 AT 5–6c
11 AT 9–3a
12 AT 9–3c
13 AT 9–3e
14 AT 9–4a
15 AT 9–4b
16 AT 9–5a
17 AT 9–5b
18 AT 2–4c
19 AT 3–4a
20 AT 3–6b
21 AT 6–5a
22 AT 8–3d
23 AT 9–3b
24 AT 9–6c

Unit 1 Lively places

Test 1

1 a Read this passage and answer the questions that follow.

The [1] sun shone brightly on the fast flowing stream. In this type of place animals have flattened shapes to cling onto rocks. This prevents them from being washed away. Plants have long flattened stems and narrow leaves. They can bend in the [2] cold rushing water.

We [3] measured the distance between two trees on the bank of the stream. Then we dropped a table-tennis ball into the water at the first tree and found [4] how long it took for it to reach the second tree. We did this three times.

(i) Which words in the passage mean the same as *environment*?

(ii) What measuring instrument would you use at each of the points 1, 2, 3 and 4 in the passage?

(iii) What was being measured in the experiment with the table-tennis ball?

(iv) Why was it a good idea to repeat this experiment three times?

b Look at these two lists. The first list describes some animals and plants. The second list gives the names of places where these live.

Animals and plants	Place
A vicuna has thick wool and small ears.	Desert
The elephant seal's body has a thick layer of fat called blubber.	Cold mountain
One type of holly points its leaves straight up. They are covered with white powder. It has very long roots.	Antarctic water
The mudskipper has eyes on the top of its head and its front fins are like mini arms.	Seashore

Match each animal/plant with its correct place. Give an explanation for your answers.

2 Examine the map and key.

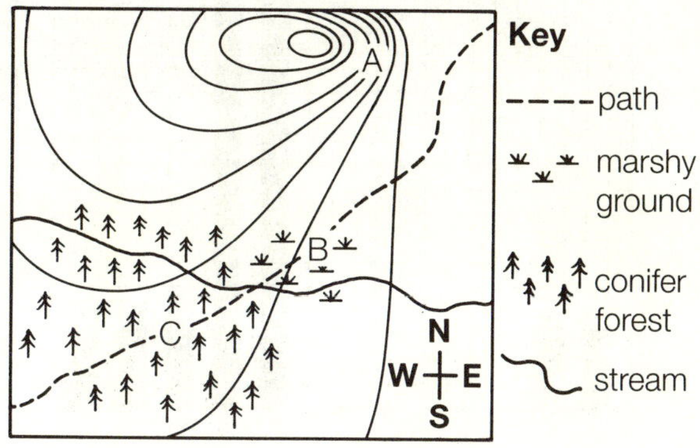

a In what direction does the path run?

b Use the key to describe:

- the slope at point A on the map
- the ground at point B
- what you would see all around you at point C.

3 a These are the weather symbols for one morning.

(i) Describe the weather shown by the symbols.

(ii) What season of the year is it likely to be? Give a reason for your answer.

b These two bar charts compare the rainfall over one year in two different places.

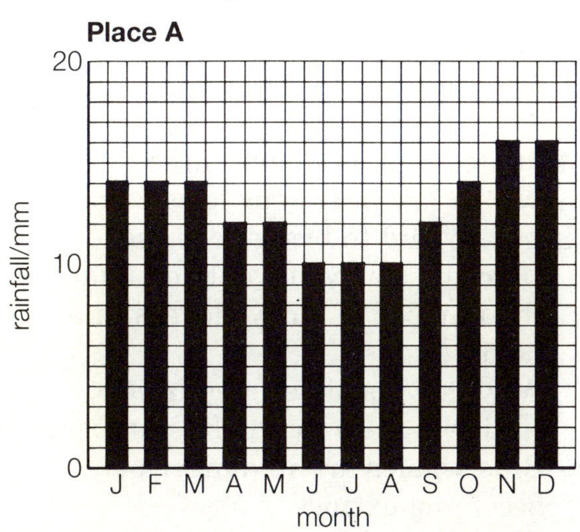

continued ▶

Place B

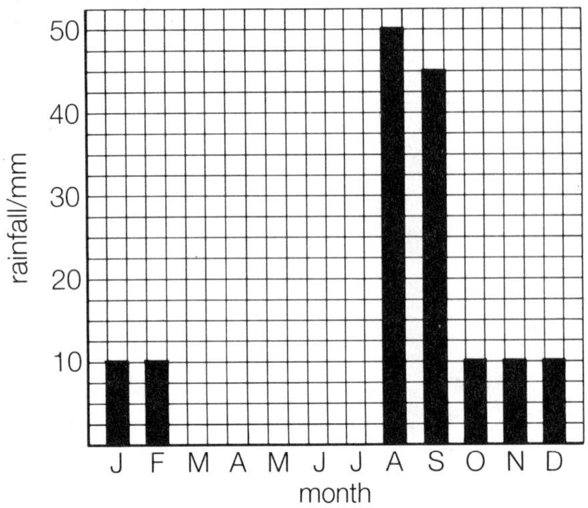

(i) Describe the pattern of rainfall in place A.
(ii) If you wanted to plant seeds in March, in which place would you plant them? Give a reason for your answer.
(iii) Which two months of the year have the highest rainfall in place B?
(iv) What is the highest monthly rainfall in place A?
(v) Apart from rainfall, what weather factor could damage crops?

c Animals and plants respond to seasonal and daily changes. Read the examples of animal and plant responses below.

A People go to sleep at night.
B Bears hibernate over winter.
C Tulips flower every spring.
D Hamsters are most active at night.
E Greylag geese migrate to Iceland.
F Cows stand under trees in hot weather.

Make a list of:
(i) responses to daily changes
(ii) responses to seasonal change.

4 Most clover plants have three leaves. A few have four leaves and these are said to bring good luck.

a Describe how you would estimate the number of lucky clovers in a field.

b Why is it sensible to **estimate**, rather than to count the number?

c Blue whales are in danger of becoming extinct.
What does this mean?

5 a What happens in photosynthesis?

b Which of these statements is an example of a food chain?

A Any food not eaten is put in the bin, collected by refuse collectors and then dumped.

B Grass grows in the sun and is eaten by insects, which starlings feed on.

C Milk from a cow is turned into cream, butter and cheese.

D First peas were put on the plate, then a sardine and then a piece of a larger fish.

E Light energy is used by plankton which are the food of the blue whale.

c Read this description then answer the questions that follow.

The rabbit was munching grass when it was caught by a fox. The fox dragged the dead rabbit back to its cubs. Soon there was little left but fur and bones. But these were not wasted. Soil invertebrates and microbes used these bits for food. Eventually everything decayed away. Essential minerals were returned to the soil. This allowed grass and other plants to grow.

(i) Name the predator in the passage.
(ii) Name the prey.
(iii) Why are soil microbes important?

d Give one advantage and one disadvantage of using artificial fertilisers.

6 a Look at the two lists. The first list gives examples of types of pollution. The second list shows possible sources of pollution.

Type of Pollution	Sources of pollution
A Air	**1** Oil spilling from a wrecked oil tanker
B Water	**2** Jumbo jet taking off
C Noise	**3** Farmers burning stubble in fields
D Soil	**4** Cars using petrol containing lead
	5 Dumping rubbish in hedges
	6 Spraying chemicals on crops to kill insects
	7 Using aerosol spray cans
	8 Allowing bigger lorries to use the roads

continued ▶

Match each source of pollution with the type of pollution. Each number can be used more than once.

b Choose one source of pollution from the list above and explain how it harms the environment.

c What does *conservation* mean? Describe one example of conservation.

7 These four drawings show stages in the formation of soil. The pictures are not in the correct order.

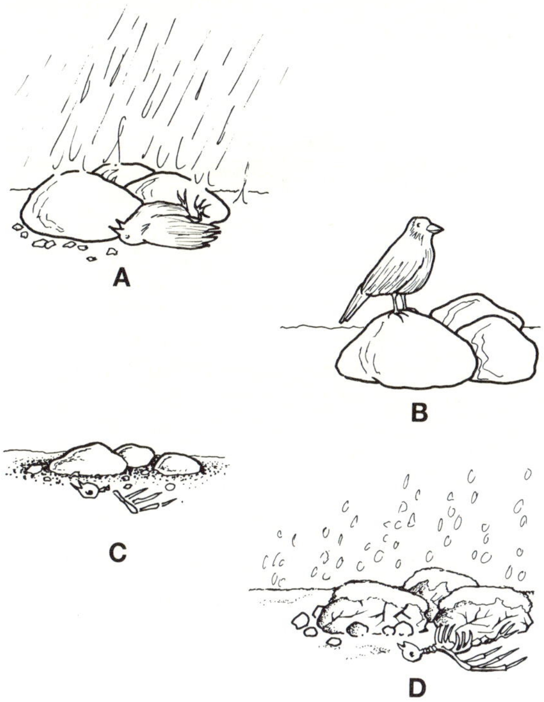

a Write down the letters of the drawings in the correct order.

b Describe how soil is formed in drawings A and D.

c New landforms can be made by earthquakes, volcanoes and movements of the earth's crust. Describe how any two of these can produce new landforms.

Extension questions

8 a List three ways in which fossils can form.

b Describe one of the ways in which a fossil may form.

9 Joan and George were comparing the drainage of two different soil samples. They were given the apparatus shown in the diagram.

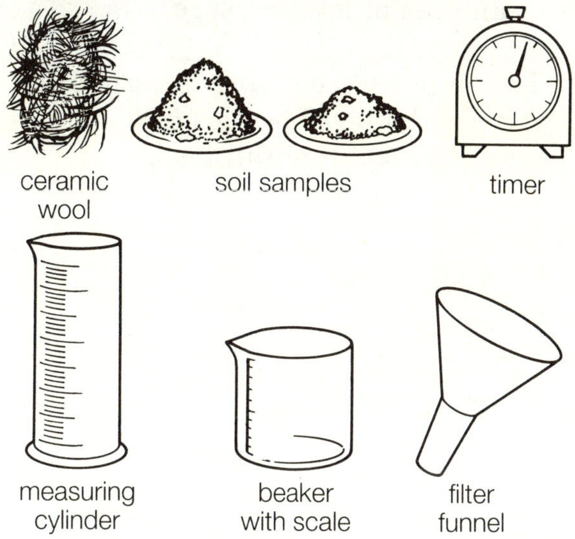

a Explain how they would use each of the following:

- measuring cylinder
- beaker with a scale on it
- timer.

b What two features of the soil would have to be the same to make the experiment fair?

c Why do gardeners and farmers need to test the acidity of the soil.

10 a Decide which word of each pair in italics is correct in the passage below.

Wind is *air/cloud* that moves because of differences in *time of day/air pressure*. Wind coming from the *north/south* usually brings colder weather. When the wind blows from sea to land there is a *lower/higher* chance of rain. The weather is usually unsettled or poor when the air pressure is *low/high*.

Write down the correct version of the passage.

b Three lows are shown in the diagram. Low A produces the highest wind speeds.

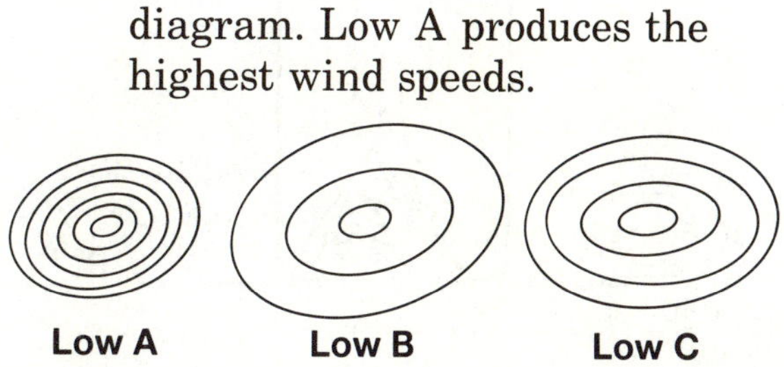

continued ▶

(i) Which low has the lowest wind speed?
(ii) How can you judge the wind speed by looking at a diagram of an area of low pressure?

11 Two pupils were trying to estimate the population of beetles in a small woodland using pitfall traps.

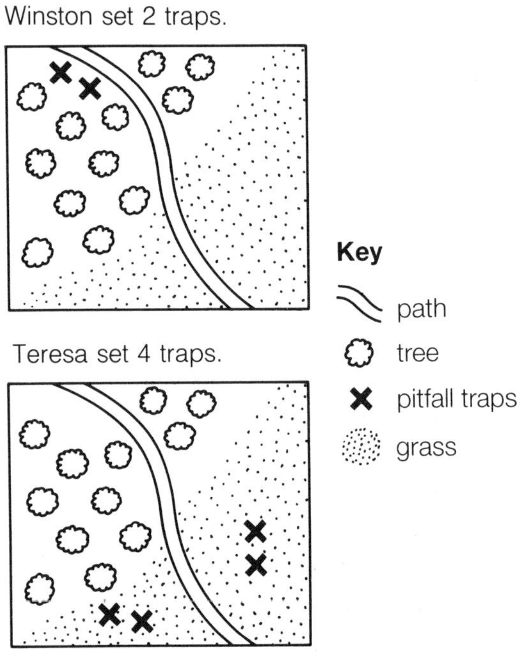

It is unlikely that either Winston or Teresa will make a good estimate.

a Give two ways in which Winston's sampling method could be improved.
b Give two ways in which Teresa's sampling method could be improved.

12 The plant in this experiment is carrying out photosynthesis.

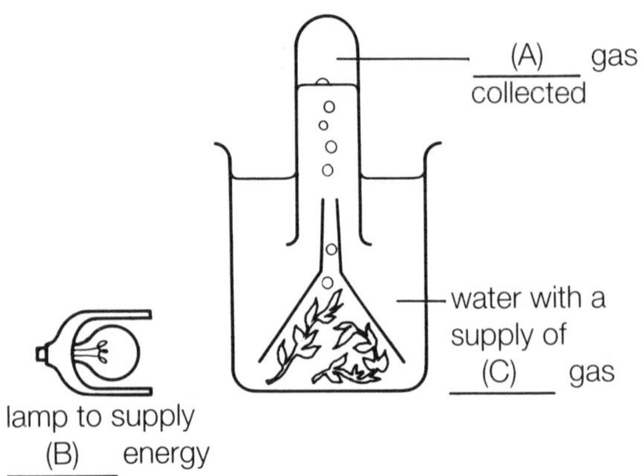

a What words should be written at points A, B and C on the diagram?
b What would happen to the number of bubbles per minute if the lamp was brought closer?
c How could you alter the design of the experiment to study the effect of a change in temperature on photosynthesis?

13 The diagram below shows a mayfly larva. It uses its gills for breathing. The table shows the rate at which its gills beat in three different water samples.

Water sample	Gill beats per minute
A	70
B	200
C	140

a Which water sample is likely to contain most oxygen?
b Which sample is likely to have the highest water temperature? Explain your answer.

Unit 1 Lively places

True or False 1

Name ____________________

Put a tick after the statements that are true. Put a cross after the statements that are false.

1 **a** A squirrel hibernates whenever it has made a store of food. ☐
b Some animals only hunt at night. ☐
c Animals do not alter their behaviour when the weather changes. ☐

2 **a** Two similar environments 1000 km apart are likely to have similar plants and animals. ☐
b Heather grows in acid soil so it will grow well in sandy soil. ☐
c A freshwater fish like the roach could live in salt water. ☐

3 **a** Fertilisers improve the growth of crops. ☐
b Fertilisers cause pollution in rivers. ☐
c Using fertilisers will allow a bigger crop to be grown in a small field. ☐
d Repeated use of fertilisers is good for the soil. ☐
e Using fertilisers makes food more expensive. ☐

4 **a** A bee visiting a flower is a predator. ☐
b Predators are always meat eaters. ☐
c When an animal is eaten by another, it is the prey. ☐

5 **a** There are no animals in danger of becoming extinct in Britain. ☐
b Conservation is needed to protect rare wild plants. ☐
c There are no dodos alive. The dodo is an extinct bird. ☐

6 **a** Human activity can cause changes in the local environment. ☐
b Tall chimneys prevent smoke from damaging the air. ☐
c Chemicals dumped in the ocean cause no pollution because the ocean is so big. ☐
d Chemicals passed into rivers do not cause pollution because they are carried away. ☐

7 **a** Sand-blasting buildings improves the environment. ☐
b Conservation talks improve the environment. ☐

8 **a** Noise pollution damages buildings. ☐
b Putting garden compost in the soil causes pollution. ☐
c Air pollution can be prevented by cleaning buildings. ☐
d Air pollution helps plants because it kills some types of fungus. ☐
e Oil pollution in water kills seabirds and fish. ☐

9 **a** Building a leisure centre on waste ground will always be a bad idea. ☐
b Using a lake for sailing will cause permanent damage to that environment. ☐
c Human activity will always affect the environment badly. ☐
d Planning decisions should always consider the effect on the environment. ☐

10 **a** Mining for coal and iron is necessary to maintain our lifestyle. ☐
b Pollution from mining can be safely ignored. ☐
c It is possible to control and reduce pollution from power stations. ☐

continued ▶

Name ____________________

11 a Weathering helps keep buildings clean. ☐
b Cold, wet weather can cause cracks in stone and bricks. ☐
c The landscape is not permanently altered by the weather. ☐
d Weathering takes hundreds of years to change the shape of a mountain. ☐

12 a The only difference between soils is the size of the stones present. ☐
b The type of soil that forms depends on the rock it is made from. ☐
c Wind, rain and temperature change all cause the weathering of rock. ☐

13 a This is the weather symbol for windspeed and direction ☐

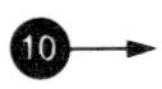

b This is the weather symbol for temperature  ☐

c This is a weather symbol that describes the sky  ☐

14 a Wind is moving air. ☐
b Wind is caused by the movement of trees and cars. ☐
c A compass is a device for measuring wind speed. ☐
d A warm day in summer has a temperature of about 23 °C. ☐

15 a All plants require sunlight and water to grow. ☐
b Plants are unlikely to be badly affected by very heavy rainfall. ☐
c Weather is the most important factor in farming. ☐
d Flooding is a disaster because it washes away the rich topsoil. ☐

16 a There is very little natural change in the landscape. ☐
b Our landscape changes very slowly. ☐
c The earth's crust formed mountain ranges. ☐
d Movement of the earth's crust causes volcanoes and earthquakes today. ☐
e The earth's crust is no longer moving. ☐
f Erosion can change the path of a river. ☐
g Sand and pebbles can be carried long distances in rivers. ☐

17 a Earthquakes can make large pieces of land sink or rise. ☐
b Volcanoes produce fire and smoke but have little effect on the landscape. ☐

Extensions

18 a A true fossil always shows the whole plant or animal. ☐
b The bones of animals can become fossils by mineral replacement. ☐
c Fossils are only found in sedimentary rock. ☐
d There are no fossils being formed today. ☐

19 a Leaves, stems, roots and flowers are all plant organs. ☐
b Food is made in the leaf of a plant. ☐
c Unlike animals plants have no organs. ☐

20 a Plants carry out photosynthesis to reproduce. ☐
b During the day plants are useful in hospitals since they make oxygen. ☐

continued ▶

Name ____________________

c Without plants there could be no animals on earth. ☐

d The word equation for photosynthesis is water + carbon dioxide → sugar + oxygen. ☐

e Plants carry out photosynthesis all day and all night in summer ☐

f Plants that lose their leaves in winter cannot carry out photosynthesis then. ☐

21 a Some gases are lighter in weight than others. ☐

b Fairground balloons float because they contain a lighter-than-air gas. ☐

c We cannot feel air because it has no weight. ☐

22 a Colour is an important property of soil. ☐

b Soil acidity can be measured with newspaper. ☐

c Soil drainage depends on how deep the soil is. ☐

d Size of soil particles has no effect on soil properties. ☐

23 a An empty cup has air in it. ☐

b There is no air below ground level. ☐

c There is no air above cloud level. ☐

d When a lid is put on a plastic box, the box will have no air in it. ☐

24 a The strength of the wind is a more important weather factor than the direction of the wind. ☐

b The speed of movement of a low affects how quickly the weather will change. ☐

c Wind coming from the sea to land brings rain. ☐

d A low usually brings better weather than a high. ☐

Unit 1 Lively places

Name ____________________

Complete each sentence. Put the correct words in each blank space.

1 The place around you is called your ____________________.
Three examples are

● ____________________ ● ____________________ ● ____________________.

2 Things that affect where an animal or plant can live are the

____________________ and geographical factors such as ____________________

and ____________________.

3 Soils are different because they are formed by the ____________________

of different ____________________.

Farmers improve their soil by adding chemicals called ____________________.
Adding too much chemical can damage the environment by causing

____________________.

4 Important weather measurements are

● ____________________ ● ____________________ ● ____________________.

Weather can cause natural disasters for farmers such as

____________________ and ____________________. The movement of

____________________ over Britain causes weather changes.

5 Population means the ____________________ of any living thing. It would

take too long to find the population by counting all living things. An

____________________ of the population is made by taking several

____________________ and counting the number in these.

Plant populations can be sampled using a ____________________.

If the whole population is killed the animal or plant becomes

____________________.

continued ▶

Name ____________________

6 Plants and animals are linked in a food ____________________.

Green plants trap energy from the ____________________ to make

____________________.

An animal that eats another animal is called a ____________________. The

animal that is eaten is called the ____________________.

7 We need to protect the environment. This is called ____________________.

The environment can be harmed by many kinds of ____________________.

For example,

- ____________________ from chimneys
- ____________________ from ____________________
- ____________________ from ____________________
- noise from ____________________.

8 There are good indicators of the level of pollution in the environment. Three examples are

- ____________________
- ____________________
- ____________________.

9 The environment we see has been formed over ____________________ of years.
Slow changes are caused by movements of the earth's crust and by the

effects of weather called ____________________ and ____________________.

Faster changes can be caused by ____________________ and

____________________.

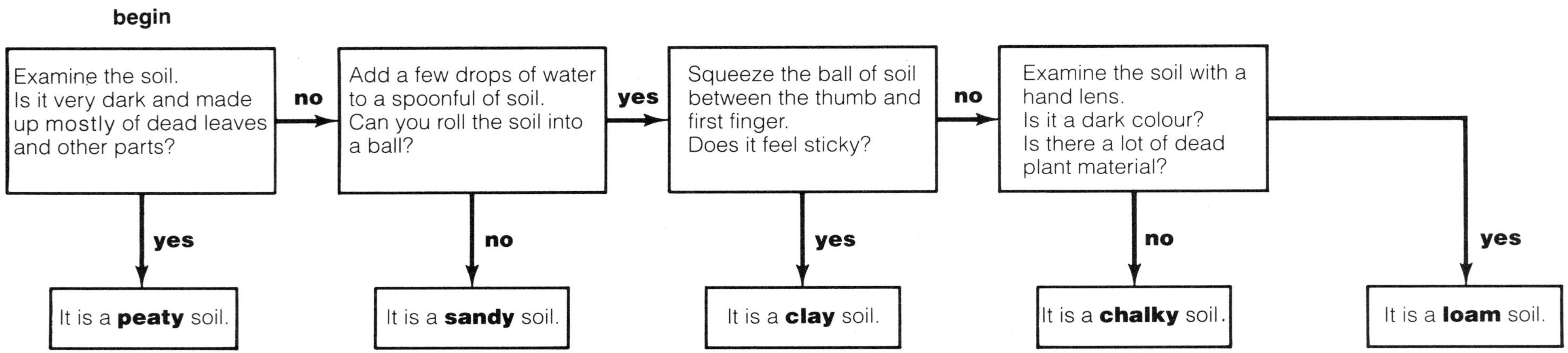
begin
Examine the soil.
Is it very dark and made up mostly of dead leaves and other parts?
no
Add a few drops of water to a spoonful of soil.
Can you roll the soil into a ball?
yes
Squeeze the ball of soil between the thumb and first finger.
Does it feel sticky?
no
Examine the soil with a hand lens.
Is it a dark colour?
Is there a lot of dead plant material?
yes
It is a **peaty** soil.
no
It is a **sandy** soil.
yes
It is a **clay** soil.
no
It is a **chalky** soil.
yes
It is a **loam** soil.

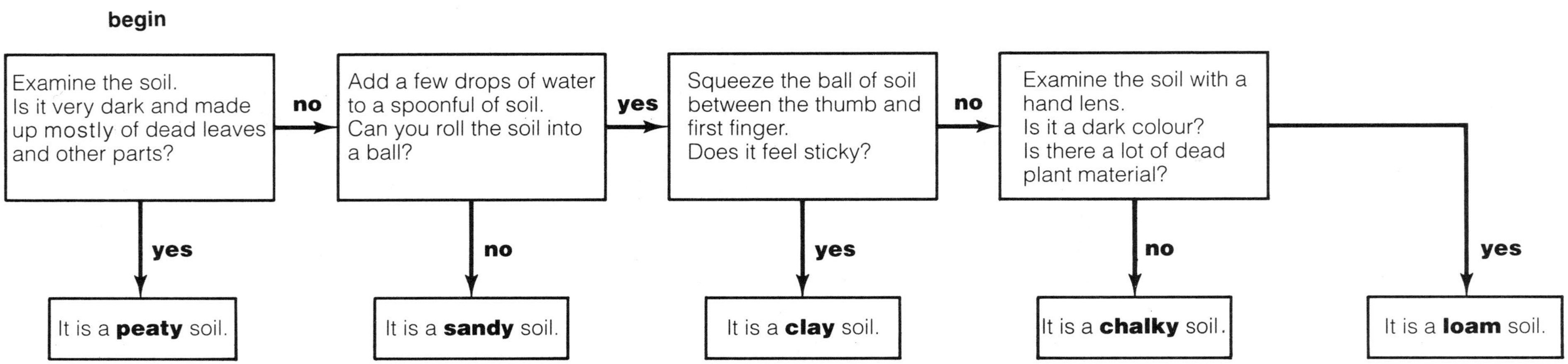
begin
Examine the soil.
Is it very dark and made up mostly of dead leaves and other parts?
no
Add a few drops of water to a spoonful of soil.
Can you roll the soil into a ball?
yes
Squeeze the ball of soil between the thumb and first finger.
Does it feel sticky?
no
Examine the soil with a hand lens.
Is it a dark colour?
Is there a lot of dead plant material?
yes
It is a **peaty** soil.
no
It is a **sandy** soil.
yes
It is a **clay** soil.
no
It is a **chalky** soil.
yes
It is a **loam** soil.

Wind chart

You can estimate the speed of the wind from some simple observations.

Description	**Observations**	**Average speed** miles per hour
Calm	Smoke rises up	0
Light air	Smoke drifts slightly	2
Light breeze	Wind felt on face, leaves rustle	5
Gentle breeze	Leaves and small twigs always moving	10
Moderate breeze	Dust and loose paper in the air	15
Fresh breeze	Small trees start swaying	21
Strong breeze	Large branches moving	28
Near gale	Whole trees moving, some resistance when walking	35
Gale	Twigs break off trees, resistance when walking	42
Strong gale	Slight damage to buildings	50
Storm	Trees fall over, buildings damaged	59

Wind chart

You can estimate the speed of the wind from some simple observations.

Description	**Observations**	**Average speed** miles per hour
Calm	Smoke rises up	0
Light air	Smoke drifts slightly	2
Light breeze	Wind felt on face, leaves rustle	5
Gentle breeze	Leaves and small twigs always moving	10
Moderate breeze	Dust and loose paper in the air	15
Fresh breeze	Small trees start swaying	21
Strong breeze	Large branches moving	28
Near gale	Whole trees moving, some resistance when walking	35
Gale	Twigs break off trees, resistance when walking	42
Strong gale	Slight damage to buildings	50
Storm	Trees fall over, buildings damaged	59

Weather chart

Date	Temperature °C	Wind direction	Wind speed	Cloud conditions

Weather chart

Date	Temperature °C	Wind direction	Wind speed	Cloud conditions

Weather chart

Date	Temperature °C	Wind direction	Wind speed	Cloud conditions

Soil organisms

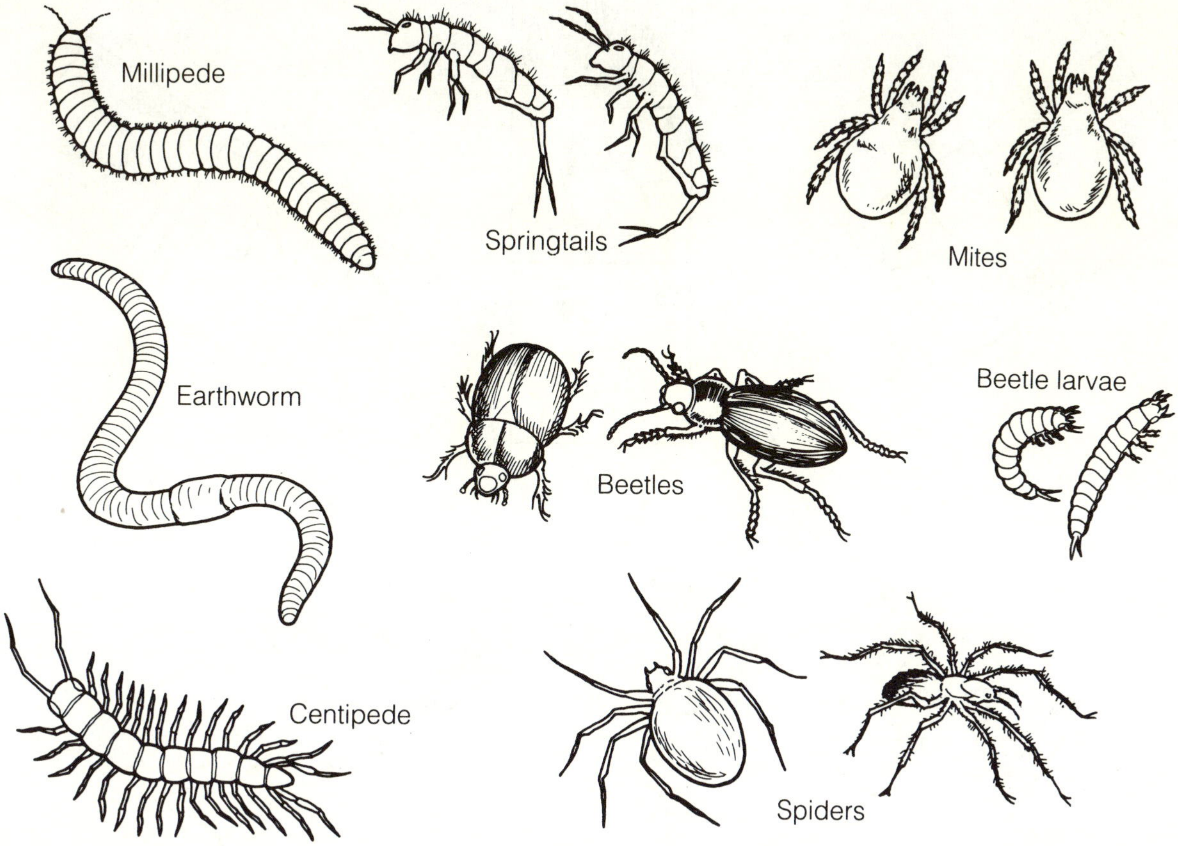

Soil organisms

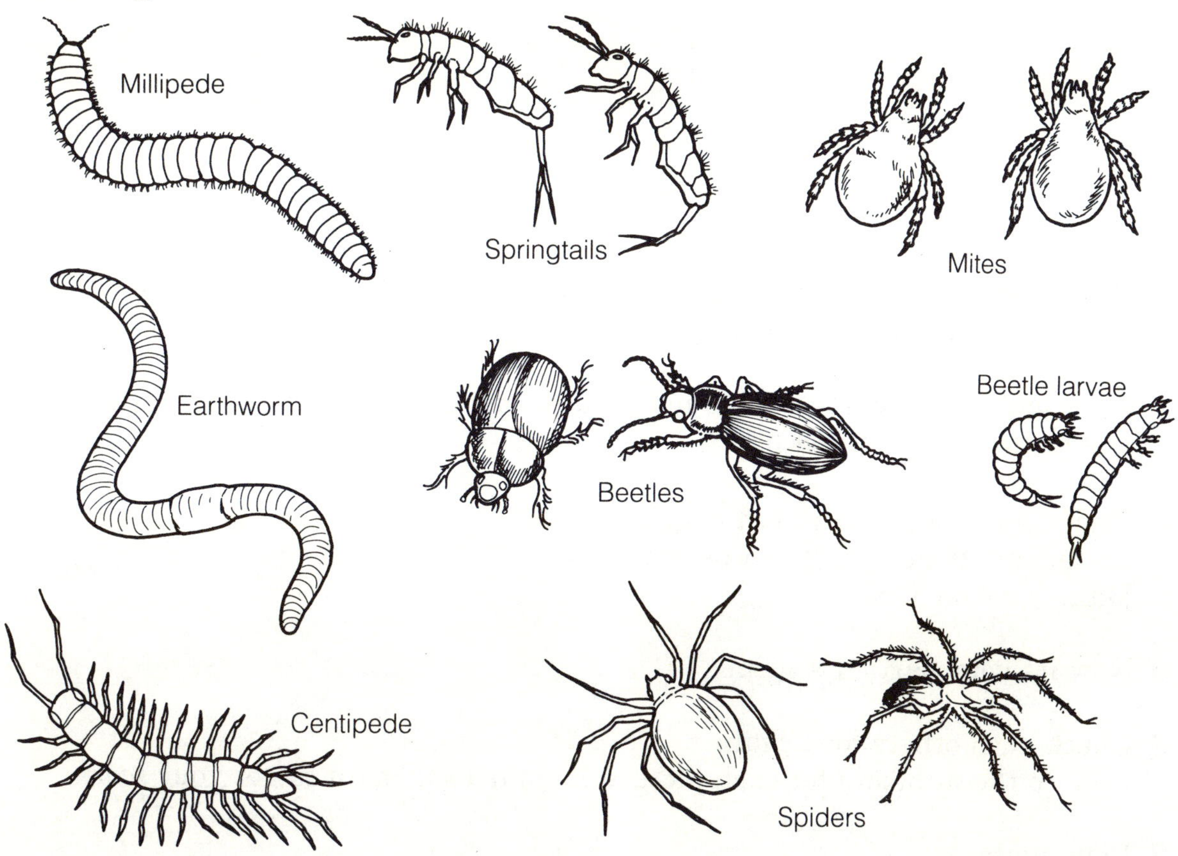

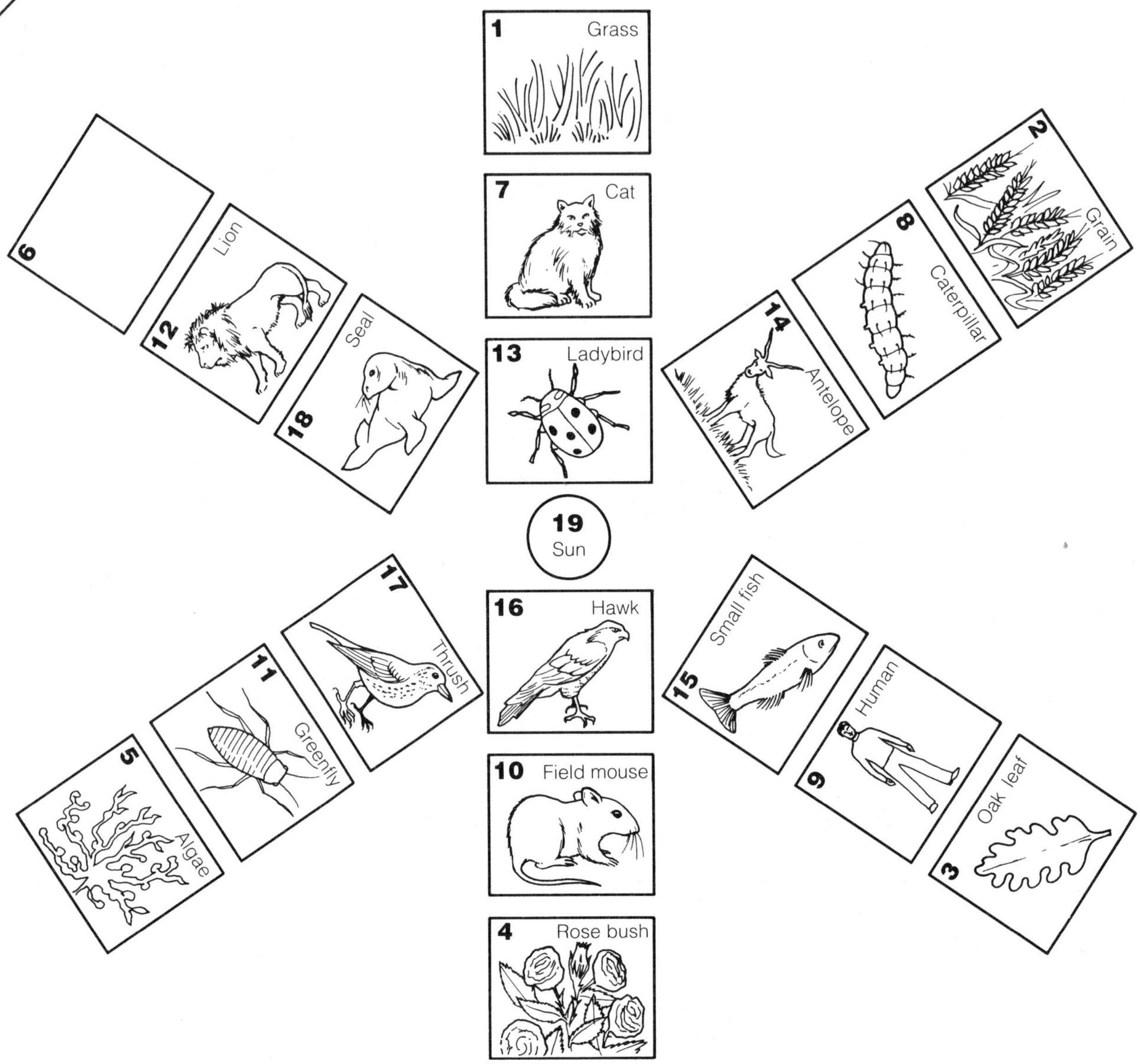

Rules

1. Play with a partner.
2. Throw the die. The number tells you where to start. If you throw a 6, you may choose any number from 1 to 5.
3. Work out the **longest** possible food chain that includes this plant. Write your food chain in the correct order.
4. Underline a predator in red pencil.
   Underline its prey in green pencil.
   Make a colour key.
5. Now its your partner's turn.
6. Check each others food chain.
   Add up the numbers for each picture in your food chain to get your score.
7. Play again.

Understanding Science Conservation Award Scheme

Application form

Level of award applied for: Bronze/Silver/Gold

Name(s) of applicant(s):

Write down the number of points scored for each task that you complete, then add up the total number of points gained

Task	Points scored
1	
2	
3	
4	
5	
6	
7	
8	
9	
10	
11	
12	
13	
14	
15	
16	
17	
18	
19	
20	
21	
Total	

Teacher's signature

Understanding Science Conservation Award Scheme

Application form

Level of award applied for: Bronze/Silver/Gold

Name(s) of applicant(s):

Write down the number of points scored for each task that you complete, then add up the total number of points gained

Task Points scored
1
2
3
4
5
6
7
8
9
10
11
12
13
14
15
16
17
18
19
20
21
Total

Teacher's signature

Understanding Science Conservation Award

By the power invested in me I hereby award

name

the order of Conservation Volunteer at the

Gold/Silver/Bronze level

for services to the environment

signature

date

Understanding Science Conservation Award

By the power invested in me I hereby award

name

the order of Conservation Volunteer at the

Gold/Silver/Bronze level

for services to the environment

signature

date

Unit 2 Substances

Describing elements and compounds

The first three topics develop the skills of finding information about substances and organising it in a structured way. Experimental observations and facts from reference books about exemplar elements are compiled into a detailed description under the headings of 'appearance', 'properties' and 'uses'. The periodic table is introduced as another structured way of presenting information. The next four topics concern the concept of making and breaking compounds in chemical reactions. Some general knowledge of the periodic table, the nature of an element and of a compound is presented as the necessary foundation for later work (such as AT6, levels 6 and 7 and AT8, level 7 of the National Curriculum). Specific facts about hydrogen, oxygen, copper, iron, magnesium, zinc, rust (defined as iron oxide), acids and alkalis are also noted in preparation for work on AT7, levels 6 and 7. The final three topics comprise a practical investigation, an oral exercise that also requires the finding and organising of information, and a short reading exercise. In addition to meeting the general demands of Attainment Target 1, this unit deals specifically with the development of AT1, levels 4c, 4h, 4i, 4j.

Core and Reinforcement	Extension
2.1 Describing substances	*AT 3–6a*
Find out about the appearance, burning, melting point and uses of oxygen and hydrogen (using experiments and books). *page 26*	Practise the test for oxygen and use it to find out whether oxygen is produced in three experiments *page 134*
Observe, measure and record accurately. Collate information in a given format.	Follow instructions. Use a given procedure to test for oxygen in unfamiliar experiments.
2.2 Organising information *AT 6–3b, 4b*	
Find out information about several metals and organise it into the given categories of appearance, properties and uses. *page 28*	Design, do and report upon experiments to compare the strength of several metals. *page 135*
Observe, measure and record accurately. Collate information in a given format.	Extract information from a labelled diagram. Devise an experiment which is a fair comparison.
2.3 Periodic table	*AT 6–3b*
Use the periodic table provided. *page 30*	Test some properties of metal and non-metal elements. *page 136*
Extract information from the periodic table. Translate from element name to symbol.	Devise and carry out experiments to test given properties. Recognise patterns in experimental data.
2.4 Elements make compounds *AT 8–6c*	
Make water from its constituent elements. Break up copper chloride and water using electricity. *page 32*	Electroplate a coin. *page 137*
Communicate observations in a written report. Translate an observation into a word equation.	Communicate observations in a written report.

Core and Reinforcement

2.5 Rust—An important compound

Identify rust using an indicator.
Use three methods of surface coating to prevent rusting. *page 34*

Observe.
Follow largely diagrammatic instructions.
Explain the technology of simple rust prevention.

2.6 Acids and alkalis *AT 6-5b*

Use a number of indicators to identify acid and alkali, and universal indicator to determine the pH of household solutions. *page 36*

Follow instructions and observe.
Record information in a self-designed table, given the number of columns.

2.7 Chemical reactions *AT 7-4a, 6c*

Carry out several changes and identify the aspects which make them chemical reactions. *page 38*

Follow instructions and observe.
Recognise instances of given criteria from observations.

2.8 Problem—Stick with milk

Make a glue from milk.
Investigate the effect of changing the reactants in the procedure. *page 40*

Follow instructions.
Extract information from a diagram.
Devise an experimental procedure that fulfils the given requirements.
Draw a conclusion from self-sought results.

2.9 Talkabout—Metals

Prepare and deliver a short talk on the appearance, properties and uses of one of six metals. *page 41*

Extract relevant information from given sources.
Explain some technological applications of a metal.
Communicate observations logically and concisely.

2.10 Readabout—The earth's resources *AT 6-3a; AT 7-4b, 5a*

Read a short passage about resources.
Interpret/compile small flow diagrams to describe how selected resources are used. *page 42*

Extract information from a given passage.
Translate from a flow diagram to a written description.
Translate from knowledge to flow diagrams.

Extension

AT 7-5c

Estimate the amount of oxygen in the air by burning and rusting experiments. *page 138*

Estimate sensibly.
Recognise and explain the unreliability in a given experimental procedure.

AT 6-5b

Make an indicator from plant material and use it to identify acids and alkalis. *page 139*

Follow instructions and observe.
Record information in a self-designed table, given no help.

AT 7-4a, 6c

Carry out a sequence of chemical reactions beginning with limestone. *page 140*

Follow a sequence of procedures and observe.
Apply given criteria to observations.

Equipment
required for each pupil group

Notes

2.1—Describing substances

- Two stoppered tubes of oxygen

Provide oxygen in labelled test tubes. Alternatively, allow pupils to fill their own tubes from a Winchester bottle by displacement with water (as shown below).

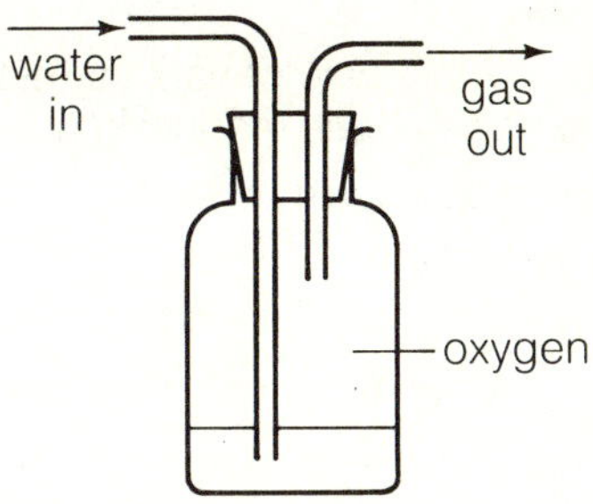

- Wooden splints
- Bunsen burner and heatproof mat
- Safety glasses
- Access to data book with melting points of elements
- Access to junior encyclopaedia/reference book/textbook with information about uses of oxygen and hydrogen
- Two stoppered test tubes of hydrogen
- Test-tube holder

Oxygen's melting point is −218°C.
It is used to help people breathe (hospital, diving) and help things burn (oxy-acetylene and blast furnace).
Provide hydrogen in labelled tubes. Make in the prep room **not** in the lab—using zinc and 2 M hydrochloric acid (consult the department's laboratory manual).
Hydrogen's melting point is −259°C.
It is used to make margarine, to weld metals, to make ammonia (fertilisers, explosives, dyes) and was used as a rocket fuel.

Extension

- Stoppered tube of oxygen
- Bunsen burner and heatproof mat
- Wooden splint
- Fresh lemonade
- Small cubes of raw potato
- 10 vol hydrogen peroxide solution
- Safety glasses
- Baking powder (sodium hydrogencarbonate)
- Vinegar (2 M ethanoic acid)

Make with a Sodastream, if available

2.2—Organising information

- Safety glasses
- Two 2 cm strips of iron (or wire)
- Two 2 cm strips of magnesium ribbon
- Sandpaper
- Access to balance
- Access to data book with melting points
- Sharp nail (to scratch metal with)
- Hot water in a beaker
- Battery, bulb and 3 connecting wires
- 2 M hydrochloric acid
- Test tube and rack
- Bunsen burner and heatproof mat
- Tongs
- Two 2 cm thin strips of zinc foil
- Two 2 cm thin strips of copper foil

The description is of copper metal.
Iron melts at 1540°C. Magnesium melts at 650°C.
Pupils must not look directly at burning magnesium. The light is intense and it contains some UV. You may wish to issue blue glass to pupils for this observation.
At this point, the teacher may wish to show pupils the appearance of the alkali metals and their reaction with water. Use sodium and lithium. Set up the experiment behind a safety screen. Pupils should wear safety glasses. Cut a small piece from the metal with a scalpel on a paper towel. The shiny metallic surface will tarnish quickly. Teaching points here are the softness of the metal, the dull coating of oxide/peroxide compared with the shiny metal inside and the mark left on the paper by the oil in the container. Add a pea-sized piece of metal to water in an open pneumatic trough. Note fizzing but do not attempt to collect or light the hydrogen

Equipment
required for each pupil group

Notes

gas. Test pH with paper and show that the water has been changed by the metal.
Alternatively, show a video sequence which illustrates these reactions.

Extension

- Safety glasses
- About 10 cm of thin wire of various metals; e.g. copper, nichrome, steel, magnesium, aluminium
- Clamp stand plus G-clamp
- Child's sand bucket
- 100 g masses
- Sponge or polystyrene to catch the falling bucket
- Strips of metal, if possible the same as in the first experiment

Fix the clamp stand to the bench.

2.3—Periodic table
No equipment required

Extension

- Samples of copper, iron, aluminium, zinc, sulphur, carbon, iodine (solid chunks if possible)
- Battery/power pack
- Connecting leads
- Crocodile clips
- Bulb
- Hot water at about 80°C
- Heat-sensitive paper/thermometer (strip)
- Small test tube (to hold element being tested)
- Mortar and pestle

Alternatively, could use hot plate with small wide-necked glass container acting as a receptacle for element being tested.
Care: iodine sublimes at 114°C.

2.4—Elements make compounds

- Pre-filled gas jar of chlorine
- Tongs
- Dutch metal (used as thin 'copper' foil)

Prepare chlorine according to standard laboratory manual (from a small amount of potassium permanganate crystals and concentrated hydrochloric acid).
The experiment should be conducted in a fume cupboard. Push the metal into the chlorine with the tongs.
The teacher could also demonstrate the reaction of aluminium and iodine in a fume cupboard. Use equal amounts (about a spatula-full) of powdered aluminium and powdered iodine. The aluminium must be fairly new otherwise it will have oxidised. The iodine can be ground in a mortar and pestle. Mix the powders on top of a tin lid. Pile up into a volcano shape. To initiate the reaction, add a few drops of water to the tip of the volcano.

- Water indicator paper is cobalt chloride paper.

This can be made by soaking filter paper in a solution of cobalt(II) chloride and drying in an oven. The blue paper is cut up into small pieces and kept in a desiccator until required. It turns from blue to pink in the presence of water.

- **Dry** test tube of hydrogen
- Copper(II) chloride (green solid)

Equipment
required for each pupil group

Notes

- Two carbon rods

To keep rods apart use a petri dish lid with two holes in it.
Gases can be collected from water more easily if the electrolysis is conducted in a plastic beaker which has the electrodes fitted to its base.

- 100 cm^3 beaker
- Connecting leads and power pack (6V DC)
- Crocodile clips
- Bunsen burner, heatproof mat and spills
- Safety glasses

Extension
- Copper(II) sulphate solution (about 0.5 M)
- Nickel(II) sulphate solution (about 0.5 M)
- Copper and silver coins
- Materials for circuit (as in 2.4)
- Safety glasses

2.5—Rust—An important compound
- Small iron nails

To make rust indicator solution dissolve a few crystals of potassium hexacyanoferrate in 50 cm^3 of water. Put in a small dropper bottle.
Colour change is from pale yellow/green to dark blue/green.

- Sandpaper
- Rust indicator
- Salt water
- Test tubes and rack
- Access to display of rusty objects

Car parts are an excellent source.

- Three spillage trays, one for each nail treatment
- Three pairs of tongs
- Unwanted tin of paint
- Expanded polystyrene block

Nails can be stuck in polystyrene to dry.

- Small beaker of motor oil
- Small beaker of plastic powder
- 10 cm lengths of wire
- Bunsen burner and heatproof mat
- Copy of Rusting picture quiz cartoons (**R2.5**-p.198)

Extension
- Two boiling tubes
- Two beakers
- Wax taper (6 cm length)
- Coarse iron filings
- Vinegar

Rusting can be accelerated by soaking the iron filings in vinegar.

- Plasticine
- Holder for the boiling tube
- Bunsen burner and heatproof mat
- Labels

2.6—Acids and alkalis
- Safety glasses
- 1 M hydrochloric acid (labelled acid)
- 1 M sodium hydroxide (labelled alkali)
- Selection of four or five indicators in dropper bottles to include universal indicator and phenolphthalein
- Two test tubes and test-tube rack

Equipment

required for each pupil group

Notes

- Access to books which have information on uses of acids
- Household liquids in dropper bottles, including tea (very weak), coffee (very weak), lemonade, bleach, baking powder, lime juice, vinegar plus about 5 others
- Small pieces of universal indicator paper

Pupils could take a few pieces home.

- Spotting tile
- Coloured pencils or crayons

Extension

- Chopped red cabbage (or red petals or beetroot)

Most coloured petals will produce an indicator when boiled in water. Red cabbage liquid has several colour changes.

- 100 cm³ beaker
- Bunsen burner and heatproof mat
- Same selection of household liquids as above
- Tripod stand and gauze mat
- Dropper bottle

2.7—Chemical reactions

- Safety glasses

Reaction 1

- Copper(II) carbonate

Turns from green to black.

- Test tube and holder
- Bunsen burner and heatproof mat

Reaction 2

- Marble chip

Gas produced. Heat given off.

- Test tube
- 1 M hydrochloric acid in dropper bottle

Reaction 3

- Magic bottle contains 200 cm³ of 0.5 M sodium hydroxide solution with 6 g of glucose dissolved in a stoppered conical flask

On shaking, the colour turns from clear to blue. The blue will fade but will reappear when shaken again.

- 0.5 cm³ of methylene blue is added

An alternative is to add a tablet of resazurin or 1 cm³ of indigo carmine instead of the methylene blue. Colour changes are different.

Reaction 4

- Piece of granulated zinc
- Copper(II) sulphate solution

Copper sulphate solution should be only weakly blue.

- Test tube or small beaker

Heat produced, blue colour disappears, brown copper forms.

Reaction 5

- Cobalt(II) chloride solution

Purple solid formed.

- Sodium carbonate solution
- Test tube

Reaction 6

- Piece of calcium metal

Care: Teacher should keep the bottle of calcium. Gas produced.

- Wooden splint
- Test tube and rack

Equipment
required for each pupil group

Extension
- Marble chip
- Bunsen burner and heatproof mat
- Tripod stand and wire gauze
- Dropper
- Straw
- Filter funnel and filter paper
- 100 cm^3 glass beaker
- Conical flask
- Stirring rod
- Safety glasses

Notes

Use as limestone.

2.8—Problem—Stick with milk
- Pint of full-fat milk
- Water bath at 50°C (or hot water)
- Vinegar in dropper bottle
- Filter funnel and filter paper
- 2 M ammonia solution
- Beaker
- Several 10 cm squares of card
- Clamp stand
- Thread
- Hanger and slotted masses (10 g)

2.9—Talkabout—Metals
- Access to books which have information about the appearance, properties and uses of iron, titanium, aluminium, tin, uranium and gold

2.10—Readabout—The earth's resources
No equipment required

It may be necessary to introduce the idea of a flow diagram.

Assessment 2

The questions are designed to assess the skills and knowledge developed in the unit, as shown in the table. A selection of questions would be appropriate for a unit test.

Topic	*Core*	*Extension*
2.1	1, 2, 3	14, 15, 16
2.2	4, 5	17
2.3	6, 7	21
2.4	8, 9	—
2.5	10	19
2.6	11, 12	18
2.7	13	20
2.10	22	—

Answers

1 Hydrogen pops with a lit splint. Doesn't relight a glowing splint. Oxygen makes a lit splint brighter. Relights a glowing splint.
2 **a** B, **b** B **c** C.
3 Description organised in three paragraphs on appearance, properties, uses.
4 **a** (i) Sentence 3, (ii) sentence 2; (iii) sentence 1.
b Stands up to weather well, it can be cut and shaped, it is pleasant looking (*any two*).
c It dissolves in rain water.
d Natural.
5 **a** Light; **b** strong;
c cheap, strong, doesn't rot (*any one*);
d attractive, doesn't dissolve in water;
e good conductor.

6 a Ca, P, Mg, Fe.
b Phosphorus is a non-metal whereas the others are metals.
7 a Rust, water,
b Oxygen, hydrogen, nitrogen, helium (*any two*).
c Iron, silver, copper.
d Hydrogen + oxygen → water *or* iron + oxygen → rust.
e Fe, Ag, O, H, N, Cu, He (*any three*).
8 Z is iron sulphide; X and Y are iron/sulphur.
9 a Electrical
b Potassium iodide is the compound, the others are elements.
10 a Rust is not strong, it flakes off.
b Paint or oil it (*or* use grease or plastic coating).
c Iron + oxygen → iron oxide (rust).
11 a Different colour in acid and in alkali.
b Acid.
c Alkali.
d It is neutral.
12 Pure water pH7, conc. hydrochloric acid pH1 (actually less), vinegar about pH3, conc. sodium hydroxide pH14, ammonia pH10, salt water pH7.
13

	New substance?	**Energy change?**	**Reaction?**
a	X	✓	X
b	✓	✓	✓
c	X	✓	X
d	X	✓	X
e	✓	✓	✓

14 a **(i)** 'Chlorine is a green gas';
(ii) 'Reacts with very many substances;
(iii) 'It was used in the First World War as a weapon' *or* 'It is used to kill microbes in water';
(iv) Salt, disinfectants, pesticides, plastics (PVC), solvents (tetrachloroethane) (*any one*).
b It is a *compound* containing sodium and chlorine
c Kills microbes, poisonous.
d Destroys ozone layer.
15 a Put a glowing splint into oxygen gas, it will relight.
b Combustion.
c A compound containing two or more elements, one of which is oxygen.
16 a Oxygen helps the organism to get energy from food. The mouse survived for a day.
b Oxygen, water vapour.
c Oxygen.
17 Likely to get an experiment based on the work on page 135 of pupils' book.
Other methods possible. Each should (i) be feasible, (ii) control as many other variables as is reasonable.
Answer should indicate method, perhaps in a diagram, and describe what the meaning of the likely results is.
18 a (i) pH7; (ii) any pH number below 7.
b Lunch at 12.30 p.m., dinner at 6 p.m.
c Drops.
d The pH dropped so acid was made.
e Acid is produced each time you eat, this can cause decay.
19 a There is an energy change (heat produced etc.); also a change in appearance; new substances made (smoke).
b Oxygen.
c Smother/cover the flames with foam.
d Combustion means that a substance joins with oxygen to release heat energy and make a new substance (called an oxide).
20 a Compare answers with class notes.
b New substances are made; the limestone has a different pH than the limewater.
21 See page 136 of pupils' book.
22 See page 42 of pupils' book.

True/false 2

Each statement is marked as either true or false by the pupil. This gives a rapid assessment of a pupil's grasp of the Attainment Targets covered in the unit. The following list gives the Attainment Targets covered by each set of statements.

1	AT 6–3a	7	AT 7–5a
2	AT 6–3b	8	AT 7–6c
3	AT 6–4b	9	AT 8–6c
4	AT 6–5b	10	AT 3–6a
5	AT 7–4a	11	AT 7–5c
6	AT 7–4b		

1 You are given two test tubes full of a colourless gas.
Describe how you would find out if the gas was hydrogen or oxygen.

2 The diagrams show three possible ways of collecting a gas.

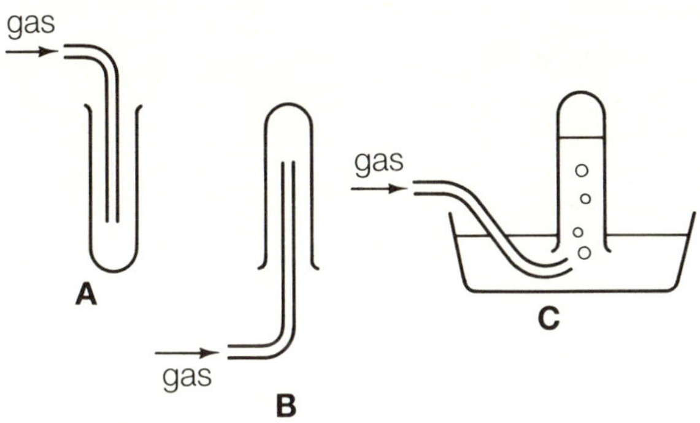

a Which way would you use to collect hydrogen, which is a light gas?
b Which way would you use to collect ammonia, which is a light soluble gas?
c Which way would you use to collect carbon dioxide, which is a heavy insoluble gas?

3 A really good description will be full of useful details.
Write a good scientific description of water. Organise your description under the headings *appearance, properties* and *uses.*

4 Read the following scientific description of limestone.

1 Limestone can be cut and shaped to form pleasant-looking blocks of building stone.
2 Limestone is soft and can dissolve in rain water, but it does however stand up to the weather well.
3 Limestone is a white solid which sometimes contains small fossilised sea creatures in it.

a Which sentence is about the (i) appearance, (ii) properties, (iii) uses?
b Give two reasons why limestone is used for building houses.
c Give one reason why limestone buildings would not last for thousands of years.
d Is limestone a natural or a synthetic material?

5 A substance is used for a particular job because it has a property which fits the job.
Which property is important in each of the following cases?
a Hydrogen is used to fill weather balloons.
b Steel is used to build cars.
c Plastic is used to make dustbins.
d Glass is used to make vases.
e Copper is used to make electrical wires.

6 The table shows part of the label of a packet of crisps.

Nutritional information	Per 100 g
Calcium	120 mg
Phosphorus	380 mg
Magnesium	178 mg
Iron	20 mg

Use a periodic table to answer the following questions.
a What are the chemical symbols for calcium, phosphorus, magnesium and iron?
b The substances listed are all elements. However, one of them is a different kind of element from the other three. Which one? Explain your answer.

7 Look at the following list of substances:

- iron
- silver
- oxygen
- rust
- hydrogen
- nitrogen
- copper
- helium
- water

Use a periodic table to answer the following questions.
a List the compounds.
b List two gases.
c List the metals.

continued ▶

d Write a word equation which connects together three of the substances.

e Write the symbol for three of the elements.

8 Look at the following word equation:

substance X + substance Y → substance Z

The names of the three substances are iron sulphide, iron and sulphur. Which is which?

9 The following word equation describes a chemical reaction:

potassium iodide → potassium + iodine

a What kind of energy could cause this chemical reaction?

b Identify each substance as either an element or a compound.

10 Rusting can only happen when oxygen and water are able to get at the iron metal. The iron will then form iron oxide. The iron oxide flakes off and the metal underneath begins to rust.

a Why might a rusty car be dangerous?

b What could you do to protect a car from rust?

c Write a word equation for the chemical reaction that forms rust.

11 **a** How does pH indicator work?

b If a substance has a pH of 4, is it an acid or an alkali?

c If a substance has a pH of 11, is it an acid or an alkali?

d If a substance has a pH of 7, what does this mean?

12 What are the pH values of these solutions?

- pure water
- concentrated hydrochloric acid
- vinegar (a weak acid)
- concentrated sodium hydroxide
- ammonia solution (a weak alkali)
- salt water

13 **Copy** and **complete** the table below which shows a number of possible chemical reactions.

Change observed	Is a new substance made?	Is there an energy change?	Is this a reaction?
a Bouncing a ball **b** Grilling meat **c** Melting ice cream **d** Chopping wood **e** Burning wood			

Extension questions

14 Chlorine is a green poisonous gas which reacts with very many substances. It was used in the First World War in 1915 as a weapon to kill soldiers.

Chlorine is a very important element. It is extracted from salt. On its own it is used to kill microbes in water. Chlorine atoms are also present in many disinfectants and pesticides and in other compounds like plastics (PVC) and solvents (tetrachloroethane).

Certain compounds of chlorine have been used for many years in aerosols and they are now thought to be responsible for the destruction of the world's ozone layer.

a Write down a phrase from the passage which describes

(i) the appearance of chlorine

(ii) a property of chlorine

(iii) a use for the element chlorine

(iv) a chemical compound which contains chlorine.

b Salt is called *sodium chloride* by scientists. Why do you think it has this name?

c What property of chlorine makes it useful in the treatment of water?

d What property of certain chlorine compounds is dangerous for the environment?

continued ▶

15 Oxygen is used up in both combustion and respiration. Compounds called oxides are made when substances join with oxygen.

a Describe the test for oxygen gas.
b In this test is the oxygen involved in combustion or respiration?
c What is an *oxide*?

16 The following report has been received about Planet Xwray:

We dropped a smouldering piece of cloth into the atmosphere and it flared up producing a lot of smoke. Other burning objects also flared up. When our pet mouse escaped onto the planet's surface, it ran off in search of food. It returned the next day because it was hungry. George fell over and broke his face mask. We quickly bundled him back into the shuttle and he has only a sore throat. Incidentally, the feet on the craft have begun to rust.

a What do you understand by the term respiration? Is there any evidence that the atmosphere of Planet Xwray supports respiration?
b What must be present in the atmosphere if the feet of the spacecraft have begun to rust?
c What gas do you think the astronaut was testing for when he used a smouldering cloth?

17 Describe a way of comparing the strength of iron and copper. Make sure that you mention how to make the comparison **fair**.

18 Guzzling Gus is a person who sometimes eats between meals. The graph below shows how the pH of Gus's mouth changes during the day.

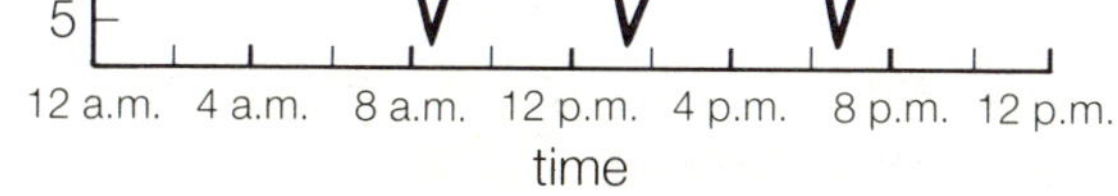

a (i) Which pH number represents neutral?
(ii) Which pH numbers represent acid?
b Gus eats breakfast at 8 a.m. When does he eat his lunch and his evening meal?
c What happens to the pH of his mouth immediately after a meal?
d Gus has eaten two chocolate bars during the day, one at 10 a.m. and the other at 3.30 p.m. What effect did these chocolate bars have on his mouth?
e Why is eating between meals likely to increase tooth decay?

19 Read this report of a fire.

Firemen were called to the M6 last week. A car had overheated and smoke was billowing out from under the bonnet. The car was smothered in foam and the fire was quickly controlled. Many of the materials in the car engine had been destroyed but the driver was unhurt.

a What evidence is there that this fire was a chemical reaction?
b What substance in the air is needed to help things burn?
c How did the firemen try to stop this substance from reaching the fire?
d Another word for burning is *combustion*. Write a definition of *combustion* that uses all your answers to questions a–c.

20 Limestone can be changed by two chemical reactions into limewater. The word equations below describe these changes.

(i) limestone → lime + carbon dioxide gas
(ii) lime + water → limewater
Limestone is neutral in water.
Limewater will turn universal indicator purple.

a Write the two word equations as full sentences, adding any details that you remember from the experiment.
b What evidence is given that this process is a chemical change?

21 Iron and carbon are both common elements. Write down two ways in which they are similar and two ways in which they are different.

22 Using two examples, explain why the earth's resources (raw materials) are so important.

True or False 2

Unit 2 Substances

Name ____________________

Put a tick after the statements which are true. Put a cross after the statements which are false.

1 a Human beings make all the substances that they need. ☐
b Plastic is a synthetic material. ☐
c Peat is a synthetic material. ☐
d A raw material is an uncooked material. ☐

2 a Metals are similar because they are strong. ☐
b Most metal elements are solid at room temperature. ☐
c All metals conduct heat and electricity well. ☐

3 a Iron is useful because it rusts. ☐
b Oxygen is useful because it allows respiration to take place. ☐
c Steel is useful because it is strong. ☐
d Magnesium is a light metal and would be useful for building aircraft. ☐

4 a A neutral solution has a pH of about 6. ☐
b A liquid with a pH of above 7 is an acid. ☐
c Pure water has a pH of 7. ☐
d Universal indicator goes red in pure water. ☐
e Universal indicator goes green in polluted water. ☐
f Universal indicator goes blue in alkali. ☐
g Phenolphthalein is an indicator. It is one colour in acid and a different colour in alkali. ☐

5 a There is often a change in appearance when a chemical reaction occurs. ☐
b A chemical reaction occurs when water boils. ☐
c A chemical reaction occurs when toast burns. ☐
d A chemical reaction occurs when bread is baked. ☐
e A chemical reaction can occur without any new materials being formed. ☐

6 a Natural materials can be changed into useful substances by chemical reactions. ☐
b Oil can be changed into lots of useful substances. ☐
c Coal is good for burning but not for making other substances. ☐

7 a Air contains oxygen and nothing else of use. ☐
b Most metals are separated from rock by chemical reactions. ☐
c Fossil fuels are made from dead animals and plants. ☐
d Coal, oil, natural gas and wood are all fossil fuels. ☐

8 a Most chemical reactions give out energy. ☐
b Some chemical reactions use up energy. ☐
c Burning wood is a chemical reaction. ☐
d Freezing ice cream is a chemical reaction. ☐
e Heating soup is a chemical reaction. ☐

9 a $y + mc^2 = 2d$ is an example of a word equation. ☐
b water → hydrogen + oxygen is an example of a word equation. ☐

continued ▶

Name ______________________

Extensions

10 a Oxygen and energy can be released from food. ☐

b Plants make food by respiration. ☐

c The main energy change in respiration is stored → heat. ☐

11 a When a substance burns, the chemical reaction is called combustion. ☐

b Respiration is a chemical reaction which happens in the air. ☐

c Respiration and combustion both use up oxygen. ☐

d Respiration and combustion both use up energy. ☐

Summary 2

Unit 2 Substances

Name ____________________

Complete each sentence. Put the correct word(s) in each blank space.

1 A good description is full of facts.
For example, three facts about the element oxygen are

- ____________________
- ____________________
- ____________________

Facts can be remembered better if they are organised into sets.
Facts about a substance can be organised into three sets:

- ____________________ (what it looks like)
- ____________________ (what it does)
- ____________________ (what it is used for).

2 All substances are built from elements. The elements are listed in the ____________________ table. There are ____________________ natural elements and most of these are metals. The metals are on the ____________________-hand side of the table.

3 When elements join together a ____________________ is formed.
Water is a compound. It is made by joining hydrogen and oxygen.

hydrogen + oxygen → water

(element) + (____________________) → (____________________)

Rust is also a compound. It is made by joining ____________________ and ____________________.

4 Acids are also compounds. Acids can be cancelled out and made safe with ____________________.

5 Acids and alkalis can be detected by using indicators. An indicator is a chemical which will change ____________________ when the pH changes.

6 Universal indicator has a range of colours.

When put in	pH number	Colour	Two examples
Acid	Less than ____	Red	________ and ________
Neutral solution	Exactly ____	______	________ and ________
Alkali	____ than ____	______	________ and ________

7 Elements and compounds can change into new substances. This change is called a chemical ____________________. You can spot a chemical ____________________ because it can

- make new ____________________
- transfer ____________________ to the surroundings.

Unit 3 Good health

Finding out about the body

The first eight topics in this unit introduce inter-related aspects of health and fitness. Throughout pupils are encouraged to work co-operatively and some important learning strategies are embedded in the various activities. The skills of extracting information and of translating it from one form to another are highlighted. Some general knowledge of the main body systems and their functions, and a more detailed treatment of diet and digestion, heart and lungs and describing and measuring fitness is presented. The final three topics comprise an exercise to design a board game, a discussion to generate a short radio play or advertisement and a reading exercise. The material covers Attainment Target 3 of the National Curriculum. In addition to meeting the general demands of Attainment Target 1, this unit deals specifically with the development of AT1, levels 3b, 3i and levels 4f, 4g, 4h, 4i, 4j.

Core and Reinforcement

3.1 Body systems *AT 3–4a, 5e*

Learn about the name, position and function of the main body systems.
Classify a series of health hazards into 4 sets.
page 44

Extract information from diagram and text.

3.2 Food for health *AT 3–4b, 5b*

Learn about the components of foods.
Carry out food tests to identify 4 basic components. *page 46*

Follow outline instructions to conduct a matrix of chemical tests.
Extract information from text and diagrams to complete a table.

3.3 Healthy teeth *AT 3–4b*

Learn about tooth types and tooth decay.
Examine position and function of tooth types.
Demonstrate the effect of brushing on distribution of plaque on teeth. *page 48*

Extract information and communicate ideas in continuous prose.
Communicate results of an experiment in written form.

Extension

AT 3–5e, 6a

Interpret and answer questions on a flow diagram of body systems.
page 141

Extract information from a flow diagram.

AT 3–4b, 5b

Estimate energy and protein requirements from measurement of body weight.
Calculate energy and protein content for a meal from nutritional information on food packaging. *page 142*

Carry out single and double operation arithmetic calculations.

AT 3–4b

Read and discuss a passage on the fluoride debate.
Answer questions from the passage.
page 143

Extract relevant information from graph and text.

Core and Reinforcement	Extension
3.4 The fate of food *AT 3–5c*	*AT 3–5c; AT 8–6c*
Play a bingo game to learn parts and functions of parts of the digestive system. Set up an experimental model to demonstrate the absorption of digested food from gut to blood. *page 50*	Carry out an experiment, with a control, on the digestion of fat by lipase. *page 144*
Follow a given procedure to learn the relationship between a structure and its function. Communicate the method, result and conclusions of an experiment in written form.	Follow a complex series of instructions. Apply knowledge to explain results of an experiment. Communicate method, result and conclusions in written form.
3.5 Heart and lungs *AT 3–5b, e*	*AT 3–4b, 5d, 6e*
Observe dissection of heart and lungs. Observe and note main features of each organ. Measure pulse rate and observe blood capillaries in finger. *page 52*	Read a passage and tabulated information on drug abuse. Plot a bar graph. *page 145*
Communicate facts in written and diagrammatic form from observations. Make measurements using a timer.	Extract relevant information from text and tabulated information. Translate tabulated information into a bar graph.
3.6 Fit for life *AT 3–5b*	*AT 3–5b*
Use measurements of pulse rate as an indicator of fitness and efficiency of training. Measure lung capacity. *page 54*	Complete a colour-coded activity clock to show range of activities in a single day. *page 146*
Make measurements with a timer. Carry out single operation calculations. Plot a line graph. Communicate observations in a written form.	Extract information from a table and text. Prepare a colour key.
3.7 Fit for nothing *AT 3–4b, 6e*	*AT 3–4b, 6e*
Learn about the dangers of smoking and alcohol. Observe the effects of smoke in a smoking machine. Alter the message on a cigarette or alcohol advertisement to warn of the dangers of smoking/drinking. *page 56*	Conduct a survey on pupils' understanding of the effects and dangers of alcohol. *page 147*
Communicate scientific facts and ideas in the form of continuous prose. Carry out single operation arithmetic calculations.	Devise a questionnaire. Collate and analyse data collected. Communicate results of survey in written, diagrammatic, graphical form.
3.8 Learning *AT 3–5e*	*AT 3–5e*
Carry out simple experiments on memory and learning. *page 58*	Carry out simple experiments on factors that affect reaction time. *page 148*
Extract information from a diagram. Communicate results and ideas in written form.	Plot a bar graph of data collected. Extract relevant information from text.

Core and Reinforcement

3.9 Problem—Design a game *AT 3-4b, 5b*

> Design a board game based on knowledge and understanding of fitness and health. *page 60*

Apply knowledge and understanding to devise rules and game plan for a board game.

3.10 Talkabout—Smoking and health *AT 3-4b, 5d, 6e*

> Prepare a short audio tape or drama script using information provided. *page 61*

Extract information from a variety of sources. Devise a drama based on collation of extracted information, knowledge and understanding.

3.11 Readabout—Body defences *AT 3-4b, 5d*

> Read a passage on body defences and answer questions on this. *page 62*

Extract relevant information from text.

Extension

Equipment
required for each pupil group

3.1—Body systems

- Scissors
- Glue
- Timer
- Body sheet **(R3.1A)**
- Health-hazard cards **(R3.1B)**

Notes: This topic introduces some learning strategies. Pupils should work in pairs for effective discussion. A time limit should be placed on this activity.

Extension
No equipment required

3.2—Food for health

- Small pieces of various fresh foods, e.g. biscuit, bread, apple, potato, raisin, tomato, cereal
- Clinistix
- Albustix
- Filter paper
- Dropping bottle iodine soln.
- Test-tube rack
- 4 test tubes
- Stirring rod
- Buffet-table diagram **(R3.2)**
- Coloured pencils

Notes: Pupils should work in groups of four and each group should devise its own strategy for carrying out all tests on different foods.
Benedict's solution is an alternative to Clinistix.
The biuret test is an alternative to Albustix: place liquid food in test-tube, add an equal volume of NaOH solution (10 g/100 cm^3), add 10 drops of dilute $CuSO_4$ (1 g/100 cm^3), shake test-tube—violet colour indicates protein.
Care: spilled NaOH (sodium hydroxide/caustic soda) solution will damage bench tops, clothing and skin.

Extension

- Bathroom scales (kg)
- Collection of food wrappers from prepared foods

Notes: The formulae provided give a rough guide to energy and protein needs. Pupils can then calculate the contribution that one meal makes to their needs.

Equipment
required for each pupil group

3.3—Healthy teeth

- Hand mirror
- Slice of apple
- Disclosing tablet
- Vaseline
- Toothpaste
- 2 small squares aluminium foil
- 1 light microscope
- Red pencil
- Graph paper
- Jaw diagram **(R3.3)**

Extension
No equipment required

3.4—The fate of food

- Paper/cloth bag
- Dropping bottle of iodine solution
- Clinistix
- 250 cm^3 bottle 5% glucose solution.
- 250 cm^3 bottle 5% starch solution.
- 15 cm length visking tubing
- Cotton thread
- Boiling tube
- Test-tube rack
- Spotting tile
- 2 dropper pipettes
- Bingo cards **(R3.4A)**
- Bingo caller cards **(R3.4B)**
- Digestion summary sheet **(R3.4C)**
- Scissors

Extension

- 100 cm^3 fresh milk
- 100 cm^3 fresh 5% lipase solution
- Universal indicator solution
- pH colour chart
- Marker pen
- 2 syringes (5 cm^3)
- 2 test tubes
- Beaker of warm water

3.5—Heart and lungs

- Heart and lungs
- Coloured pencils
- Stethoscope
- Dropper bottle of oil
- Timer
- Binocular microscope
- Heart diagram **(R3.5)**
- Lung diagram **(R3.5)**

Notes

Pupils should be asked in advance to bring their own toothbrush to school. Pupils should rub a little vaseline on their lips before **sucking** the tablet. Brushing teeth will remove most of the stain. Good brushing technique is required.
The aluminium foil must be unused.
Scratches visible under the microscope show that toothpaste is abrasive.

The bingo game provides a strategy for learning some basic facts.
Answers are given on the caller cards.

The principle behind the experiment is that large molecules like starch can't get through the visking tubing (gut wall), but smaller molecules like glucose can. Demonstrate by using poppet beads and a cardboard cylinder punctured with holes.

Lipase enzyme changes neutral fat in the milk into acidic fatty acids and glycerol. The pH change is seen by a colour change in the experimental test tube from green to orange/yellow.
Tube 2 is a control and will not change.
The importance of controls could be discussed with the pupils.

Normally available from a local slaughterhouse or friendly butcher. A video could be used as an alternative to dissection. Biologist colleagues can give in-service help on dissection. The activities introduce learning strategies. For the lungs, pupils could write as much as they can during the dissection, or after it. The main task then is to collate and sequence the information as a group to generate an accurate set of notes.

Equipment
required for each pupil group

Notes

Extension
- Graph paper
- Coloured pencils

The very negative effects of drug abuse should be very firmly stressed.

3.6—Fit for life
- Timer
- Coloured pencils
- Disinfectant solution
- Bell jar (or plastic container) with graduated scale from 5 to 0 litres with 0.25 l intervals
- Rubber tubing
- Training graph **(R3.6)**

The rubber tubing should be disinfected after each pupil and rinsed in clean water. Alternatively, straws can be used.
The experiment is best carried out with the bell jar in a sink to minimise spillage.
Training is only effective if heart rate is increased to a safe (as defined by given formula) higher level for about 30 minutes 3 times per week.

Extension
- Activity clock **(RE3.6)**
- Coloured pencils

Pupils should prepare an activity clock for their most active day of the week which is normally a Saturday.

3.7—Fit for nothing
- Glass U-tube with two side arms
- 2 corks to fit U-tube
- Rubber tubing to fit U-tube side arms
- Universal indicator solution
- Cotton/ceramic wool
- Filter pump
- Felt pens
- Glue
- Stencils
- Unlined white paper
- Cigarette adverts from magazines
- Alcohol adverts from magazines

Set up the apparatus as shown in the pupils' book in advance. Clean cotton wool should be used for each experiment.
Smoke is drawn through the U-tube, staining the cotton wool yellow. Some tar and moisture may be seen in the glass tubing. The indicator will go yellow showing the gases produced are acidic.

Collect adverts in advance. Pupils come up with interesting captions that have an alternative message.

Extension
- Clipboard
- Lined paper
- Coloured pencils
- Poster paper
- Graph paper

Pupils should question about 20 people. They should be encouraged to discuss how to collate, analyse and display their data.

3.8—Learning
- Retort stand
- Boss and clamp
- Small hand mirror
- Timer
- Tray 1—variety of 12–15 different objects
- Tray 2—variety of 12–15 different objects that can be grouped into four sets, such as writing implements, items of glassware, measuring devices, items of clothing, wooden objects or foods
- Star shapes **(R3.8)**

The mirror drawing can be quite addictive for some pupils. Others have enormous problems with it and may be sensitive about their inability to complete the star.

Equipment
required for each pupil group

Notes

Extension
- Reaction timer
- Computer-program reaction timer
- Ruler
- Explanation of ruler method **(RE3.8)**

Use whichever test is available.

3.9—Problem—Design a game
- A3 white paper
- Stencils
- Coloured paper
- Coloured pencils
- Glue
- Dice
- Plasticine
- Scissors
- Magazines

Pupils often produce remarkable games. The key is for each group to make a list of good and bad health points at the start.
Playing pieces can be made from cardboard or plasticine.
If time permits have the class list their criteria for a good game and vote on the best game produced.

Magazines can supply ready-made artwork for the games.

3.10—Talkabout—Smoking and health
- Tape recorder
- Blank C15 tape

Pupils enjoy this exercise but must be given a very tight time limit to produce a script based on the information available on the page.

3.11—Readabout—Body defences
No equipment required

Assessment 3

The questions are designed to assess the skills and knowledge developed in the unit, as shown in the table. A selection of questions would be appropriate for a unit test.

Topic	*Core*	*Extension*
3.1	1	8
3.2	2	9, 10
3.3	3	11
3.4	4	12
3.5	5a	13
3.6	5b	14
3.7	6	—
3.8	7	15

Answers

1 a A—lungs, B—brain, C—heart, D—stomach.
b A—5, B—1, C—2, D—3, E—3, F—4.
2 a (i) protein, **(ii)** growth/repair, **(iii)** fruit/vegetables, **(iv)** constipation/helps movement of food through gut.
b Add iodine, look for a blue-black colour to show presence of starch.
c Lack of a balanced diet *or* not enough of each of the basic food substances.
3 a (i) D; **(ii)** A, B, C, D; **(iii)** A, D; **(iv)** C; **(v)** A.
b Bacteria breaking down food.
c Gritty/scrapes the teeth clean of plaque.
4 a Most to least soluble: B, C, D, A.
b Maltose, amino acid, peptides, glycerol.
c Transport/blood system.
5 a Lungs: 2, 5, 7, 8. Heart: 1, 3, 4, 6, 9, 10
b (i) Shamim, as her pulse increases less and returns to normal faster.
(ii) 2 minutes.
(iii) They will inhale a larger volume of air, and inhale and exhale faster.
6 a (i) Tar, carbon monoxide, nicotine.
(ii) Tar—clogs the air sacs/damages tiny hairs in system; CO—prevents the uptake of oxygen by the red blood cells; nicotine—becomes addictive/may narrow arteries.
b (i) Poor balance, e.g. stumbled; lose inhibitions/become loud, e.g. shouting in street; become aggressive, e.g. lashed out/fighting; slows reactions, e.g. couldn't move quickly enough.
(ii) Liver, brain.
7 a (i) Learned: 2, 3, 4, 6. Unlearned: 1, 5, 7, 8

(ii) Controls movement, body systems, thinking, emotions, memory, co-ordination (*any three*).

8 a A—oxygen; B—carbon dioxide.
b **(i)** Breathing system/lungs;
(ii) blood/transport system.
c To supply energy for heat, growth, repair, movement.

9 a 204 kJ
b 14 g fat, 6 g protein, 3 g carbohydrate, 2 g fibre.

10 a From food/respiration.
b 42°C.
c Supply the energy to keep the body temperature steady in a colder temperature.
d As air temperature increases/decreases, body temperature increases/decreases.

11 a For: stronger enamel, prevents tooth decay, tiny amounts required (*any two*). Against: could be poisonous in long term, people have no choice.
b Correctly drawn tissues, with enamel, dentine, pulp (cavity), blood/nerve, root canal, abscess labelled accurately.

12 a Acid.
b 37°C, body temperature. Enzyme involved.
c fat → fatty acid + glycerol.
d Slower than at 20°C *or* about the same as 60°C.
e At high temperatures enzymes stop working.

13 a Supply of blood to the lungs is upset *or* pickup of oxygen is adversely affected.
b Nervous system.

14 a **(i)** the bigger the animal, the slower the heart rate (or *vice versa*).
(ii) Titmouse.
(iii) Correct plots, correct scales on axes, correct labels on axes.
b Stamina, strength, suppleness.

15 a 170 seconds.
b Repeat soon, Beatrice's time decreased most and she quickly repeated the activity.
c Ali had not learned the skill *or* had forgotten the skill.
d The same pupil should try to learn in both ways, more pupils should be used.

True/false 3

Each statement is marked as either true or false by the pupil. This gives a rapid assessment of a pupil's grasp of the Attainment Targets covered in the unit. The following list gives the Attainment Targets covered by each set of statements.

1 AT 3-4a	5 AT 3-5d
2 AT 3-4b	6 AT 3-5e
3 AT 3-5b	7 AT 3-6e
4 AT 3-5c	8 AT 3-6a

Unit 3 Good health

1 a These diagrams show the outline of four important human organs.

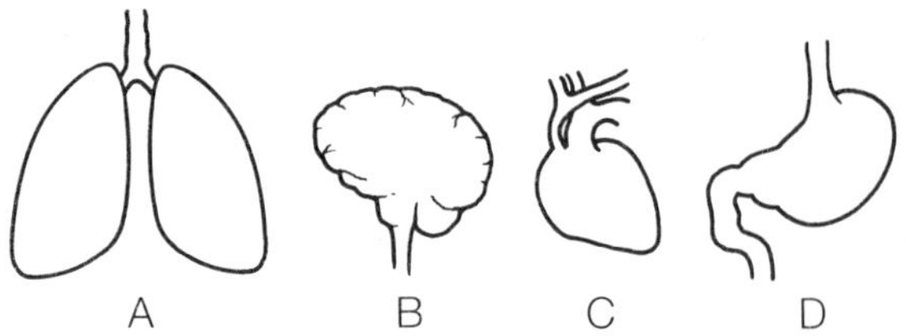

Write down the names of each of the organs.

b Look at these two lists. One list gives statements about diseases or injuries. The other is a list of organs.

Statements	Organ affected
A Pleurisy makes breathing painful.	**1** Stomach
B A gastric ulcer causes digestion problems.	**2** Bones
C Arthritis causes stiff joints.	**3** Heart
D Too much fatty food can cause the arteries to become narrow.	**4** Brain
E A pacemaker can be attached to make it pump steadily.	**5** Lungs
F Meningitis affects the nervous system.	

Match each statement with the correct organ. Each organ may be used more than once.

2 a Arthur the astronaut is about to have lunch.
Some of the labels have been rubbed off the tubes.
All of the foods contain water.

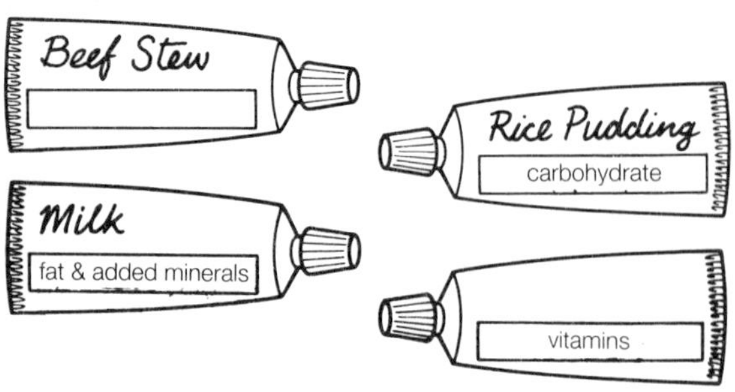

(i) What is the main basic food substance in the beef stew?
(ii) What is this basic food substance used for in the body?
(iii) What food might be in the vitamins tube?
(iv) There is a lack of fibre in this diet.
What problems might Arthur have?

b Describe how you would show that the rice pudding contained starch.

c What causes malnutrition?

3 a These drawings show the four types of human teeth.

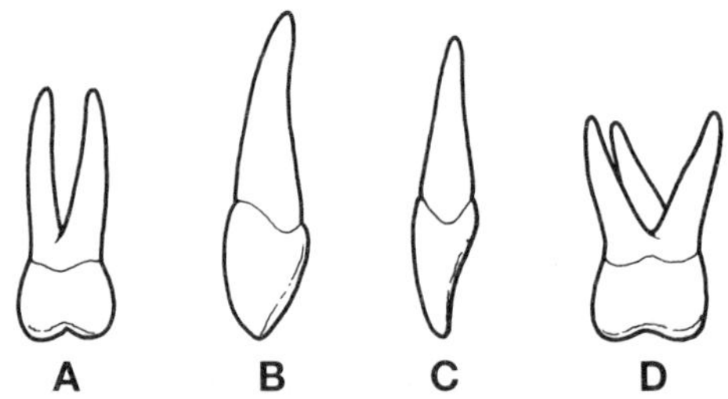

Which of the four types of teeth
(i) are found at the very back of the mouth?
(ii) have the same number on the upper and lower jaw?
(iii) are used for chewing?
(iv) act like scissors when the jaw is closed?
(v) are called premolars?

b Tooth decay is caused by acid forming in the mouth. How is this acid produced?

c Salt or fine sand can be used to clean teeth.
Explain why these substances could be used instead of toothpaste.

continued ▶

4 a These diagrams show models of four foods.

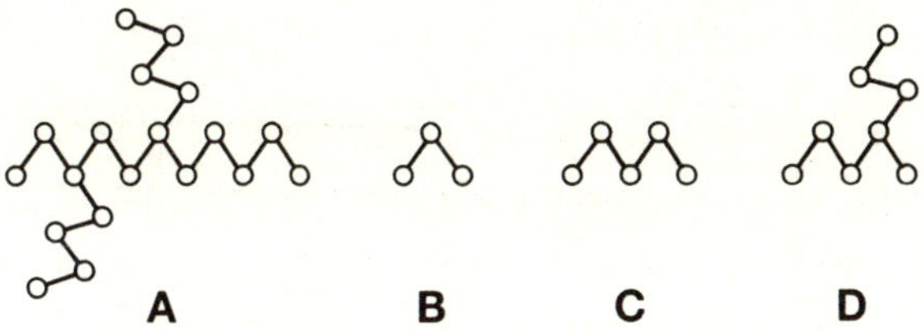

Write down the letters of each food to show the order of solubility. Write down the most soluble first and the least soluble last.

b The table gives the names of several foods and shows if they are soluble or not.

Food	Soluble	Insoluble
Lipid		✓
Maltose	✓	
Amino acid	✓	
Collagen		✓
Peptides	✓	
Glycerol	✓	
Cellulose		✓

Which foods have been formed as a result of digestion?

c Which body system takes digested food away from the gut?

5 a The list gives some information about the heart and lungs.

1 Rate 60 to 80 per minute
2 Rate 10 to 14 per minute
3 Rate can be measured from pulse
4 Acts as a pump
5 Collects oxygen
6 Made of thick muscle
7 Rings of cartilage visible
8 Has hundreds of tiny tubes
9 Valves present
10 Affected by diet

Which statements are about the lungs? Which statements are about the heart?

b The graph shows what happens to the pulse rate of two friends during the same exercise.

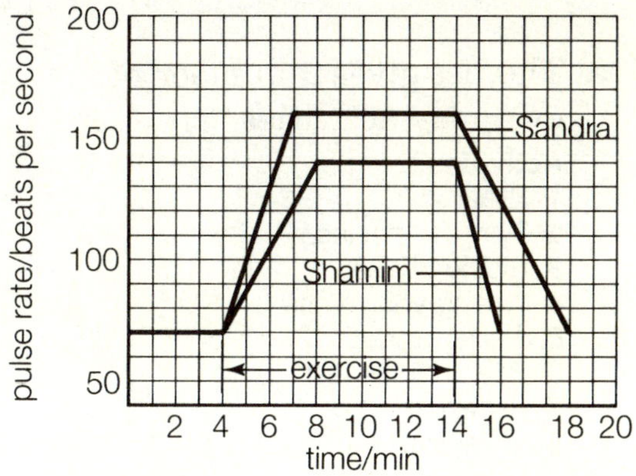

(i) Who is the fitter girl? Give two reasons for your answer?
(ii) How long after stopping the exercise does it take for Shamim's pulse to return to normal?
(iii) Both girls are training. In what two ways will their breathing system be improved?

6 a Look at this list of chemicals.

- oxygen
- tar
- carbon dioxide
- fluoride
- nicotine
- lead
- carbon monoxide
- fat

(i) Which three are dangerous chemicals that are found in cigarette smoke?
(ii) Describe the effect of any one of these chemicals.

b Read the passage and answer the questions that follow.

They came out of the pub at 10.30. Jack lost his footing on the step and stumbled. Sam laughed loudly and accidentally bumped into a passer-by. Jack's trousers had been torn and he began to swear and shout. When Sam tried to quieten him Jack lashed out with a fist and fell again. Sam couldn't seem to move quickly enough to stop him. Finally they got to the car and after trying several times managed to unlock the door . . .

(i) List four effects of alcohol, and give an example of each effect from the passage.
(ii) Name one organ in the body that alcohol is known to damage.

continued ▶

7 a The list gives a number of everyday activities.

Activities

1 Blinking
2 Tying a shoelace
3 Riding a bike
4 Writing your name
5 Falling asleep
6 Reading this test
7 Sneezing
8 Breathing

(i) Divide the activities into two groups: those which are learned and those which are not learned.
(ii) Write down three important jobs that the brain carries out, other than learning.

Extension questions

8 This is the word equation for respiration:

food + gas A → water + gas B + energy

a What are the names of gases A and B?
b Which body system is used to
(i) obtain gas A and remove gas B
(ii) bring food to the cells where respiration takes place?
c What is the energy produced in respiration used for?

9 A label on a jar of peanut butter gives the following information.

100 g of this delicious peanut butter contains

Fat	56 g
Protein	24 g
Carbohydrate	12 g
Fibre	8 g

a Carbohydrate supplies 17 kilojoules of energy per gram. How much energy is supplied by carbohydrate in 100 g of peanut butter?
b A normal serving of peanut butter weighs 25 g.
Calculate how much fat, protein, carbohydrate and fibre this supplies.

10 The graph shows how body temperature changes as air temperature changes for three animals.

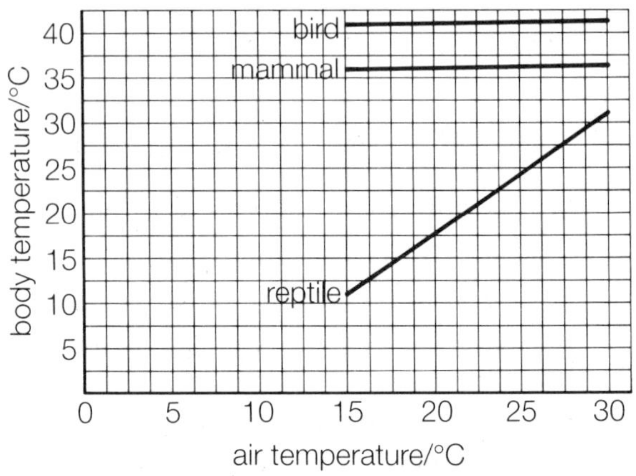

a Where does the heat energy to warm the mammals come from?
b Predict the body temperature of the bird when the air temperature is 5 °C.
c Why do birds and mammals have to eat more during the winter than they do during the summer?
d How does a change in air temperature affect the body temperature of a reptile?

11 a Fluoride is added to some water supplies and to some toothpastes. Give **two** arguments **for** and **two** arguments **against** adding fluoride to the water supply.
b Read the following passage.

Dental caries, usually called tooth decay, is a common disease. The outer layer of the tooth—the enamel—is affected first. The softer dentine below the enamel can also be affected. If the hollow inner pulp cavity is affected infection can spread down to the base of the root canal where an abscess may form. The nerve in the pulp cavity sends pain signals to the brain.

Copy the outline of the tooth. Include as much detail from the passage on the diagram as you can.

continued ▶

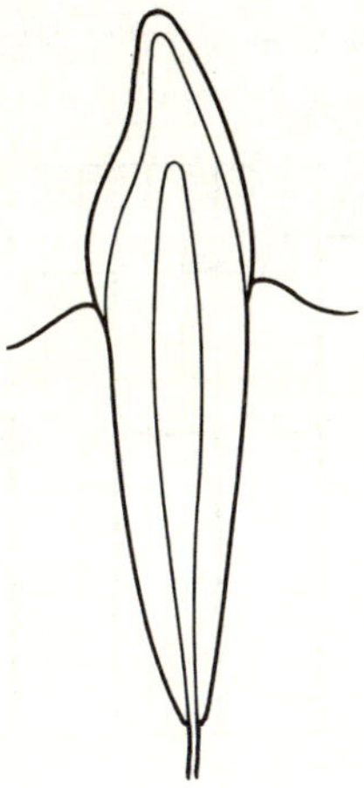

Label all of the parts.
Show the position of an abscess.

12 The graph shows the results of an experiment on the digestion of fat by an enzyme, at three temperatures.

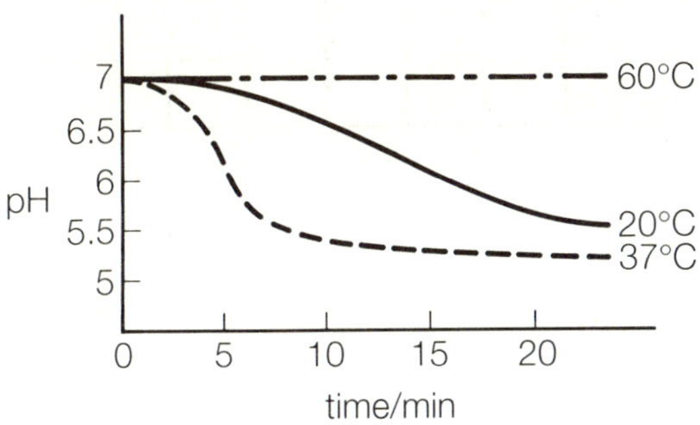

a What type of chemical caused the fall in pH?

b At which temperature was fat digested most quickly? Why do you think this is?

c Write a word equation to show what substances are formed when fat is digested.

d If the experiment had been repeated at 10°C how do you think the result would compare to those shown above?

e Biological washing powders contain enzymes to digest stains on clothing. Why are these washing powders unlikely to work very well at temperatures above 40°C?

13 The cocaine-based drug crack is very dangerous. It can cause an irregular heart-beat that can eventually lead to heart failure and damage to the breathing system. There is also a danger of bleeding in the brain and strokes, which can cause paralysis.

a How could damage to the heart cause breathing problems?

b Which system of the body is described in the last sentence of the passage?

14 a The table shows the average heart rate of some animals.

Animal	Heart rate (beats per minute)
Elephant	46
Horse	55
Human	75
Dog	120
Cat	240
Titmouse	960

(i) Describe how the heart rate is related to the size of the animal.
(ii) Which animal would you expect to have the fastest breathing rate?
(iii) **Collect** a sheet of graph paper. Draw a bar chart of the data.

b What three aspects of fitness can be improved by regular exercise?

continued ▶

15 The bar charts show the times taken for two pupils to complete a mirror drawing.

a What is the shortest time taken by Ali to complete the mirror drawing test?

b What seems to be the best way to learn a new skill like mirror drawing? Explain your answer.

c Give a possible explanation for the pattern of results shown by Ali.

d This is not a fair comparison. What variables should be kept constant to make the experiment fair?

Ali did the mirror drawing test once a week for three weeks.

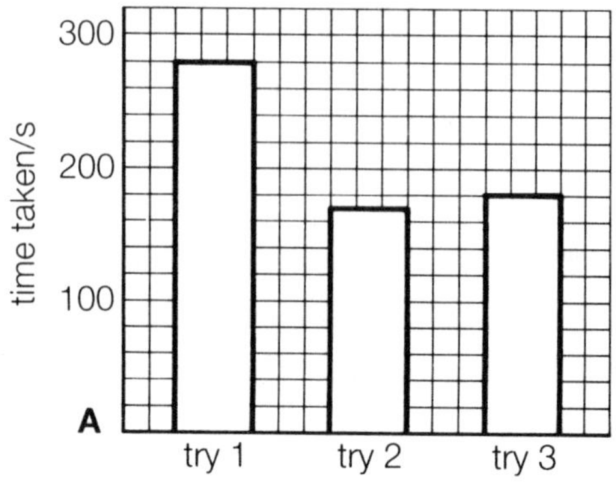

Beatrice did the mirror test 3 times in one hour.

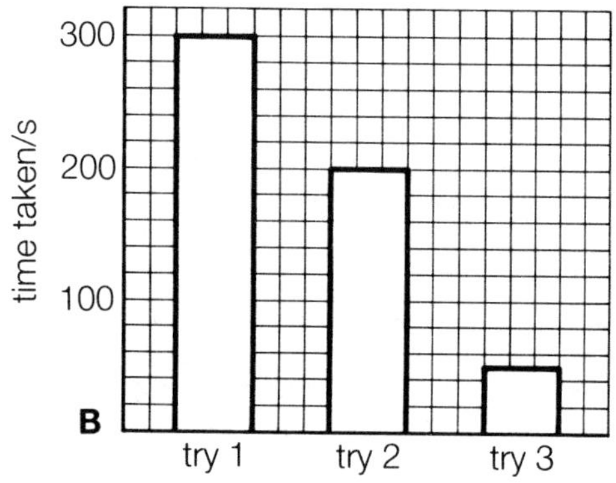

Unit 3 Good health

True or False 3

Name ____________________

Put a tick after the statements that are true. Put a cross after the statements that are false.

1 a The brain is an example of a tissue. ☐
b The lungs are part of the breathing system. ☐
c Someone with circulatory problems might be given drugs that affect the heart. ☐

2 a A meal of chips, ice cream and lemonade would provide a balanced diet. ☐
b Fibre is needed as part of a balanced diet. ☐
c Alcohol makes you alert and improves your reactions. ☐
d Everyone who smokes will cause some damage to their breathing system. ☐
e Pure sugar by itself will cause tooth decay. ☐
f White blood cells fight bacteria. ☐
g Antibodies help to digest food. ☐
h Poor posture has little or no effect on your health. ☐

3 a Vegetarians will suffer from malnutrition. ☐
b Too little of one basic food substance can be replaced by eating extra of any other basic food substance. ☐
c Exercise causes an increase in heart rate. ☐
d Over-exercising can damage your heart. ☐
e Smoking can cause circulatory problems. ☐

4 a Glucose is soluble and so does not need to be digested. ☐
b In digestion food is broken down to make it soluble. ☐
c Food is made soluble so that it can be egested from the anus. ☐
d Blood takes digested food from the gut. ☐

5 a Some microbes cause disease. ☐
b You can avoid some disease and infection by having clean habits. ☐
c The healthier you are the less sleep you need. ☐

6 a The brain controls movement. ☐
b You can learn to react faster by practising. ☐
c You can learn ways of improving your memory. ☐
d Blood is cleaned in the lungs. ☐
e The stomach is part of the nervous system. ☐
f The heart is a pump. ☐

7 a Pregnant women who smoke can damage the health of their unborn baby. ☐
b You can only get addicted to drugs, but not to alcohol. ☐
c Taking some drugs can lead to permanent brain damage. ☐
d Sniffing glue cannot cause any harm the first time. ☐

Extensions

8 a Photosynthesis is the process that releases energy from food. ☐
b Carbon dioxide and water are waste materials when energy is released from food. ☐
c All chemical energy in food is changed to heat energy in our body. ☐

Unit 3 Good health

Name ______________________

Complete each sentence. Put the correct word(s) in each blank space.

1 Cells of the body are organised into **tissues** and ______________. Four main body systems are

- ______________
- ______________
- ______________
- ______________.

2 There are seven important basic food substances. Each has a particular job to do. Some foods are a good source for one basic substance.

Basic substance	**Source**	**Use**
Fibre	______________	______________
______________	______________	Healthy bones/blood
Vitamins	______________	______________
______________	Cream, butter	______________
______________	______________	Energy
______________	Bread, potato	______________
Water	______________	______________

When you have enough of each basic food you are eating a ______________ diet. If not you can suffer from ______________.

3 Each of the four types of human teeth does a different job

Tooth	**Job**
______________	______________
______________	______________
______________	______________
______________	______________

Brushing keeps teeth healthy by removing ______________. This is a mixture of food and ______________ that produces ______________ which causes tooth ______________.

continued ▶

Name ____________________

4 When food is digested the large particles become ____________________.

They can then ____________________ in water and can pass out of the gut

into the ____________________ supply.
The six main parts of the digestive system are

- Mouth
- ____________________
- ____________________
- ____________________
- ____________________
- ____________________.

5 The heart has ____________________ chambers. It ____________________ blood around the body.

The ____________________ at the wrist is a sign that your heart is beating.

The lungs pass ____________________ from the air into the

____________________ supply.

6 Change in breathing rate and in ____________________ rate can be used as a

measure of ____________________.

A fit person's pulse rate returns to normal ____________________ after exercise.

7 Smoking damages the ____________________.
Three dangerous chemicals in smoke are

- ____________________
- ____________________
- ____________________

Two effects of smoking are

- ____
- ____.

8 Alcohol is a dangerous drug because it can slow down your

____________________, make you feel ____________________ and damage

your ____________________.

9 Learning is controlled at the ____________________ of the brain.
Three methods of learning are

- ____________________
- ____________________
____________________.

Body sheet

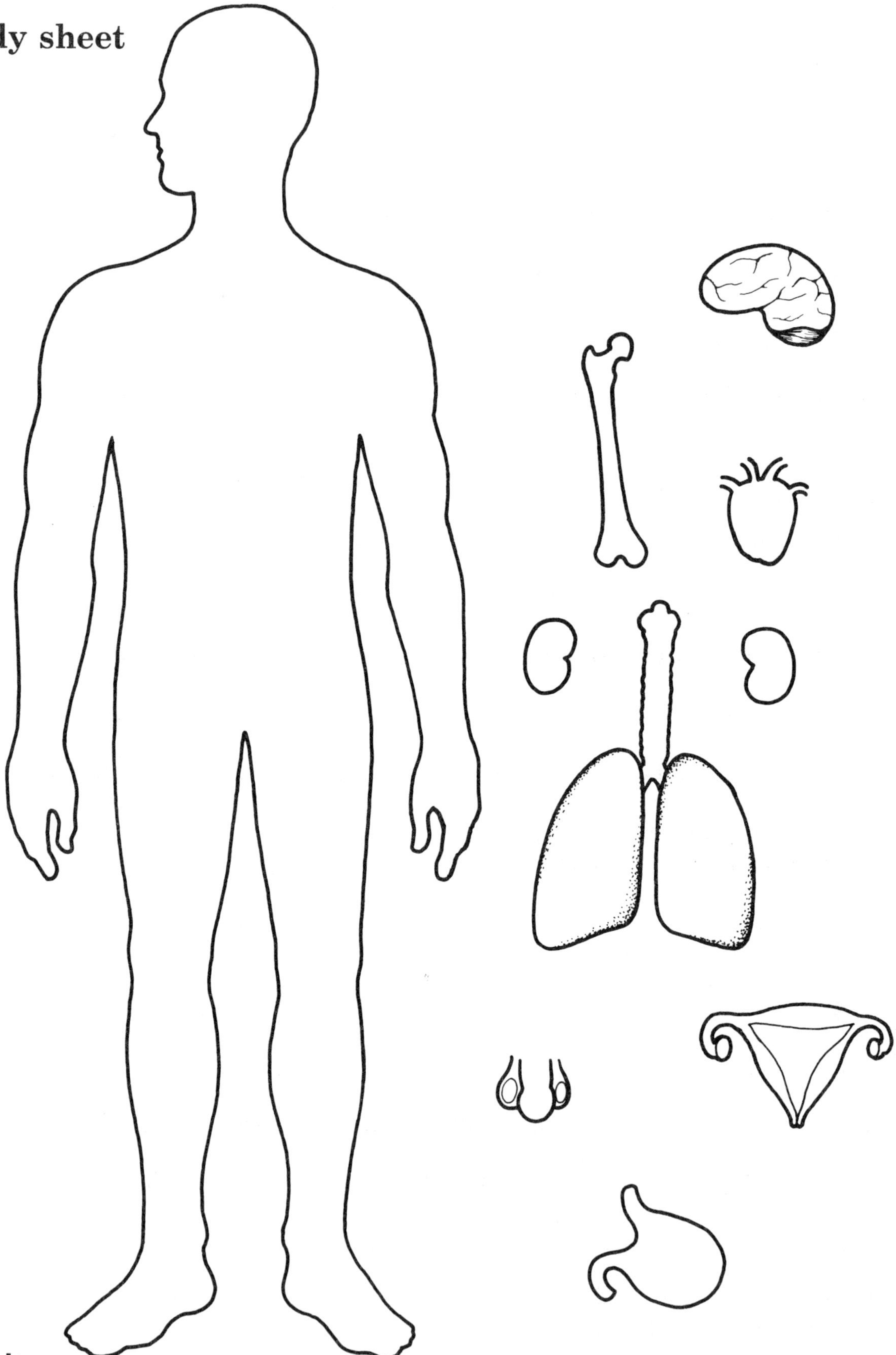

Labels

Bones	**Brain**	**Heart**	**Kidneys**
Lungs	**Sex organs**	**Stomach**	

Health hazard 1

Drinking alcohol slows down your reactions.

Health hazard 2

Meat and eggs should be carefully cooked to avoid the risk of food poisoning.

Health hazard 3

Too much fatty food can cause high blood pressure.

Health hazard 4

Smoking causes many people to cough more than normal.

Health hazard 5

Too little fibre in your diet can lead to constipation.

Health hazard 6

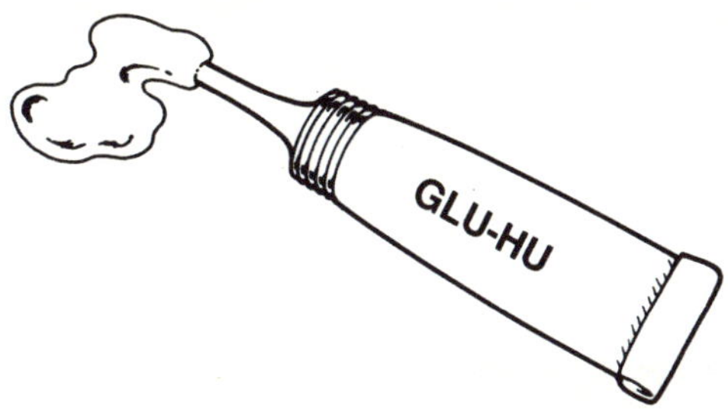

Sniffing glue can cause dizziness and can make you sick.

Health hazard 7

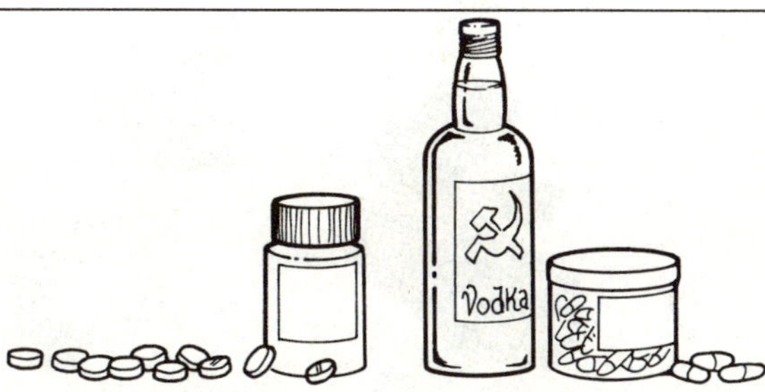

Some drugs, including alcohol, can make you aggressive and badly behaved.

Health hazard 8

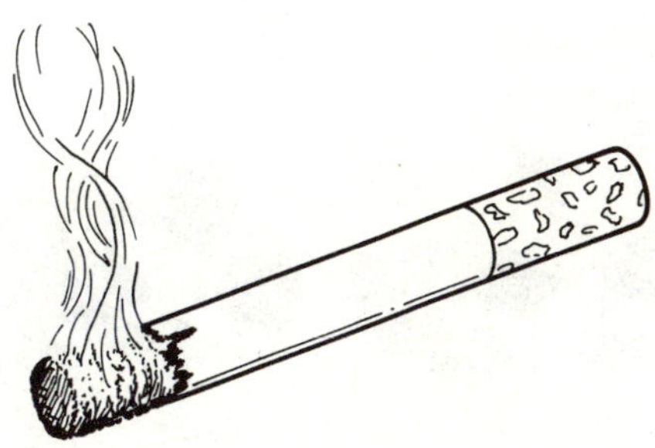

Chemicals in smoke make the heart beat faster.

Buffet table

Buffet table

Buffet table

Jaw

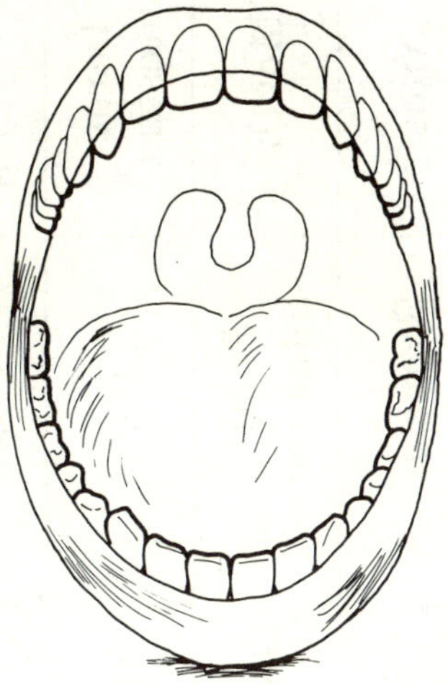

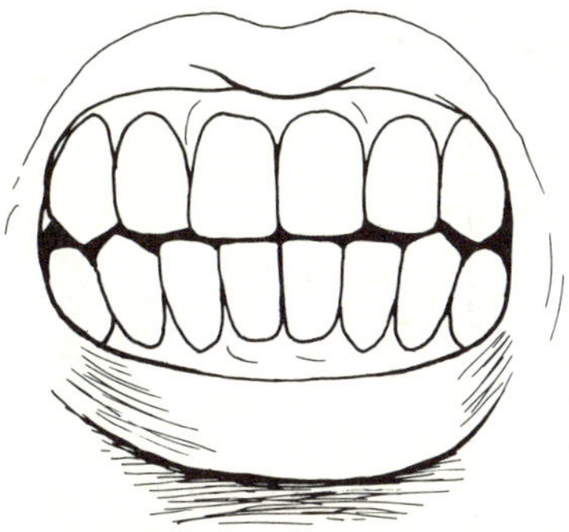

Before cleaning

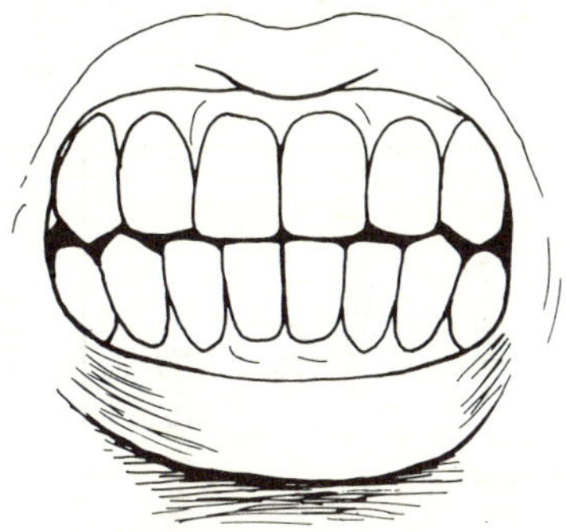

After cleaning

Jaw

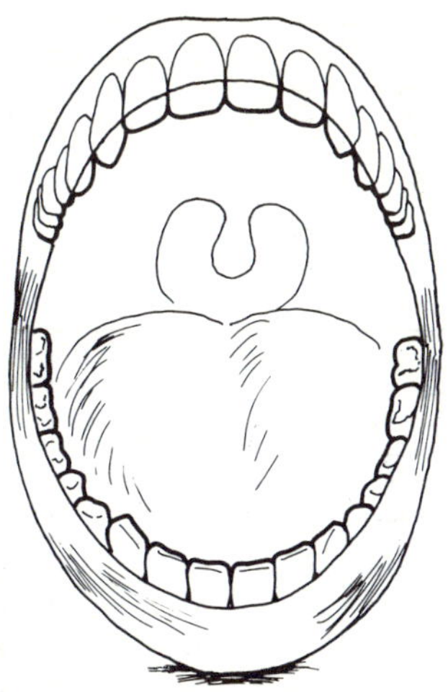

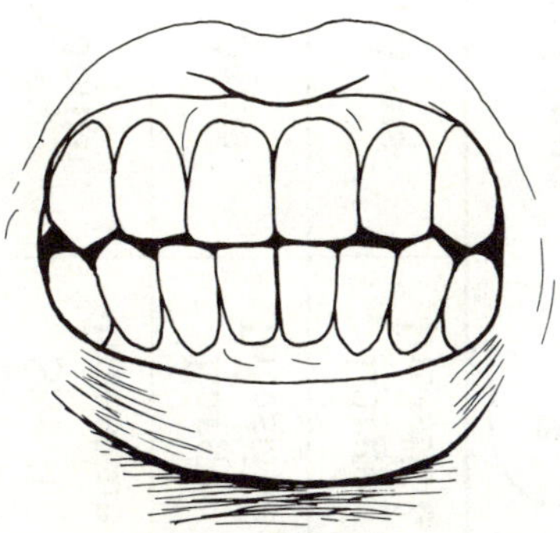

Before cleaning

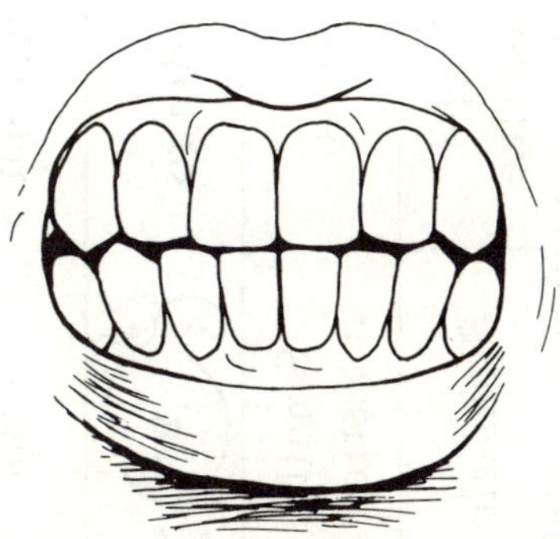

After cleaning

Digestion Bingo 1

Stomach	Small Intestine	Gullet
Small Intestine	Mouth	Stomach
Large Intestine	Anus	Mouth

Digestion Bingo 2

Mouth	Gullet	Large Intestine
Stomach	Anus	Stomach
Anus	Mouth	Small Intestine

Digestion Bingo 3

Gullet	Mouth	Small Intestine
Small Intestine	Anus	Large Intestine
Stomach	Anus	Large Intestine

Digestion Bingo 4

Large Intestine	Gullet	Anus
Mouth	Small Intestine	Gullet
Anus	Stomach	Large Intestine

Digestion Bingo 5

Small Intestine	Stomach	Anus
Gullet	Mouth	Large Intestine
Anus	Gullet	Stomach

Digestion Bingo 6

Anus	Gullet	Small Intestine
Large Intestine	Gullet	Mouth
Small Intestine	Stomach	Anus

Digestion Bingo 7

Small Intestine	Anus	Stomach
Large Intestine	Stomach	Small Intestine
Mouth	Anus	Gullet

Digestion Bingo 8

Small Intestine	Anus	Small Intestine
Anus	Large Intestine	Stomach
Gullet	Mouth	Large Intestine

Digestion Bingo 9

Gullet	Anus	Small Intestine
Anus	Large Intestine	Stomach
Large Intestine	Gullet	Mouth

Resource 3.4A

Digestion Bingo 10

Mouth	Large Intestine	Small Intestine
Gullet	Anus	Stomach
Stomach	Mouth	Gullet

Digestion Bingo 13

Small Intestine	Mouth	Anus
Stomach	Large Intestine	Small Intestine
Mouth	Gullet	Gullet

Digestion Bingo 16

Stomach	Mouth	Gullet
Large Intestine	Anus	Mouth
Gullet	Large Intestine	Small Intestine

Digestion Bingo 11

Large Intestine	Stomach	Mouth
Anus	Stomach	Gullet
Gullet	Small Intestine	Small Intestine

Digestion Bingo 14

Gullet	Small Intestine	Anus
Mouth	Gullet	Stomach
Large Intestine	Stomach	Large Intestine

Digestion Bingo 17

Large Intestine	Stomach	Gullet
Gullet	Mouth	Anus
Small Intestine	Small Intestine	Large Intestine

Digestion Bingo 12

Small Intestine	Mouth	Gullet
Anus	Large Intestine	Mouth
Small Intestine	Large Intestine	Stomach

Digestion Bingo 15

Large Intestine	Gullet	Anus
Small Intestine	Large Intestine	Stomach
Mouth	Gullet	Small Intestine

Digestion Bingo 18

Gullet	Large Intestine	Stomach
Stomach	Anus	Mouth
Small Intestine	Mouth	Large Intestine

Digestion Bingo ***Caller card 1***	**Digestion Bingo** ***Caller card 2***	**Digestion Bingo** ***Caller card 3***	**Digestion Bingo** ***Caller card 4***	**Digestion Bingo** ***Caller card 5***	**Digestion Bingo** ***Caller card 6***
Food is broken into large lumps here. *(Mouth)*	Food passes along this tube to the stomach. *(Gullet)*	Food is churned up and mixed together here. *(Stomach)*	Chemicals change large insoluble food particles into small, soluble particles here. *(Small Intestine)*	Water is removed from food and passes into the blood supply. *(Large Intestine)*	This is where waste food is stored. *(Anus)*
Digestion Bingo ***Caller card 7***	**Digestion Bingo** ***Caller card 8***	**Digestion Bingo** ***Caller card 9***	**Digestion Bingo** ***Caller card 10***	**Digestion Bingo** ***Caller card 11***	**Digestion Bingo** ***Caller card 12***
Food is covered in saliva, swallowed and partly digested. *(Mouth)*	Food is swallowed and goes down this tube. *(Gullet)*	This is where any germs are destroyed by acids. *(Stomach)*	Small soluble food particles pass from the digestive system into the blood (circulatory) system. *(Small Intestine)*	The food here will not be digested any more. It is now waste. *(Large Intestine)*	Waste is egested from here. *(Anus)*

Food is digested and made soluble in the small intestine. The soluble food passes into the blood supply.

Waste food is egested from the anus.

Food is passed from the mouth to the stomach in the gullet.

Food is broken into lumps in the mouth.

Food is mixed and stored in the stomach.

Water is removed from food. What is left in the large intestine is waste

✂ - ✂

Food is digested and made soluble in the small intestine. The soluble food passes into the blood supply.

Waste food is egested from the anus.

Food is passed from the mouth to the stomach in the gullet.

Food is broken into lumps in the mouth.

Food is mixed and stored in the stomach.

Water is removed from food. What is left in the large intestine is waste

Heart

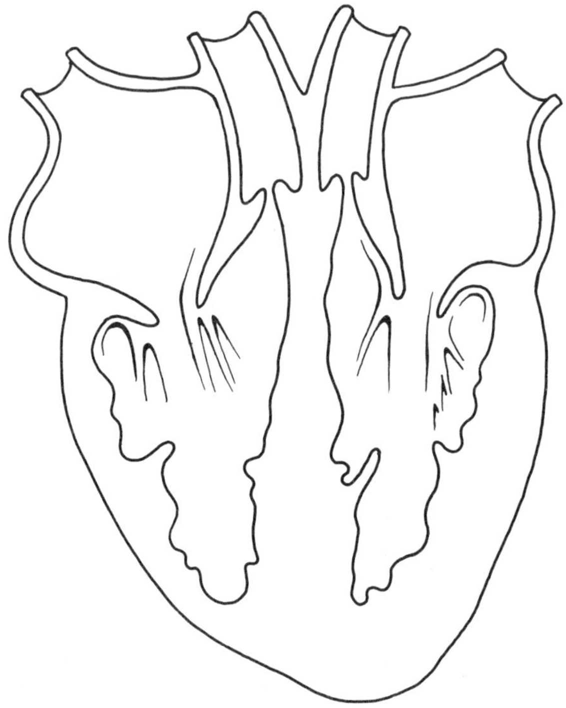

The heart ______________________ blood.

Blood returns to the heart in vessels called ______________________.

It enters the top chambers called ______________________.

Blood then passes to the lower ______________________.

From here is is pumped away from the heart
in vessels called ______________________.

Lungs

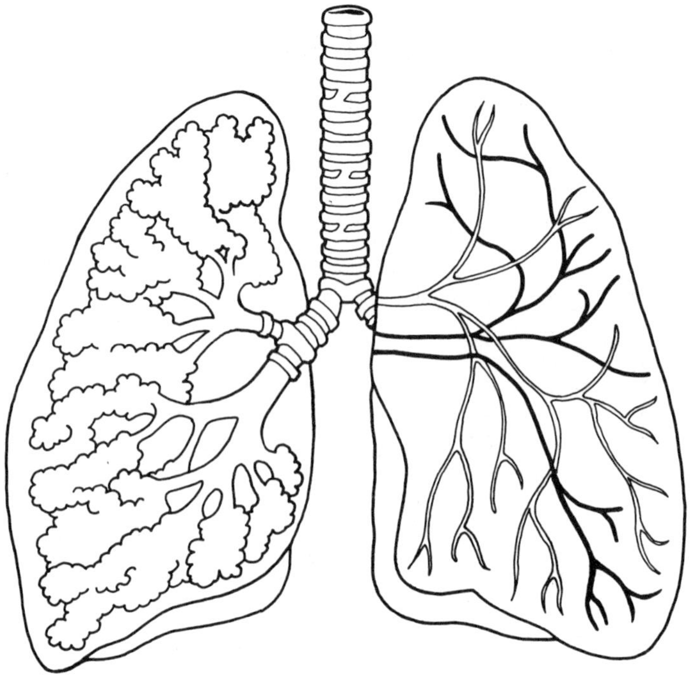

Training graph

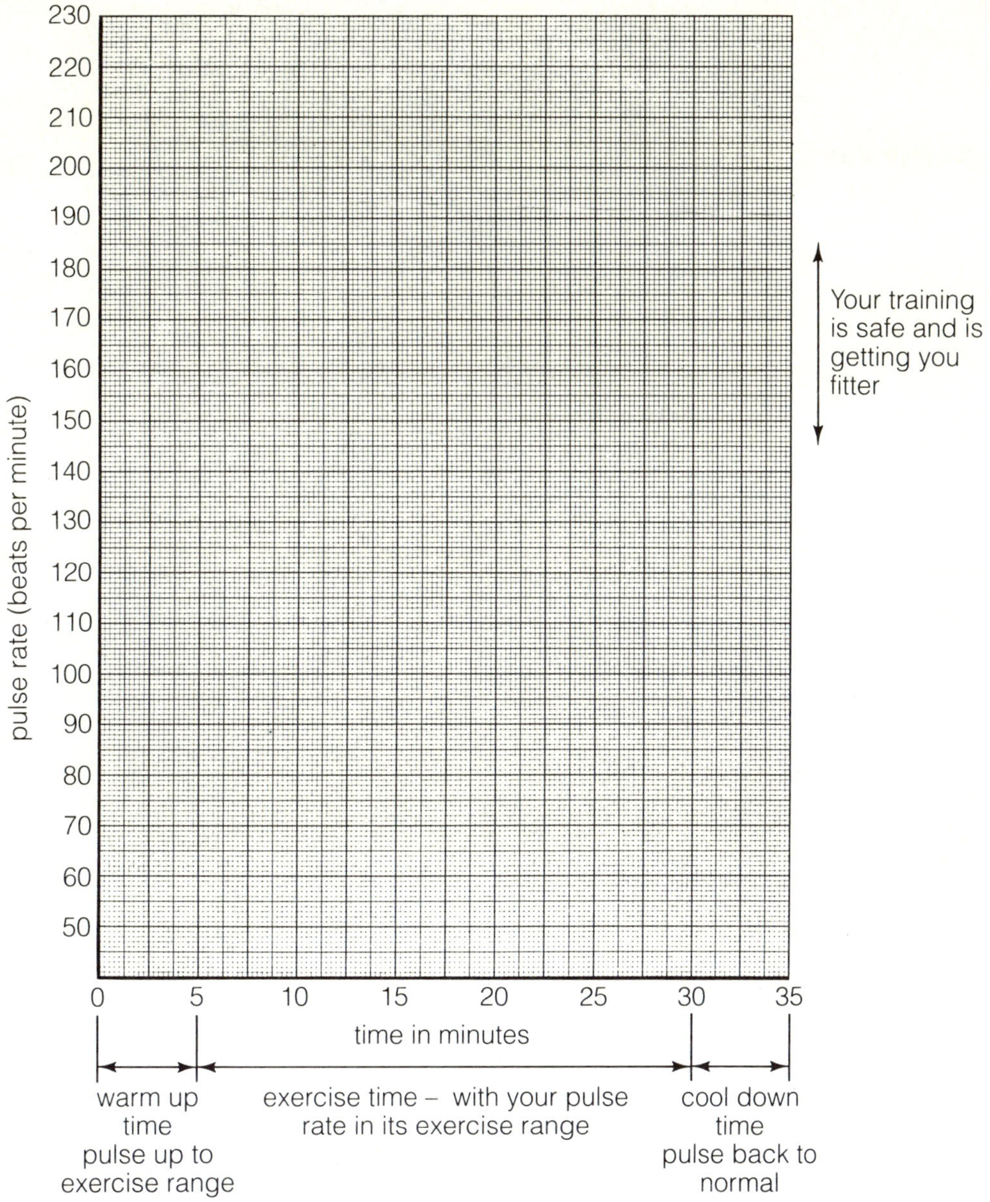

Instructions

1 Mark your resting (normal) pulse rate with a cross on the 0 time line and on the 35 minute time line.

2 Mark your 'Beginners' pulse rate on the 5 minute and on the 30 minute time line with crosses. Join these two crosses with a red pencil. Now join your normal pulse rate crosses to your line using a red pencil.

3 Repeat for your 'Intermediate' pulse rate using a blue pencil, and for your 'Fit' pulse rate using a green pencil.

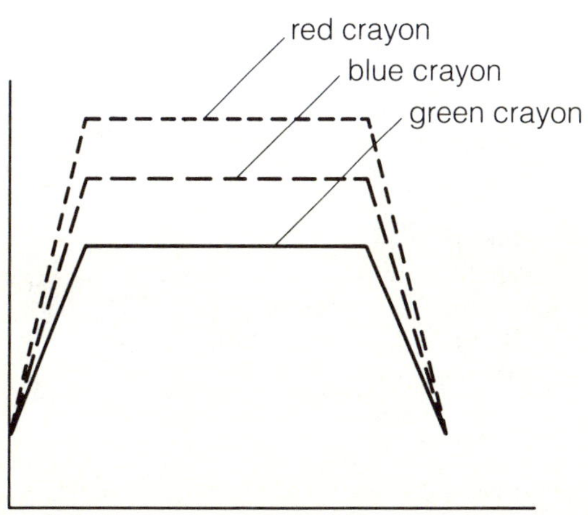

Activity clock

Colour key

Sleeping	white
relaxing	green
Light exercise	yellow
Active exercise	orange
Eating snacks	red
Eating meals	blue

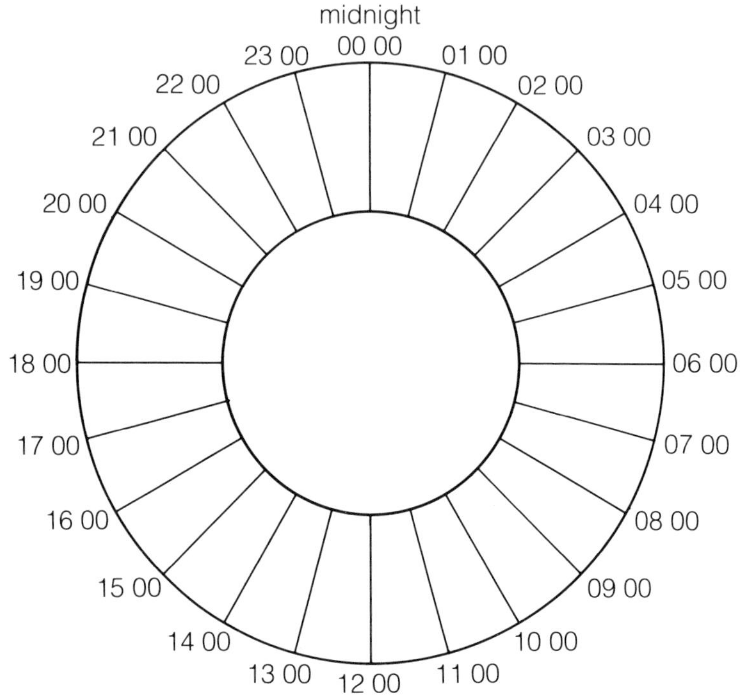

Activity clock

Colour key

Sleeping	white
relaxing	green
Light exercise	yellow
Active exercise	orange
Eating snacks	red
Eating meals	blue

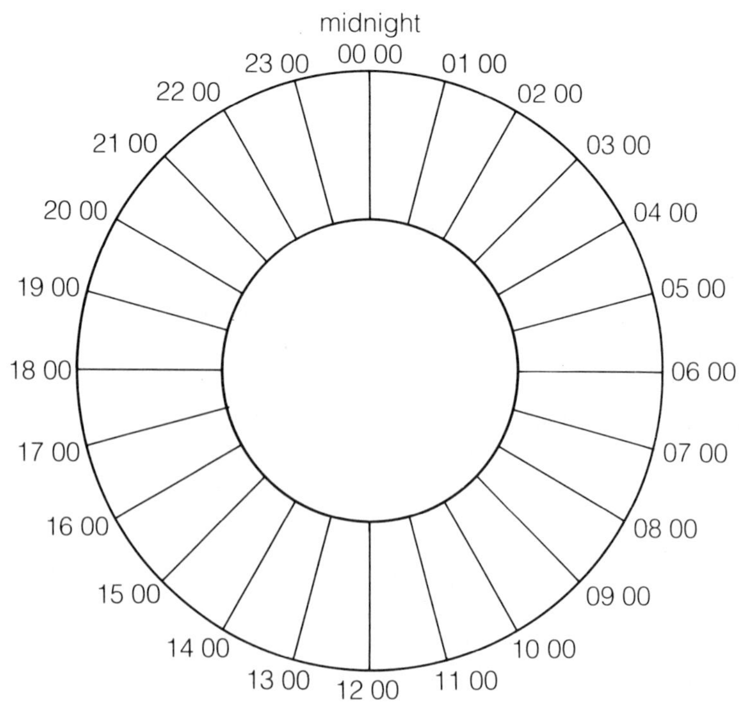

Star shapes

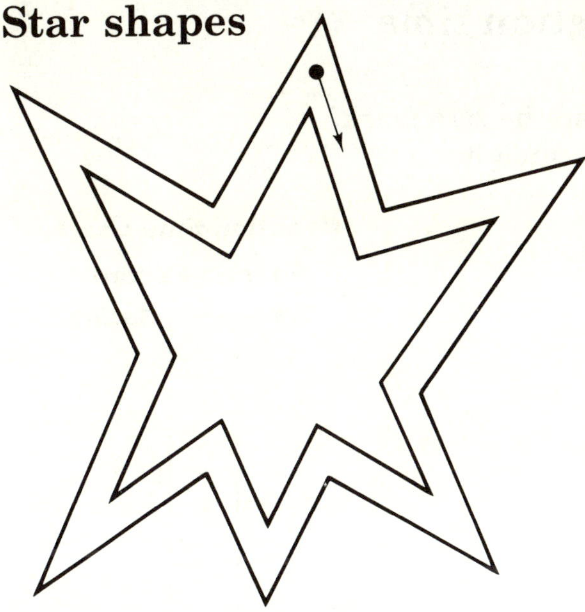

Star shapes

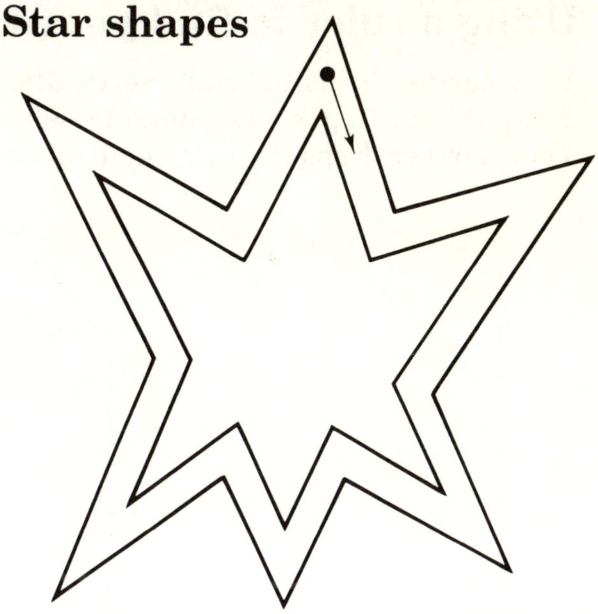

Star shapes

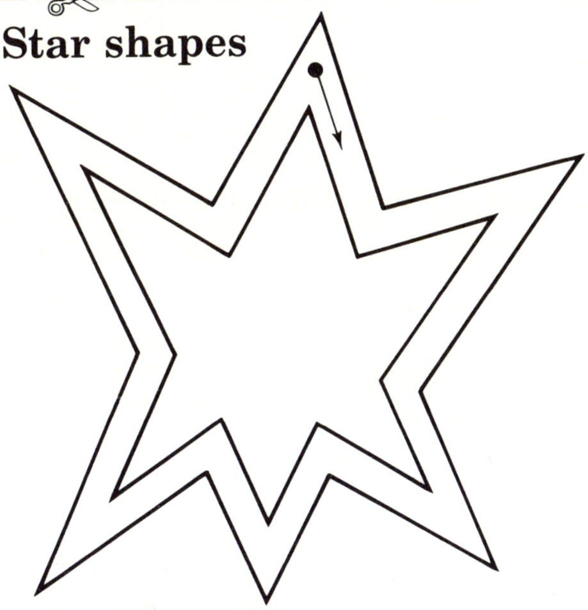

Star shapes

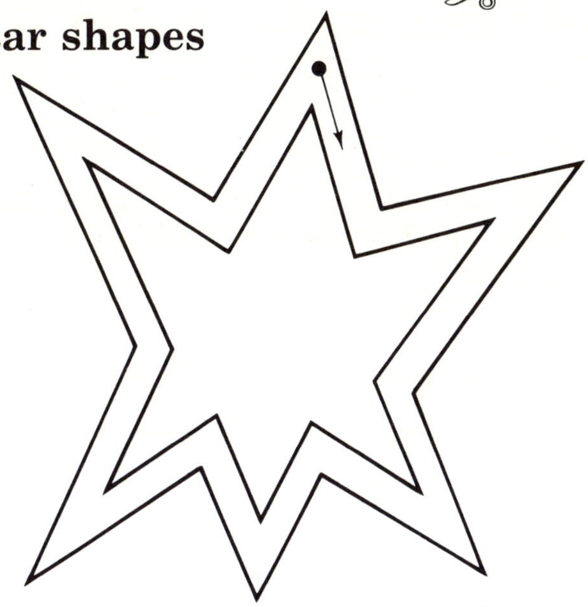

Star shapes

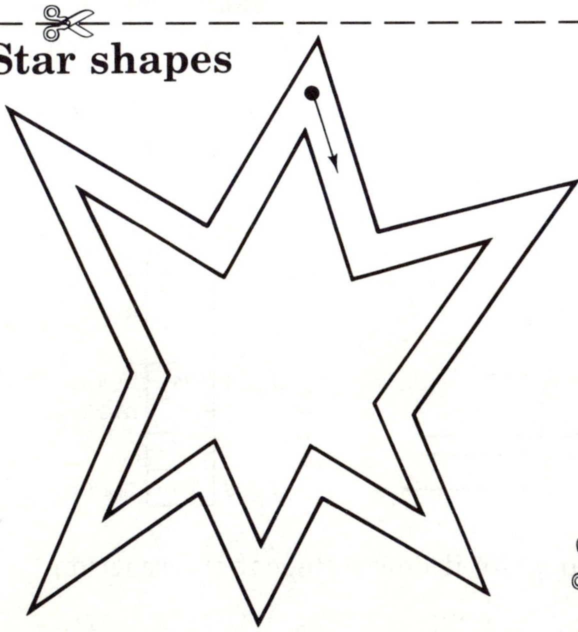

Star shapes

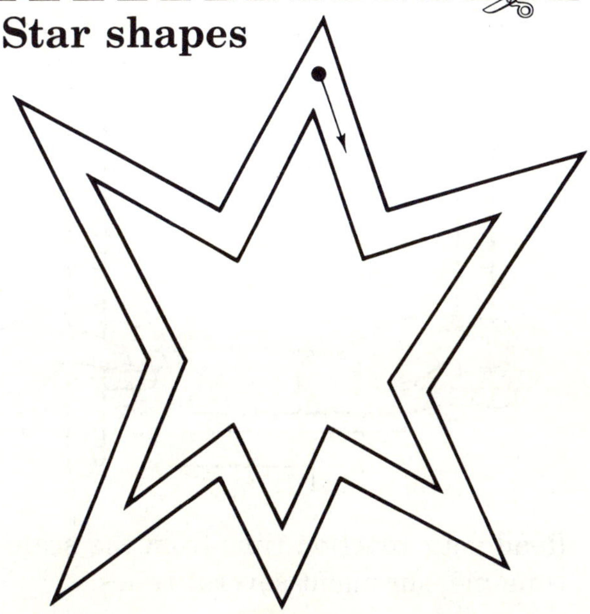

Using a ruler to find your reaction time

Your partner holds the ruler vertically.
You put your finger and thumb loosely round the zero mark.
Your partner drops the ruler and you try to catch it.

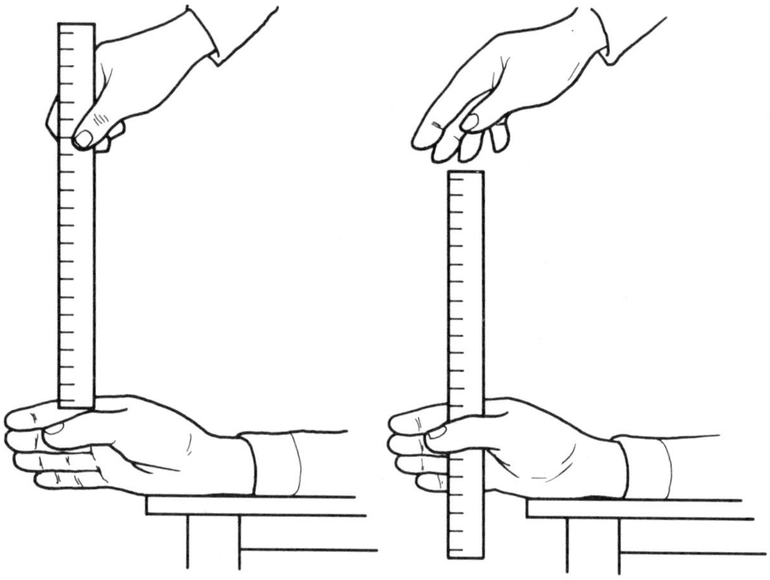

Reaction-time chart

Reaction Time	Score (cm)	Rating
0.13s	9	excellent
0.15s	11	very good
0.17s	14	good
0.18s	16	quite good
0.20s	20	fair
0.22s	24	below average
0.25s	30	poor

Read your reaction time from the scale and write it down. Repeat the reaction-time measurement several times.

Using a ruler to find your reaction time

Your partner holds the ruler vertically.
You put your finger and thumb loosely round the zero mark.
Your partner drops the ruler and you try to catch it.

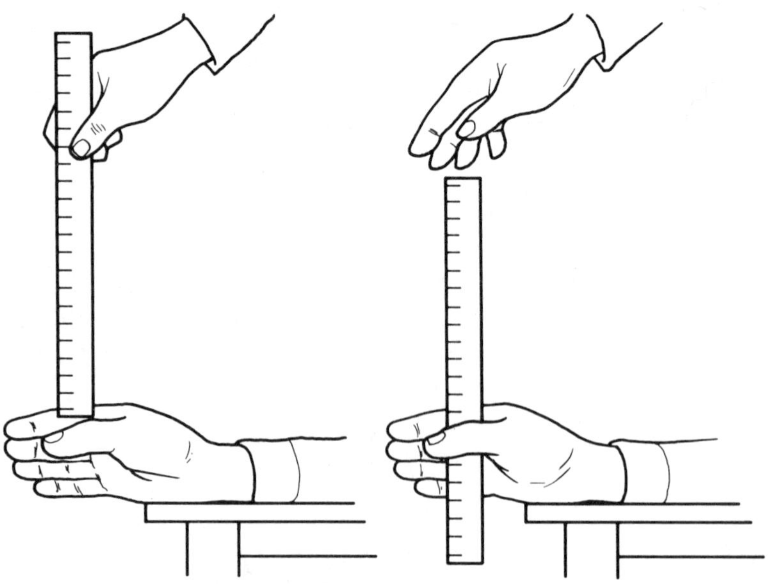

Reaction-time chart

Reaction Time	Score (cm)	Rating
0.13s	9	excellent
0.15s	11	very good
0.17s	14	good
0.18s	16	quite good
0.20s	20	fair
0.22s	24	below average
0.25s	30	poor

Read your reaction time from the scale and write it down. Repeat the reaction-time measurement several times.

Unit 4 Everyday forces

Thinking about movement and design

The first six topics in this unit deal with forces. Pupils are introduced to the concept of force. Looking for and recognising patterns in data and experimental results is also introduced. A basic knowledge and understanding of contact and non-contact forces and of balanced forces is developed in the context of familiar situations. The importance of forces in movement and in design is considered. The final three topics comprise an open-ended problem, a discussion and a short reading exercise. The material covers Attainment Target 10 of the National Curriculum and some statements from AT 6 and 11. In addition to meeting the general demands of Attainment Target 1, this unit deals specifically with the development of AT 1 at levels 4, 5a, 5b, 5c, 5d.

Core and Reinforcement

4.1 Describing forces — *AT 10–3a*

Make a plasticine model using different forces.
Identify type of force used in a number of everyday activities. *page 64*

Follow diagrammatic instructions.
Recognise examples of defined forces.

Extension — *AT 10–4d, 5c*

Measure forces with a Newton meter.
Plot a line graph of force against mass. *page 149*

Recognise a pattern in experimental data.
Process data to plot a line graph.

4.2 Forces at a distance — *AT 10–4c*

Play three games to study three non-contact forces: gravity, electrostatics, magnetism.
Identify non-contact forces in action in familiar situations. *page 66*

Recognise examples of defined forces.

Extension — *AT 10–4a; AT 11–6c*

Build an electromagnet.
Modify the given design to produce a stronger electromagnet. *page 150*

Solve a problem in a practical context.
Deduce a relationship from experimental data.

4.3 On the move — *AT 10–4a; 5a, d*

Devise ways of reducing friction between a moving object and a surface.
Identify ways of increasing friction in familiar situations. *page 68*

Devise experiments for a stated purpose.
Select appropriate materials and apparatus.
Recognise examples of friction.

Extension — *AT 10–4b, 5d*

Plot a line graph of speed against stopping distance. *page 151*

Process data to plot a line graph.

4.4 Balancing act — *AT 10–3b, 4a*

Solve a brain-teaser by trial and error experimentation.
Design a plasticine shape that will float.
Identify balanced and unbalanced forces in familiar situations. *page 70*

Explain familiar observations in terms of a scientific law.

Extension — *AT 10–4a, 5c, 6c*

Balance a lever using unequal masses.
Derive the relationship between force and distance in a balanced lever. *page 152*

Observe, measure and record accurately and systematically.
Use experimental data to recognise patterns, and to deduce relationships.

Core and Reinforcement

4.5 On the move again *AT 10–4a*

Observe changes in muscle shape to show antagonistic muscle action at a joint. *page 72*

Draw conclusions from observations.

4.6 Choosing materials *AT 6–4a; AT 10–5b*

Carry out fair tests to compare bags for flexibility, strength, hard wearing.
Identify key properties of given materials. *page 74*

Devise experiments for a stated purpose.
Draw conclusions from experimental observations and data.

4.7 Problem—Consumer report *AT 6–4a,b; AT 10–5b*

Design fair experiments to compare the properties of three different makes of a product.
Collate and present a verbal report on the results. *page 76*

Devise experiments for a stated purpose.
Select and use apparatus effectively.
Evaluate experimental design.

4.8 Talkabout—Design flaws *AT 10–3a*

Identify forces acting in four situations.
Identify possible design flaws and improvements in design for the products shown. *page 77*

Evaluate technological applications of science.

4.9 Readabout—New materials *AT 6–4b; AT 10–3a*

Read and answer questions on a passage. *page 78*

Extract relevant information from a passage.

Extension

AT 10–4a

Complete drawings of skeletons to show predicted positions of muscles for movement. *page 154*

Apply scientific knowledge in unfamiliar situations.

AT 6–4b

Identify most suitable plastic for the manufacture of specific products from given information. *page 155*

Extract relevant information from a table.

Equipment
required for each pupil group

Notes

4.1—Describing forces

- Plasticine
- Tray containing sheets of scrap paper, ball point pen, glass jar with top, container with prise-off lid (e.g. large coffee tin), screwdriver

The aim is to introduce the concept of forces.
As pupils make the castle they will use different types of force.
The tasks associated with the tray of objects rely on using 1 or 2 types of force:
open jar—pushing/twisting
open lid—pushing
pick up pen—pushing
open pen—twisting
write—pushing/pulling
crumple paper—pushing
throw away—pushing

Extension

- Newton spring balance (reading to 25 N)
- Sheets of scrap paper
- Masses (1, 1.5 and 2 kg)
- 1 dynamics trolley

Pupils may need some help in reading the scale.
The relationship between mass and weight is being explored.

4.2—Forces at a distance

- Long cardboard tube (e.g. from cling film or aluminium foil roll)
- Retort stand and clamp
- Plasticine
- Ruler
- Timer
- Polystyrene ball (2.5 or 4 cm)
- Plastic rod (polythene/acetate)
- Cotton cloth
- Iron filings in salt cellar
- Face sheet **(R4.2)**
- Bar magnet
- Petri dish top or bottom
- Sheet of filter paper

The game situation allows all pupils to explore three non-contact forces.
Pupils should deduce the relationship between strength of force and distance from games 2 and 3.

Extension

- Three 1.5 V cells
- 30 cm 24 s.w.g. insulated copper wire
- Connecting wire
- Switch
- 10 cm iron nail
- Petri dish containing panel pins

The strength of the electromagnet increases with an increase in
(i) number of coils
(ii) number of cells
The stronger the magnet the more panel pins will be picked up.

4.3—On the move

- 4 mm wide elastic band cut to 4 cm length
- 10p coin (pupil's own!)
- Metre rule
- Cloth
- Bottle of fine sand
- Bottle of chalk
- Dropping bottle of oil
- Bottle of detergent
- Paper towels

The size of elastic ensures that the coin cannot be fired far.
The elastic should be drawn back a maximum of 3 cm.
Pupils might wish to polish the bench, spread fine sand or chalk.
If oil is used pupils should clean up with detergent.
The facts that friction must be overcome to start an object moving but that it never disappears are important teaching points.

Equipment
required for each pupil group

Notes

Extension
- Graph paper

Pupils may require some support in drawing the line graph.

4.4—Balancing act
- 30 cm ruler
- Pivot (1 cm test tube/dowel rod)
- Elastic band
- 14 small masses (1p coins, iron nuts)
- 1 larger mass
- Plasticine
- 400 cm^3 beaker

The see-saw must balance with both ends off the bench.
Use the elastic band to hold the ruler in place.
To solve the puzzle: put seven on each side. If they balance the pupil left out is heavier. If not, put three pupils from the heavy side onto each side of the see-saw. If they balance the pupil left out is the heavier one. If not, . . . and so on.
To make the plasticine float the pupil must increase the surface area, so spreading the force.

Extension
- 7 small masses (1p coins etc.)
- 30 cm ruler
- Pivot (test tube/dowel rod)
- Elastic band

Set up the see-saw as before. Pupils should place the masses on the middle of the whole number lines of the ruler. This makes the pattern easier to see. To balance the see-saw the product of mass (number of coins) × distance from the pivot should be the same for both sides of the see-saw.

4.5—On the move again
No equipment needed

When a leg bends back at the knee the muscle at the front of the thigh relaxes, the muscle at the back contracts, exerting a pulling force.

Extension
- Red and green pencils
- Skeleton cut-outs **(RE4.5)**

Pupils are asked to consider the idea of movement brought about by antagonistic muscle action. If this is understood they will draw muscles in sensible, (if not anatomically accurate) positions.

4.6—Choosing materials
- 1 kg mass
- Paper carrier bags (the type used for takeaway meals work well)
- Plastic carrier bags (the thin free types given by supermarkets work well)
- 100 g masses
- Mass carrier
- Coarse sandpaper
- Wooden block

Pupils could be asked in advance to bring their own bags.
The three tests described can be done quickly and are repeatable.
Tearing the side of the bag with masses on a mass carrier requires sufficient masses per class.
Pupils might suggest testing strength by finding the load capacity.
This would require several kilogram masses.

Extension
No equipment required

Equipment
required for each pupil group

Notes

4.7—Problem—Consumer report

- Consumer magazines, e.g. *Which?*
- Three makes of clear tape
- Three makes of paper clip
- Three makes of clothes peg
- Sheets of scrap paper
- Bulldog clip
- Metal mass hanger
- Consumer test information sheet **(R4.7)**
- 100 g masses
- 10 g masses
- Piece of material e.g. cotton about 20 cm × 7.5 cm
- Scissors
- Graph paper
- Poster paper
- Coloured pencils
- OHP transparencies, if required
- OHP pens
- Tape recorder and blank C15 tape, if required.

Pupils could be asked to spend some time looking at a particular report.
Pupils could consider how easily each product breaks, e.g. tearing the tape, breaking the clips by repeated bending, breaking the pegs by twisting each arm (with care).
An alternative to the oral presentation is to have pupils record their report on tape.

4.8—Talkabout—Design flaws

- Range of coat hangers, cutlery, ring pull cans and different kinds of hard-to-open packaging.

The items shown in the pupils' book could be made available to encourage discussion.

4.9—Readabout—New materials

This reading exercise could be set as homework. It might lead to some discussion of new materials used in other contexts, such as the home (new furniture foams, Teflon-2 coatings, fabrics etc.), in buildings (glass fibre, carbon fibre, precast concrete etc.), in communications (fibre optics) and many others. This could generate a poster.

Assessment 4

The questions are designed to assess the skills and knowledge developed in the unit, as shown in the table. A selection of questions would be appropriate for a unit test.

Topic	*Core*	*Extension*
4.1	1	7
4.2	2	8
4.3	3	9
4.4	4	10
4.5	5	11
4.6	6	12

Answers

1 1—pushing, 2—twisting, 3—pulling, 4—tearing, 5—pulling, 6—twisting.

2 a Contact: weight, friction, tearing. Non-contact: magnetism, electrostatic, gravity.

b **(i)** Magnetic force can act from a distance through the paper *or* magnet does not have to be in contact with iron to exert a force.
(ii) The closer a magnet is to iron the stronger the force it exerts *or* the magnetic force only works within a certain distance of the fridge.

c **(i)** Gravity; **(ii)** magnetism;
(iii) electrostatics/static electricity.

3 a Heat energy.

b **(i)** The surface is rough *or* the surfaces will rub against each other as they move.
(ii) The oil smooths the area between the two surfaces *or* the place where the surfaces meet is smoother/less rough.

c **(i)** Position *1* (climber and air), *nuisance* friction.
Position *2* (joints and bones), *nuisance* friction.
Position *3* (boots and ground), *useful* friction.

Position *4* (shoulder and knapsack), *nuisance* friction.
(ii) most to least useful: B, D, C, A.
(iii) Hillwalker would slip; rain/icy/slippery conditions.

4 a A—stay the same, B—stay the same, C—increase, D—decrease.
b B, F, G.

5 a Muscle A, **(i)** bone 2, **(ii)** back/to right/up.
Muscle B, **(i)** bone 3, **(ii)** back/to right/up.
Muscle C, **(i)** bone 4, **(ii)** up.
Muscle D, **(i)** bone 6, **(ii)** forward/to left.
b **(i)** F; **(ii)** E.
c Pulling force.

6 a **(i)** Any workable arrangement of the given apparatus, with the mass carrier attached to the thread.
(ii) Any two variables stated as controlled; e.g. length of threads, thickness of threads, *or* 1 variable controlled and idea of repeating experiment.
b Elastic band—pulling/twisting, corkscrew—twisting/pulling, spade handle—pushing, bottle opener—pushing, guitar string—pushing/pulling

7 a **(i)** Pulling force/weight; **(ii)** Newton meter/spring balance;
(iii) 4.5 newton.
b $X = 5\,N$, $Y = 15\,N$

8 a **(i)** increases the strength; **(ii)** any number between 34 and 37.
b **(i)** switch current on to pick up iron;
(ii) switch current off to drop iron into lorry.
c Door bell, relay switch, TV, radio, cassette player (*any three*).

9 a The rougher the surface the sooner the car stops—a relationship between the surface (rougher/more friction) and the extent of the stopping distance should be expressed.
b 1.2 m
c Stopping distance would increase, because the friction has been reduced.
d Stopping distance would increase.

10 a A—up; B—up; C—stay still; D—up.
b A—250 N, B—750 N, C—100 N.
c A—**(i)** 2, **(ii)** 1; B—**(i)** 3, **(ii)** 4; C—**(i)** 1, **(ii)** 3.

11 a Fewer press-ups were completed in each successive minute *or* more press ups in the first than the second than the third minute.
b Muscles became tired *or* no more energy.
c Ali.
d 16

12 Magnet to remove iron chips; charged rod to remove plastic chips; water to remove floating wood; copper chips remain.

True/false 4

Each statement is marked as either true or false by the pupil. This gives a rapid assessment of a pupil's grasp of the Attainment Targets covered in the unit. The following list gives the Attainment Targets covered by each set of statements.

1	AT 10-3a	7	AT 6-4a,b
2	AT 10-3b	8	AT 10-4b
3	AT 10-4a	9	AT 10-4d
4	AT 10-4c	10	AT 10-5c
5	AT 10-5a	11	AT 11-6c
6	AT 10-5d		

Unit 4 Everyday forces

1 What type of force is acting at each of the numbered points in these drawings?

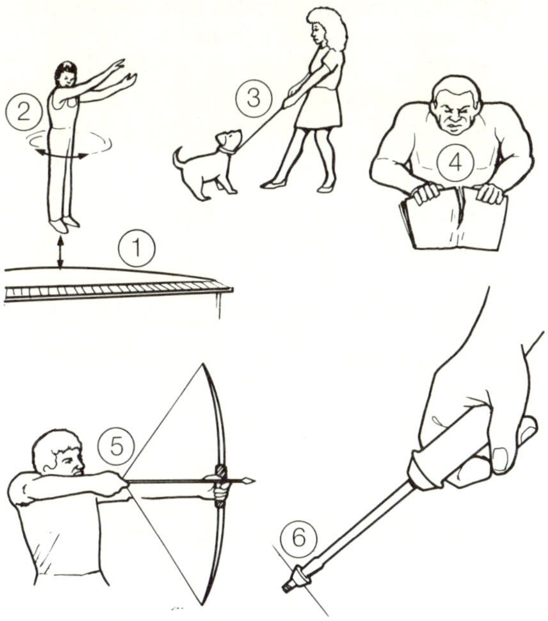

2 a Look at this list of forces.

- weight
- magnetism
- electrostatic
- friction
- gravity
- tearing

Divide the forces into two groups: those which are contact forces and those which are non-contact forces.

b Fridge magnets can be used to hold sheets of paper from a message pad on a fridge door. Here are the results of an experiment to see how many sheets of paper could be held on by a magnet.

Number of sheets	Held successfully?
1	Yes
2	Yes
3	No
4	No

(i) How can the magnet hold paper on a fridge door?

(ii) What conclusion can you make from the results of the experiment?

c Name the force that

(i) attracts objects to the centre of the earth

(ii) attracts an iron nail

(iii) attracts bits of paper to a rubbed plastic comb.

3 a What type of energy is produced when friction acts?

b Surfaces that feel smooth look rough under a microscope. The drawings show what you might see.

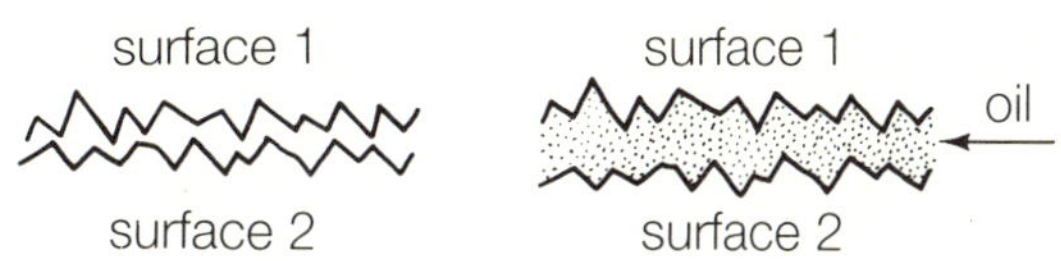

(i) Why will there be friction between the moving surfaces shown in the first drawing?

(ii) Describe how the oil in the second diagram will reduce friction.

c (i) Friction can be either useful or a nuisance in everyday situations.

When you are hillwalking . . .

continued ▶

Copy the table below. **Complete** the first two columns of the table. Then decide if the friction is either useful or a nuisance.

Position	Friction acting between ...	Is friction useful or a nuisance?
1	______ and air	
2	Joints and bones	
3	______ and ground	
4	Shoulder and ______	

(ii) The soles of four types of footwear are shown in the diagram. Write down the letters of the boots starting with the most useful for hillwalking and ending with the least useful.

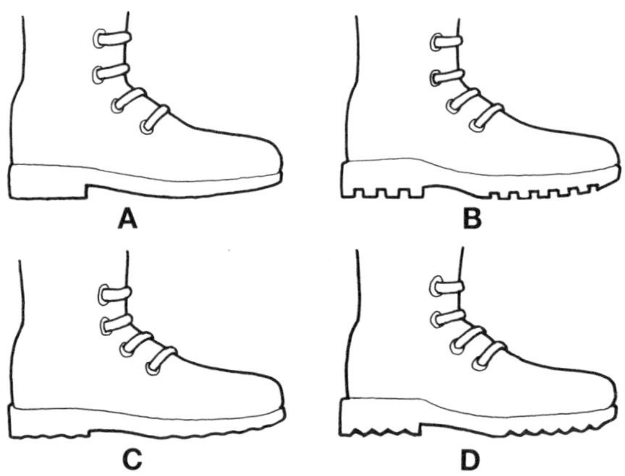

(iii) What would happen if there was suddenly no friction between the ground and the boots? What ground conditions would reduce the friction?

4 a Decide if the speed of the model car will increase, decrease or stay the same in each of these diagrams.

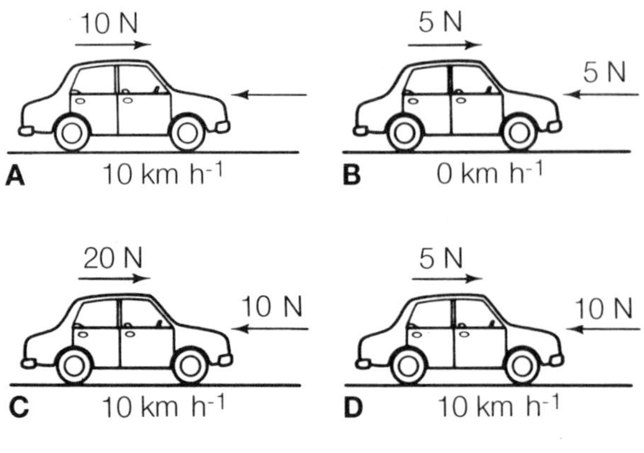

b Which of these statements describe balanced forces?

A The raft sank like a stone.
B The ball sat motionless on the penalty spot.
C She jumped from the plane and started to fall, faster and faster.
D The parachute filled with air and she slowed down.
E The roller coaster suddenly raced down the track.
F He stood still on the thin ice.
G She held the spring hard against the bench.

5 The diagram shows the bones and some of the muscles of the human leg.
The bones are labelled 1 to 6.
The muscles are labelled A to F.
An × shows the end of the muscle where there is no movement.

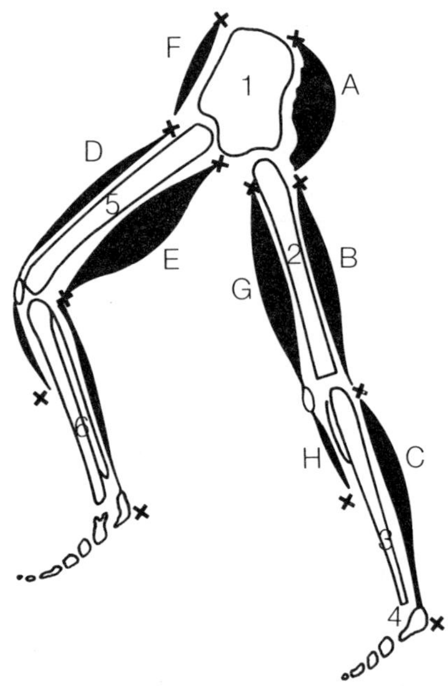

a For muscles A–D write down
(i) the bone that it moves
(ii) the direction of the movement.

b Which muscle works in the opposite way to
(i) muscle A
(ii) muscle D?

c What type of force do muscles produce?

continued ▶

6 a You are given the apparatus shown in the diagram.
(i) Design an experiment to compare the strength of cotton, polyester and nylon threads.

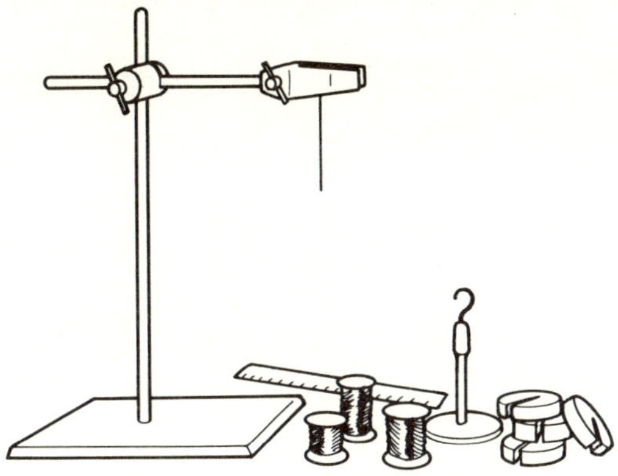

(ii) What would you do to make the comparison fair?

b A pencil lead needs to be able to withstand pushing forces. What types of force should each of the following objects be able to withstand?

- Elastic band
- Corkscrew
- Spade handle
- Bottle opener
- Guitar string

Extension questions

7 a Examine this drawing.

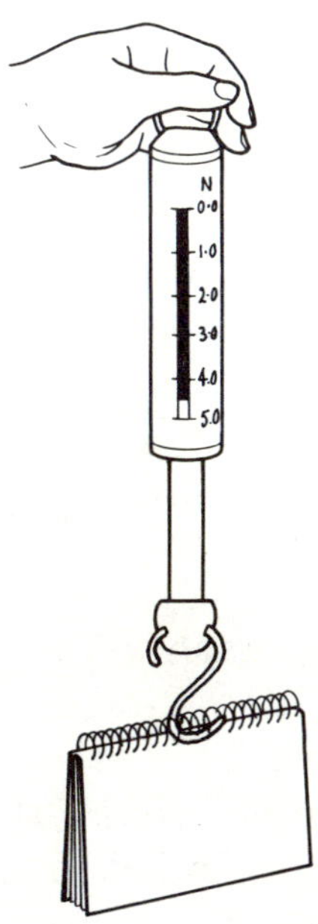

(i) What force is being measured by this instrument?
(ii) What is the name of the instrument?
(iii) Write down the reading shown and the units of measurement.

b The table shows a comparison of weight and mass.

Object	Mass	Weight
3 year old boy	15 kg	150 N
Bag of sugar	1 kg	10 N
Textbook	0.5 kg	*X*
Bag of potatoes	1.5 kg	*Y*

What are the values of *X* and *Y*?

8 a A pupil made an electromagnet to pick up pins. She then tested the effect of putting more cells in the circuit. Her results are shown in the table.

Cells in circuit	Pins picked up
1	7
2	15
3	22
5	?

(i) What effect does adding more cells have on the strength of the electromagnet?
(ii) How many pins would you expect the electromagnet with five cells in the circuit to lift?

b Describe how you would use an electromagnet to
(i) collect the iron from a pile of rubbish
(ii) transfer the iron to a lorry.

c Name three household objects which contain electromagnets.

continued ▶

9 The bar chart shows the stopping distances of a wind-up car on three different surfaces.

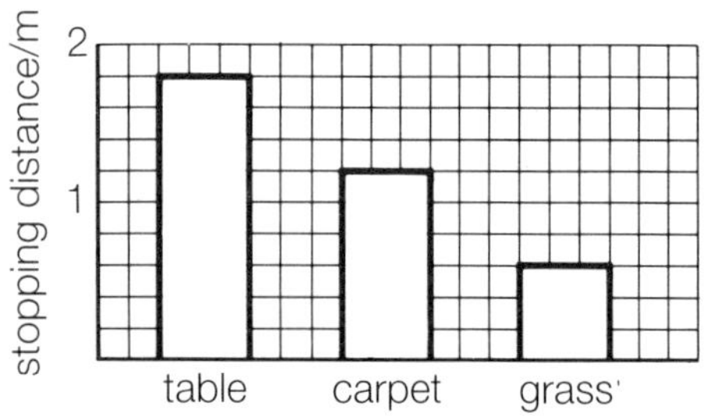

a Suggest a reason for the pattern of results shown by the bar chart.
b What was the stopping distance of the car on the carpet?
c If the wooden table top was polished what effect would this have on the stopping distance of the car?
Give a reason for your answer.
d What would happen to the stopping distance if the car was travelling faster?

10 a Four see-saws are shown in the diagram.

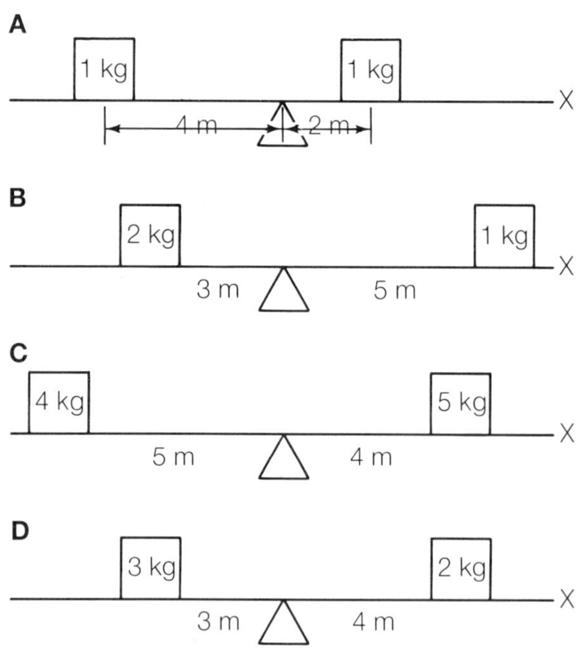

For each of the see-saws decide whether end X will move up, move down or stay still.

b The diagram shows three ways of trying to just move a boulder weighing 250 N, using a crowbar and a pivot.

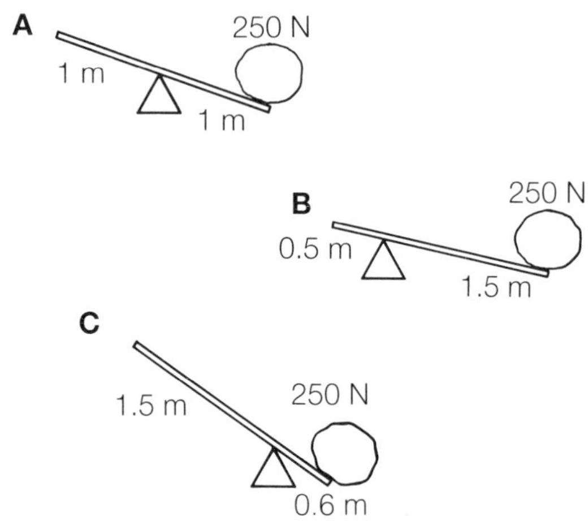

What force in newtons would be required at the end of the crowbar in each diagram?

c These three machines all use levers.

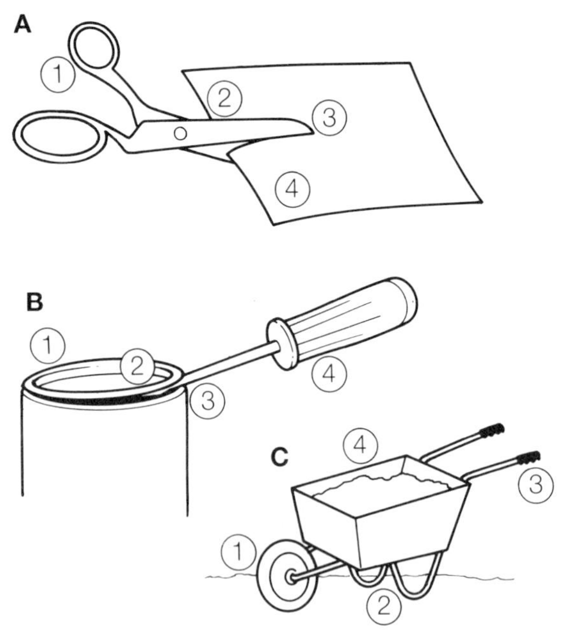

For each machine, write down the number at
(i) the pivot
(ii) the place where the force should be applied to operate the machine.

continued ▶

11 Three pupils were asked to do as many press-ups as they could in one minute. They were then allowed to rest for one minute before repeating the exercise. They had a further minute's rest and then did a final minute of press-ups.
The results are shown in the table.

Pupil	Press-ups completed		
	1st minute	2nd minute	3rd minute
Alex	16	12	4
Nicky	19	15	10
Ali	19	17	12

a What is the pattern in these results?
b Give an explanation for this pattern.
c Who seems to have the strongest muscles?
d What is the average number of press-ups completed by Ali in a minute?

12 This table gives some properties of four different materials.

Material	Floats?	Attracted to magnet?	Attracted to charged rod?
Plastic	Yes	No	Yes
Copper	No	No	No
Iron	No	Yes	No
Wood	Yes	No	No

You are given a mixture of plastic chips, copper chips, iron chips and wooden chips. Describe how you could separate this mixture into its four different parts.

Unit 4 Everyday forces

Name ______________________

Put a tick after the statements that are true. Put a cross after the statements that are false.

1 a A force is needed to stop a moving object. ☐
b A change in shape is always caused by a force. ☐
c No force is required to turn the pages of a book. ☐

2 a An object sinks when its downward force is less than the upwards force of the water. ☐
b Spreading the weight of an object over the water surface helps it to float. ☐
c Heavy objects cannot float in water. ☐

3 a The greater the force acting on an object the faster it will move. ☐
b A fast-moving car is not affected by the pushing force of wind when it comes from the side. ☐

4 a Gravity is a force that attracts objects to the centre of the earth. ☐
b On the moon the force of gravity is much lower than on earth and it is possible to jump higher. ☐
c In low gravity, a ball thrown in the air would fall faster than in high gravity. ☐

5 a When forces are balanced there can be no movement. ☐
b If you run your finger along a straight line at a steady speed balanced forces are acting. ☐
c Balanced forces are acting when any object floats. ☐

6 a The force of friction acts against a moving object. ☐
b When friction acts there is a drop in temperature. ☐
c Friction helps to prevent an object from slipping out of your hand. ☐

7 a Materials are chosen for particular jobs because of their properties. ☐
b Rubber is soft and flexible. These are examples of properties. ☐
c Soya bean, sunflower and vegetable oil are examples of properties of margarine. ☐

Extensions

8 a The faster an object moves the quicker it can stop. ☐
b Fast-moving cars should stay close behind each other for safety. ☐
c The faster an object moves the greater the force required to stop it quickly. ☐

9 a Weight is a force. ☐
b Force is measured in newtons. ☐

10 a Pushing forces can be measured in units called kilograms. ☐
b Distance can be measured in centimetres using a metre rule. ☐
c Time is measured in seconds. ☐

11 a The magnetic effect of an electromagnet can be turned on and off. ☐
b An electromagnet can be made from a nail and a piece of wire. ☐
c The strength of an electromagnet can be changed by changing the electric current. ☐

Unit 4 Everyday forces

Name ____________________

Complete each sentence. Put the correct word(s) in each blank space.

1 Forces can cause an object to

- start or ________________
- change direction and to change ________________.

2 Pushing, pulling, tearing and ________________ are all examples of ________________ forces.

3 Magnetism, electrostatics and ________________ are examples of ________________ forces. The force of gravity pulls objects towards the ________________ of the earth.

4 When forces are balanced an object does not move at all or it moves at a ________________ speed.
An object will float on water if the forces on the object pushing ________________ are ________________ by the force of the water pushing upwards.

5 Friction is a force that ________________ movement. When friction acts ________________ energy is produced.
Two examples of friction being useful are

- ____
- ____.

6 For movement at a joint ________________ sets of muscles are needed.

A muscle can produce a ________________ force when it ________________.

A muscle cannot produce a ________________ force when it relaxes.

7 Good design depends on choosing materials that are

- ________________
- ________________
- ________________.

Face sheet

Face sheet

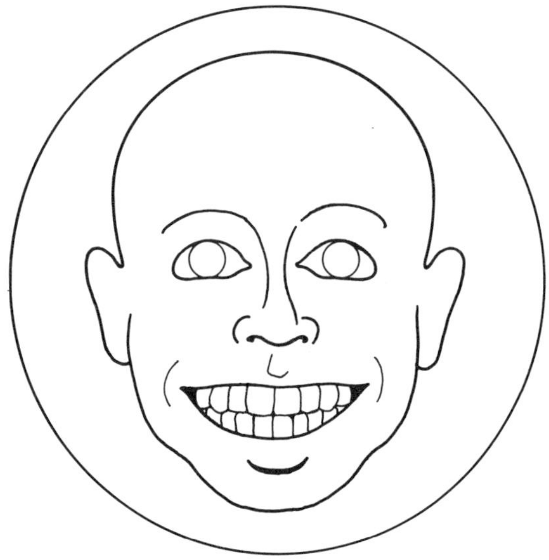

Face sheet

Face sheet

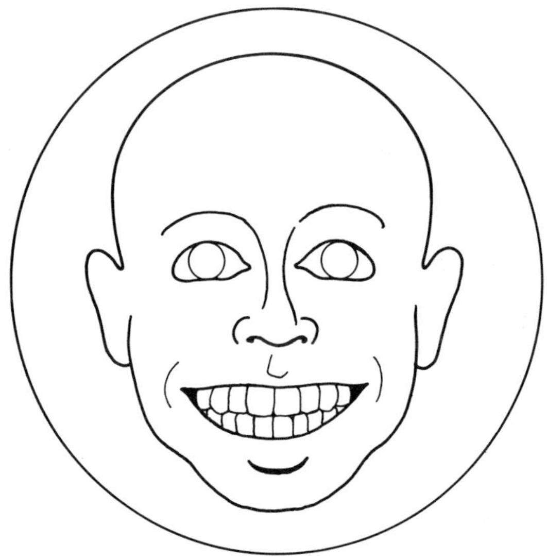

Face sheet

Face sheet

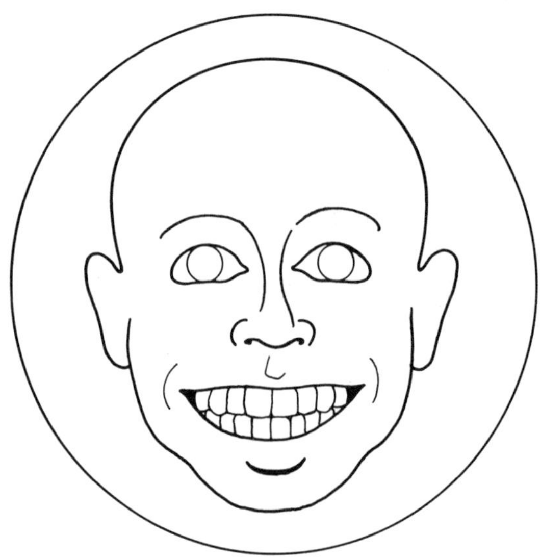

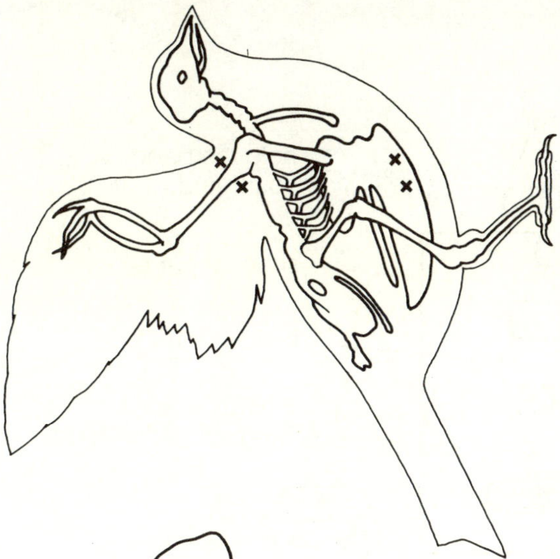

Flap a wing

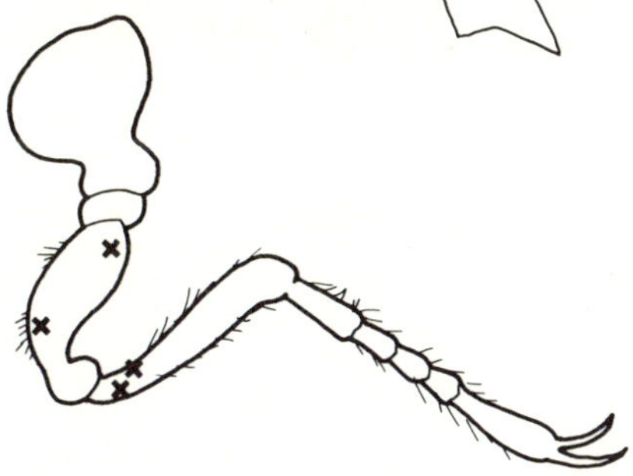

Shake a leg

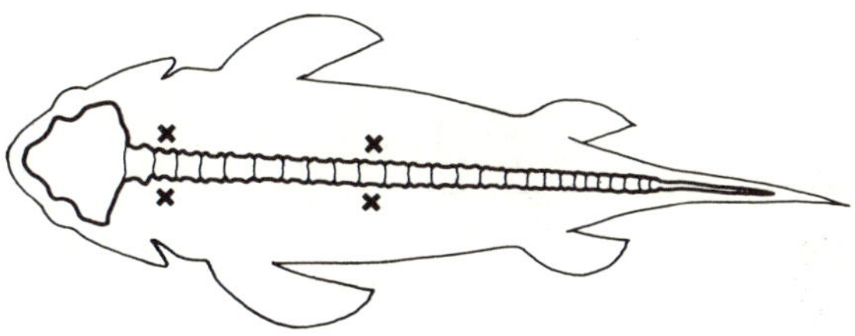

Flick a tail

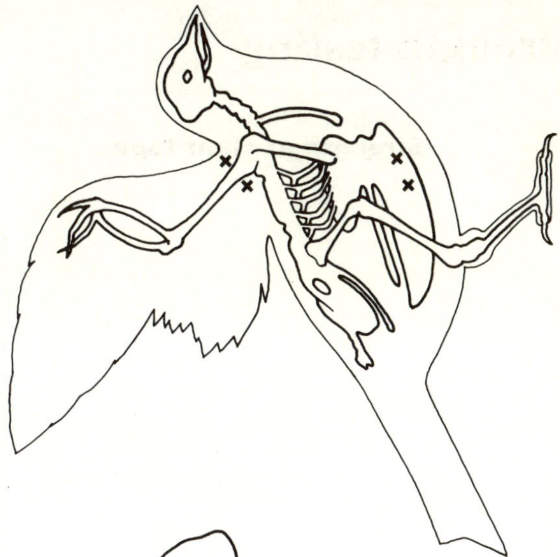

Flap a wing

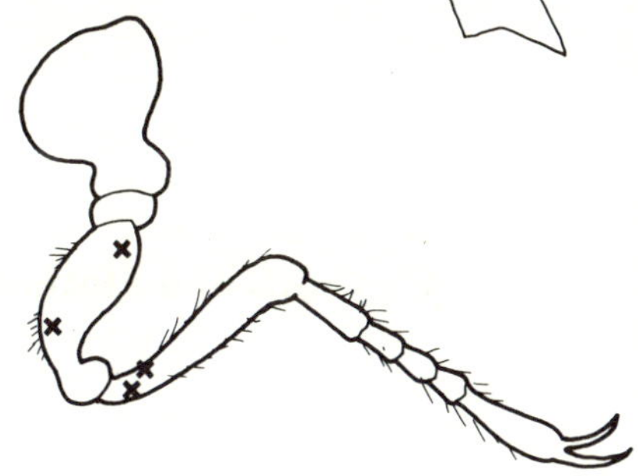

Shake a leg

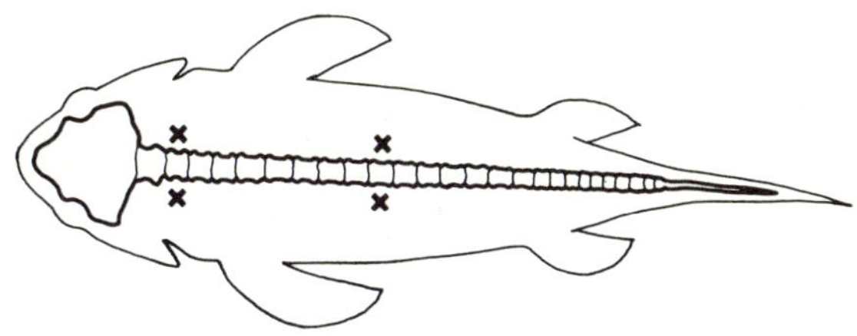

Flick a tail

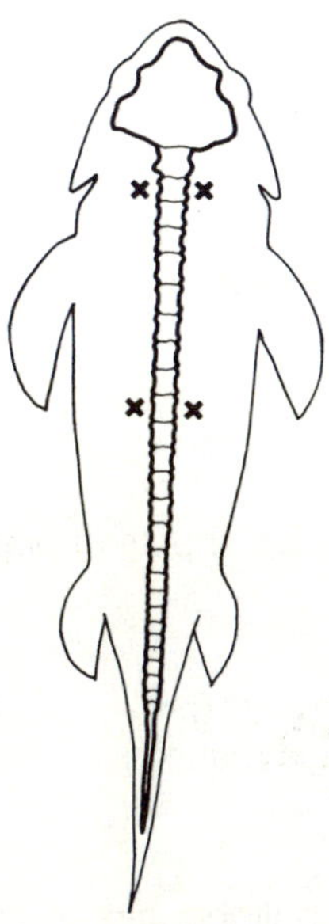

Flick a tail

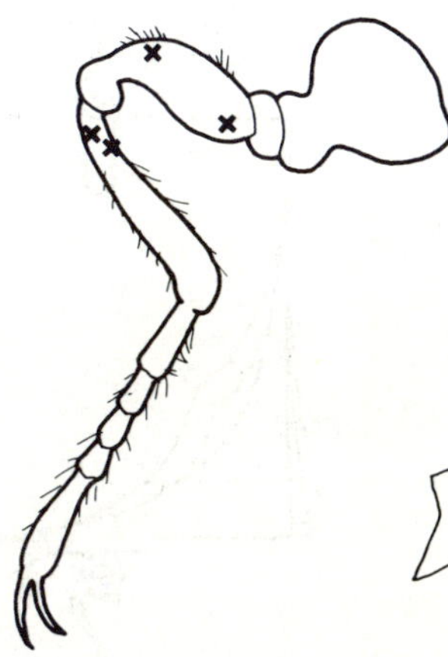

Shake a leg

Flap a wing

Strength testing

How to test the
Strength of clear tape

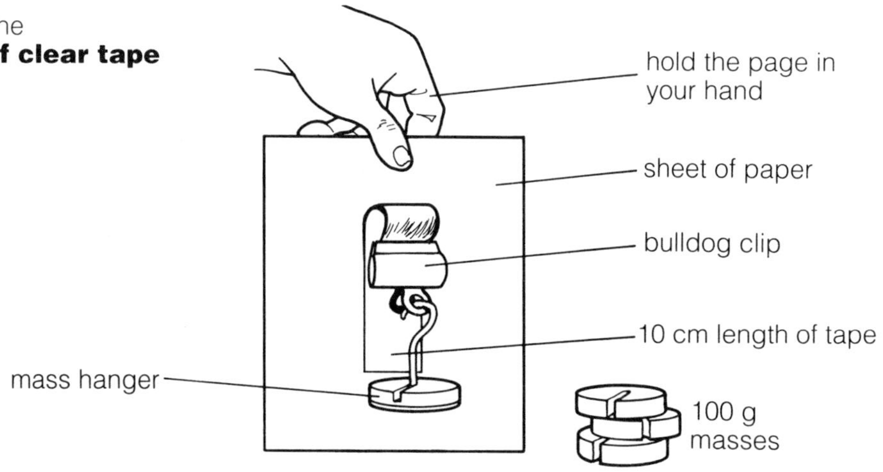

How to test the
Strength of a clothes peg

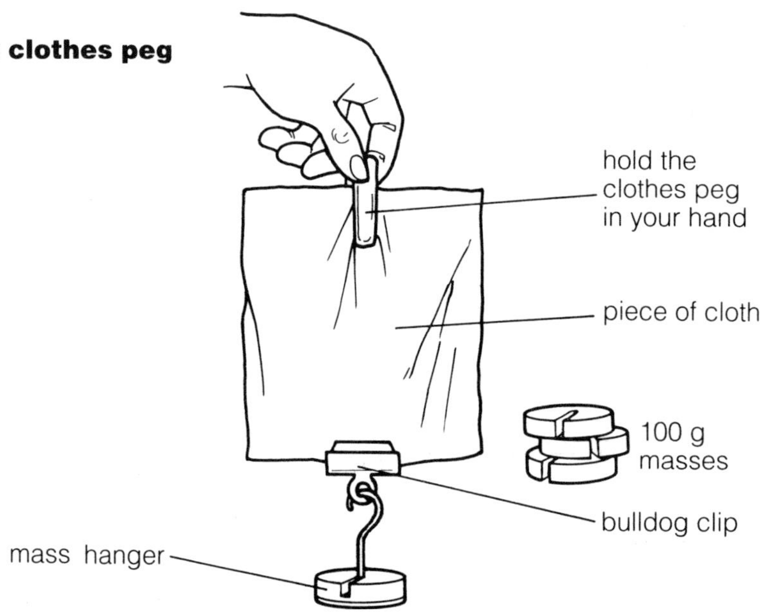

How to test the
Strength of a paper clip

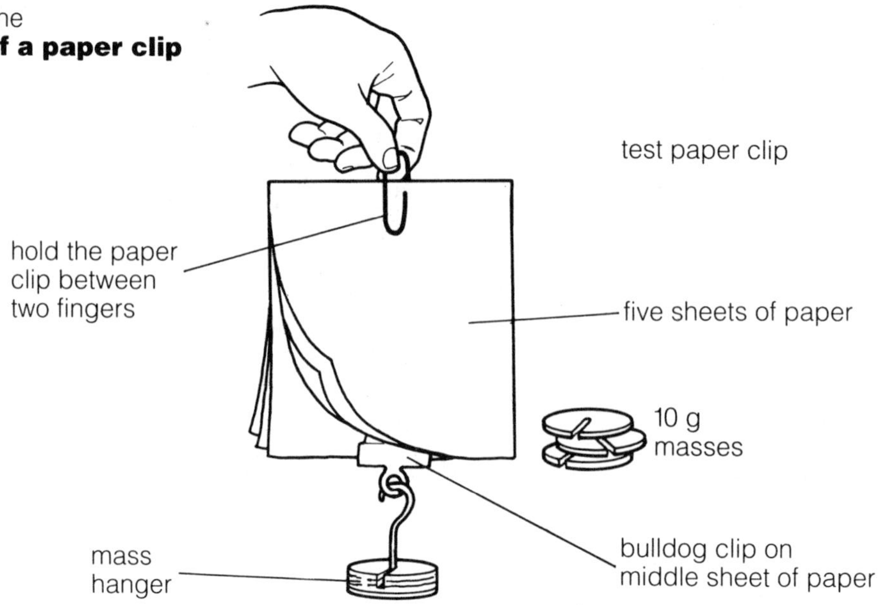

Unit 5 Tiny ideas

Thinking about particles

The first nine topics introduce pupils to the nature and purpose of scientific hypotheses. The importance of collecting observations, finding patterns in information and attempting plausible explanations is stressed. (The approach builds on earlier work in Book 1, Unit 6.) The skills of hypothesising and predicting are first illustrated and then practised in the context of particle theory. This theory is developed as an example of a scientific model which offers a likely explanation of some experimental observations. The model is then used to make predictions. Pupils will find such work difficult and so the nature of the model is treated more fully than its detail. Of course some basic knowledge is also given concerning the size, movement and spacing of particles, the arrangement of particles in solids, liquids and gases and the changes in arrangement which lead to expansion and contraction of objects. The key concepts of small size, movement and spacing can be consolidated by using the resource sheets provided at the end of the unit. The final three topics comprise an investigation, a group discussion activity and a short reading exercise about an historical subject. In addition to meeting the general demands of Attainment Target 1, this unit deals specifically with AT 1, levels 3a, 3h, 4b, 4i, 4j, 5d.

Core and Reinforcement

5.1 Scientific thinking *AT 16–3b; AT 17–5a,b*

Conduct several practical activities and try to explain what happens.
Discuss one activity and collaborate to produce a poster which summarises a likely explanation for what happens. *page 80*

Follow instructions given in a diagram.
Observe.
Suggest a scientific explanation for an unfamiliar observation.
Communicate ideas in written form and by discussion.

5.2 Finding patterns

Match fingerprint halves by observation.
Find a pattern in the results of heating a bimetallic strip and of flame tests on selected solids. *page 82*

Recognise a pattern in experimental data.
Apply a recognised pattern in data to predict the result of a related experiment.

5.3 Bits and pieces *AT 8–4a*

Conduct two experiments where a coloured solid is dissolved in water.
Describe a pattern in the results given guidance.
Try to explain the pattern given guidance. *page 84*

Observe.
Recognise a pattern in experimental data.
Communicate a recognised pattern in written form, given help.
Explain phenomena given help.

Extension

5.1

Conduct several experiments with two magnets.
From a number of statements, choose the most appropriate description of the results and the most likely explanation. *page 156*

Follow instructions.
Observe.
Recognise a valid and an invalid conclusion.

5.2

Find patterns in the names and colours of selected (ionic) solids. *page 157*

Recognise several patterns in data.
Apply a recognised pattern in data to predict other related data.

5.3 *AT 17–5a*

Solve three pictorial puzzles by asking good questions of the teacher (class activity). *page 158*

Extract relevant information from verbal communications.
Recognise a pattern in information.
Make decisions based on examination of evidence.

Core and Reinforcement	Extension
5.4 Likely explanations *AT 8–4a; AT 17–5a,b*	*AT 8–5a*
Use a game to explore the nature of hypothesising. Use the idea of particles to explain the appearance of solid from a dried solution. *page 86*	Build models of molecules from model atoms. *page 159*
Recognise that the practice of science is subject to limitations. Evaluate data critically. Recognise valid patterns in data. Explain an observation in terms of small particles.	Translate information from a diagram to a model.
5.5 Moving particles *AT 8–4a; AT 17–5a*	*AT 8–4a*
Use nose to detect movement of ammonia particles. Look at Brownian motion in hot milk and in smoke. *page 88*	Use pH paper to show the movement of ammonia particles. *page 160*
Follow instructions. Observe. Suggest a scientific explanation for observations.	Follow instructions. Observe. Communicate observations in a given table.
5.6 Spaced-out particles *AT 8–4a*	*AT 8–4a*
Use agar impregnated with indicator to show the movement of particles. Infer the existence of spaces between particles by considering experimental evidence and by analogy. *page 90*	Note the different rates of diffusion of two solids through water. Watch a **demonstration** of the diffusion of bromine or iodine through a partial vacuum. *page 161*
Communicate an experimental result in a labelled diagram and a written description. Explain observations in terms of particles.	Communicate an experimental result in a labelled diagram and a written description. Explain observations in terms of particles.
5.7 Making a hypothesis *AT 16–4a*	*AT 16–4b*
Explore several hypotheses about the phases of the moon. Summarise a hypothesis about particles. *page 92*	Draw bar graphs to illustrate information about the planets in the solar system. Derive a hypothesis from the bar graphs. *page 162*
Recognise a pattern in given data. Form a hypothesis based on this pattern. Extract information from self-sought sources. Explain unfamiliar observations in terms of self-sought scientific information.	Translate information from a table to a bar graph. Recognise patterns from graphical data. Form hypotheses based on these patterns.
5.8 Making predictions *AT 8–6a; AT 17–6a*	*AT 6–4e*
Use given hypotheses to make predictions. Test the predictions by experiment. *page 94*	Observe, discuss and summarise the properties of solids, liquids and gases. *page 163*
Predict experimental results using hypotheses. Recognise that the practice of science is subject to limitations. Classify substances into three groups according to properties.	Classify substances into three groups according to personal criteria. Communicate scientific ideas logically.

Core and Reinforcement

5.9 Model predictions

AT 6–4d; AT 8–6a,b; AT 17–6a

Use the particle model to predict the ease of compression of solid, liquid and gas and the effect of heating and cooling on a piece of metal. *page 96*

Predict experimental results using a particle model.

5.10 Problem—Build a fire alarm

Use earlier knowledge to design and build an automatic fire alarm. Guidance is given if necessary. *page 98*

Devise and build an apparatus which applies scientific knowledge to meet a given specification.
Communicate a design in a labelled diagram.

5.11 Talkabout—Good questions *AT 17–5a*

Solve four pictorial puzzles by asking good questions of an individual (group activity). *page 99*

Extract relevant information from verbal communications.
Recognise a pattern in information.
Make decisions based on examination of evidence.

5.12 Readabout—Forbidden ideas

AT 17–4a, 6a, 7a

Read a short passage about the ideas of Copernicus and Galileo concerning the position of the sun at the centre of the solar system. *page 100*

Extract relevant information from given and self-sought sources.

Extension

AT 6–4d; AT 8–6b; AT 17–6a

Investigate the expansion of liquids when heated. Design an experiment to investigate their contraction when cooled. *page 164*

Follow instructions.
Devise and carry out an experiment for a given purpose.

Equipment

required for each pupil group

5.1—Scientific thinking

- Sundial instruction sheet **(R5.1A)**
- Polystyrene tile
- Card
- Sharp knife
- Compass
- Activity cards **(R5.1B)**

Activity 1

- Hen's egg (uncooked)
- Slotted masses (100 g) and carrier

Notes

The activities are designed to encourage discussion about the results. At this stage it is not important to reach a right answer although the pupils' ideas should relate to the observations.
Set up two sets of activities 1, 2, 4, 5, 6 as stations experiments. Demonstrate activity 3.

Equipment
required for each pupil group

- Blu-Tack or Plasticine
- Clamp stand

Activity 2
- Dry ice
- Beaker
- Insulated gloves

Activity 3
- Syrup tin or similar with tight lid
- Safety glasses
- Bunsen burner and heatproof mat
- Safety screen
- Tripod stand and wire gauze

Activity 4
- Three 20 cm^3 plastic syringes with the end sealed, containing air, water and wood (dowel)

Activity 5
- Bottles of solid:
  wax—labelled A
  phenyl salicylate (salol)—labelled B
  urea—labelled C
- Tin lid and tripod stand
- Bunsen burner and heatproof mat

Activity 6
- Bimetallic strip
- Bunsen burner and heatproof mat

Activity 7
- Vacuum pump
- Oil can or similar (plastic is best because the can reforms its original shape)

Activity 8
- **Blunt** razor blade
- Tweezers
- Beaker

- Poster paper
- Coloured pencils/pens

Notes

Pupils should work in pairs.

Each report should be completed before the pair begin the next activity.
There are two replacement activities in the resource sheets for flexibility.

Posters should be titled, dated and put on the wall. The ideas on them can then be referred to during the unit as the pupils' explanations develop.

Extension
- Magnet stand with 2 ring magnets, one magnet has a blank label on its north pole and the other a blank label on its south pole
- Cling film or similar

Answers to questions are **1** Carmel, **2** Barry and Delia, **3** Albert, Barry and Delia.

5.2—Finding patterns
- Fingerprint halves **(R5.2)**
- Bimetallic strip
- Bunsen burner and heatproof mat

Equipment
required for each pupil group

- Access to ice
- Beaker
- Set of solids for flame testing:
  copper(II) chloride
  lithium chloride
  sodium chloride
  copper(II) carbonate
  lithium sulphate
- Bottles of sodium sulphate & copper(II) sulphate
- Flame test rods
- Spotting tile

Notes

Extension

- Bottles of
  cobalt(II) chloride
  ammonium chloride
  sodium dichromate

Seal the bottles with tape

5.3—Bits and pieces

- Potassium permanganate crystals
- 5 test tubes and rack
- Beaker
- Sodium carbonate crystals
- Copper(II) sulphate crystals
- Petri dish
- Spatula (or wooden splint)
- Mustard powder

The grains of mustard powder can be seen dispersed in the water. The number decreases obviously at each dilution.

Extension

No equipment required

These lateral-thinking exercises are best used with the whole class. Refuse to give any answer to a question apart from yes or no.
The good question is the one which leads to more information (which is relevant).
Solutions:
1 The elephant was parachuting and the chute failed to open in time.
2 The man used a block of ice which has since melted.
3 Mark Anthony is a goldfish. Cleopatra knocked over his bowl in her sleep.

5.4—Likely explanations

- Clue cards for murder game **(R5.4)**
- Envelope marked *Right answer* containing a blank card
- Clean evaporating basin
- Bunsen burner and heatproof mat
- Tripod stand
- Salt water in a bottle labelled 'Bottled water'
- Safety glasses

The pupils should be given a time limit.
There is no correct explanation given to these clues (although there are several possible ones).
Discuss with the class how each explanation was worked out. Stress the importance of looking for a pattern and then trying it out on other clues.

Equipment required for each pupil group	**Notes**
Extension	
● Set of molecular models (e.g. Molymod)	If possible use: black, 4 holes—for carbon; white, 1 hole—for hydrogen; red, 2 holes—for oxygen. Give pupils a colour key if different colours are used.
5.5—Moving particles	
● Watch glass containing concentrated ammonia solution	Keep covered when not in use. Do not allow pupils to sniff the fumes directly.
● Coloured pens/pencils	
● Dilute **full-fat** milk, hot (almost boiling)	Dilute the milk until it is a watery grey colour. Heat until steaming. The milk must be full fat otherwise there will not be enough fat globules. When examined with a microscope the fat globules can be seen to jiggle around randomly. There may also be convection currents. The hotter the milk, the more obvious is the Brownian motion.
● Microscope	
● Microscope lamp	
● Slide	
● Cover slip	
● Dropper	
● Smoke cell with power supply (12V d.c.)	Set this up while pupils are looking at the milk. The smoke cell can be filled by a dropper with smoke from several burning wooden spills. Use low power to look for the smoke at the sides of the cell about half way down it.
● Vaseline and glass seal for cell	
Extension	
● 2 M ammonia solution	
● Cotton wool	
● Tweezers	
● Marker pen/pencil (for glass)	
● Small pieces of universal indicator paper (or red litmus)	
● Boiling tube	
● Heatproof mat	
● Access to timer	
5.6—Spaced out particles	
● Petri dish with agar jelly and indicator	Prepare agar dish in advance. Add 3 g of agar to 100 cm³ of water and dissolve by heating gently and stirring. When hot remove heat source and add a few cubic centimetres of universal indicator solution. The agar can be poured into petri dishes and left for an hour to set. More concentrated agar solution will set more quickly.
● Cork borer	
● Tweezers	
● Dropper bottle of 0.5 M hydrochloric acid	
● Dropper bottle of 0.5 M sodium hydroxide	
● Alcohol (or methylated spirit)	
● Two 100 cm³ measuring cylinders (plastic)	
● 250 cm³ measuring cylinder (plastic)	

Equipment
required for each pupil group

- Sufficient long-grain rice
- Sufficient large dried peas
- Tray

Notes

After use, pupils should separate the peas from the rice using the tray.

Extension
- Iodine crystals
- Potassium permanganate crystals
- 2 test tubes and rack
- Bromine diffusion apparatus

Great care is needed with bromine. Check details and safety precautions before using the apparatus. An alternative is to use a sealed tube which is partially evacuated and contains iodine crystals. If the crystals are heated **gently** they sublime and the vapour diffuses very quickly to the opposite side of the tube. It then forms crystals again.

5.7—Making a hypothesis
- Expanded polystyrene ball painted half black
- Particles summary diagram **(R5.7)**
- Kinetic model

A variable electric motor causes vibration at the bottom of an enclosed tube. Small polystyrene balls represent particles.

Extension
- Graph paper
- Coloured pencils/pens

5.8—Making predictions
- Horoscope page from a paper or magazine for the coming week
- Coin
- Two balls made from different materials, e.g. wool, plastic, wood, or of different sizes
- Stoppered bottles containing:
  100 cm^3 of water (labelled B)
  gas from gas tap (labelled C)
- Single block of wood of volume 100 cm^3 (e.g. 10 × 5 × 2 cm) or small cubes of wood whose total volume is 100 cm^3 (labelled A)
- Ten substances set up around the room—four solids, four liquids and two gases (e.g. **1** plastic, **2** water, **3** milk, **4** empty bottle labelled air, **5** brick, **6** glass, **7** oil, **8** candle wax, **9** tea, **10** boiling kettle labelled steam). Each substance should be numbered

Photocopy for class use.

Pupils can refill by turning gas tap on and counting to five.

Extension
- About 20 further examples of solids, liquids, gases

Include problematic ones like toothpaste, hair mousse, body spray, sponge, powder.

5.9—Model predictions
- 20 cm^3 plastic syringe
- Large rubber stopper
- Wooden dowel which fits body of syringe

The class model will have to be well organised.

Equipment
required for each pupil group

Experiment 1

- Bunsen burner and heatproof mat
- 2 clamp stands with nichrome wire

Experiment 2

- Tongs
- Safety glasses
- Ball and ring
- Bunsen burner and heatproof mat

Experiment 3

- Iron pin breaker (commercial supplier)
- 2 bunsen burners and heatproof mat
- Ice
- Cloth
- Safety glasses

Extension

- 250 cm^3 conical flask with stopper and long glass tube
- Market pen/pencil
- Access to hot water in a basin
- Access to ice

5.10—Problem—Build a fire alarm

- Bimetallic strip
- Bunsen burner and heatproof mat
- 6 V d.c. electric bell or similar
- Power supply and connecting wires for bell
- Access to clamp stands
- Two crocodile clips
- Nail
- Clue cards **(R5.10)**

5.11—Talkabout—Good questions

No equipment required

5.12—Readabout—Forbidden ideas

No equipment required

Notes

The wire is wound around the clamps and the stand bases can be stabilised with weights.
A small weight can be added to the middle of the wire to stretch it.

The bar has to be heated strongly, preferably with two bunsen burners. Tighten nut. Cover the pin with a cloth and cool the bar, using ice if necessary. Pupils should wear safety glasses.

The water level is more obvious if a very dilute solution of potassium permanganate is used in the flask instead of water.

Clue cards should be given one at a time and in sequence.
A points system could be linked to the number of clues released to each group.

Solutions

A The man had hiccups. The barman gave him such a fright that the hiccups were cured.
B This is a picture of an early sextant. It is used in navigation.
C This is a picture of a modern electron microscope. It is used to see and take pictures of very small objects.
D The person is too short to reach the necessary lift button.

Equipment
required for each pupil group

Notes

5.13—CONSOLIDATION (R5.13)

The ideas in the unit need consolidation. The resource sheets will provide material for this if required.

Activity 1

- Incense stick
- Bunsen burner and heatproof mat

Activity 2

- Boiling tube with stopper and glass tube
- Small amount of potassium permanganate solution

Activity 3

- Same size blocks of metal, plastic, wood.

Activities 4 and 5

- Same as for Activities 4 and 5 in Topic 5.1

Activity 6

- Straw
- Access to warm water
- Crystals of potassium permanganate
- Spatula

- Poster paper
- Coloured pens/pencils

Earlier posters should be available for discussion. Discuss the two sets of posters, emphasising the differences in the quality of the explanations.

The authors are indebted to the writers of the scheme, 'Approaches to Teaching the Particulate Theory of Matter' (1987) *Children's Learning in Science Project,* Centre for Studies in Science and Mathematics Education, University of Leeds. Many approaches in this unit were suggested by this very useful material.

Assessment 5

The questions are designed to assess the skills and knowledge developed in the unit, as shown in the table. A selection of questions would be appropriate for a unit test.

Topic	*Core*	*Extension*
5.1	2	27
5.2	4, 5, 17	20
5.3	1, 17	—
5.4	3, 7	19, 21
5.5	6, 17	—
5.6	8	22
5.7	9, 10, 11	23
5.8	12, 13, 18	24, 25
5.9	14, 15	25, 26
5.10	16	—

Answers

1 Explanations should include: substance *breaks up* into *tiny particles* which *move/spread*.
2 A—2, B—3, C—1.
3 a Three weeks later I received a cheque . . .
b This money only appeared because a black cat . . .
c No, results need to be consistently repeatable.
4 a Red; **b** orange.
5 C, D.
6 a All labelled substances should be mentioned in the description.
b A white smoke forms in the middle of the tube.
c Move.
7 a Particles must be able to move out of the balloon.
b Smoke hit by moving air particles.
c Particles of scent move.
d Dye is made of tiny particles which spread/move.
8 Bad as there is empty space between particles (oxygen anyway is part of air).
9 a A likely explanation for some observation(s).
b Any reasonable experiment.
10 a Appearance of lit up part of the moon.
b Appearance changes because moon moves around the earth.
11 a Hypothesis A, result D.
b Hypothesis E, result G.

12 Hypothesis was that there was a pattern in the behaviour of the elements and the prediction was what unknown elements would look like.

13 a Any reasonable answer (room temperature assumed).

b (i) P is gas, Q is solid, R is liquid; **(ii)** P; **(iii)** P.

14 a Any size between 65 and 70 mm.

b Any size between 65 and 60 mm.

15 Particles move more so the spaces between them increase; this causes the lid to expand and become looser.

16 Refer to Readabout (topic 5.12).

17 Account should be substantially correct and include something on each of a–e

18 a Wire will sag.

b A coloured solid is left behind.

c The tyre bursts (or expands out of shape).

19 a Title which links rabbit temperature with variable place.

b Rabbit temperature is constant.

c Rabbit is keeping its body temperature constant, or other reasonable explanation.

20 a Yellow. Explanation should refer to pattern in the given information.

b White. As for **a**.

c There is no information about the colour associated with copper.

21 a Small particle

b Atoms (two or more) joined together

c CCl_4

d

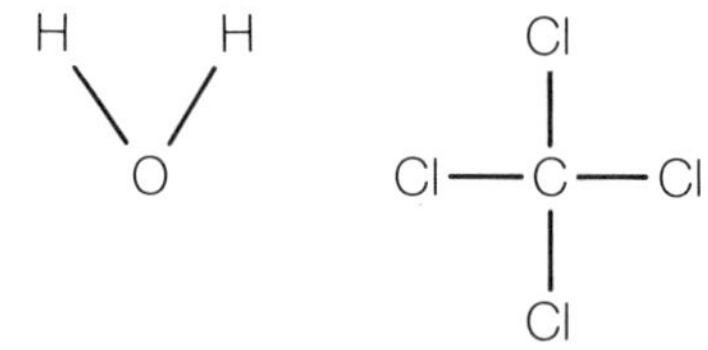

22 a Spread out/intermingle.

b Any suitable sentence.

23 Any word using some or all of the following letters: M, V, E, M, J, S, U, N, P.

24 One possible explanation is that the solid has changed to a gas. The particles therefore take up more space. There are other explanations.

25 a B, C, D, F. **b** A, B, C, D. **c** A, C, D, E.

26 All words given should be used correctly (in context).

27 Sundials use the changing length and direction of shadows cast by the sun to tell the time.

True/false 5

Each statement is marked as either true or false by the pupil. This gives a rapid assessment of a pupil's grasp of the Attainment Targets covered in the unit. The following list gives the Attainment Targets covered by each set of statements.

1 AT 6–4c
2 AT 6–4d
3 AT 8–4a, 6a
4 AT 8–6b
5 AT 16–3b
6 AT 16–4a
7 AT 17–4a
8 AT 17–5a
9 AT 17–5b
10 AT 17–6a
11 AT 17–6b
12 AT 6–4e
13 AT 8–5a
14 AT 16–4b
15 AT 16–4c

Unit 5 Tiny ideas

1 A substance is put into a bath that is full of water. After a few days the substance has coloured all the water. Write an explanation of this which mentions **particles**.

2 Match the following experimental results with the correct explanations.

Experimental result	Explanation
A If you heat water in a closed tin then you can blow the lid off	**1** The particles react with oxygen
B You cannot press in the plunger of a syringe that is full of water.	**2** The particles become more spaced out.
C Paper burns when it is heated.	**3** The particles are very close together.

3 Read this report about an experiment.

My Mum said that it was a sign of good luck if a black cat ran in front of you. I decided to experiment. One day I waited until the neighbour's black cat was prowling about on the pavement. I grabbed my bike and cycled down the street just after the cat had crossed it. Sure enough, three weeks later I received a cheque for sixty pounds from my uncle. This money only appeared because a black cat is a sign of good luck.

a Which sentence describes a possible **result** of the experiment?

b Which sentence describes the writer's explanation of the result?

c Do you think this explanation is a likely one? Give your reason(s).

4 This table shows the colours of a flame when various compounds are put in it.

Name of compound	Colour of flame
Copper(II) chloride	Green
Strontium chloride	Red
Sodium chloride	Orange
Copper(II) sulphate	Green

a What do you think the colour of the flame would be if strontium sulphate was put in it?

b What colour would the flame be with sodium sulphate?

5 Alexander compared the strength of different glues by measuring what mass each glue could hold. Here are his results.

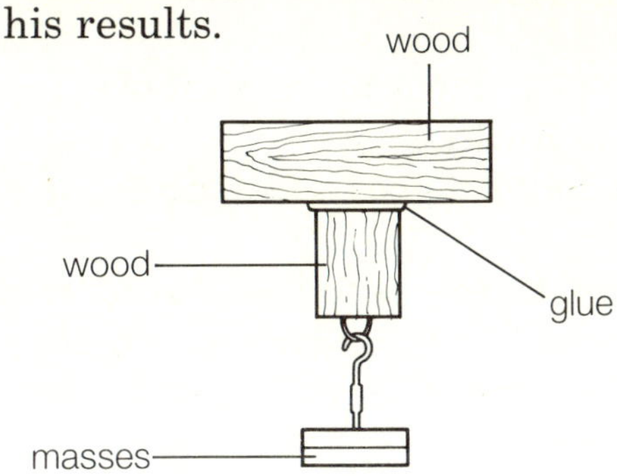

Glue	Type of glue	Mass held
Amaglue	Type A	250 g
Blogstic	Type A	300 g
Clobber	Type B	1090 g
Dullcoat	Type B	1020 g
Eggcoat	Type A	270 g

Which of these sentences describe a pattern in the results.

A Each glue held a different weight
B Clobber was the strongest glue
C Type A glues held less weight than type B glues
D Glues of a similar type held a similar weight
E Two glues had coat as part of the name

6 The experiment shown in diagram A is set up. The results are shown in diagram B.

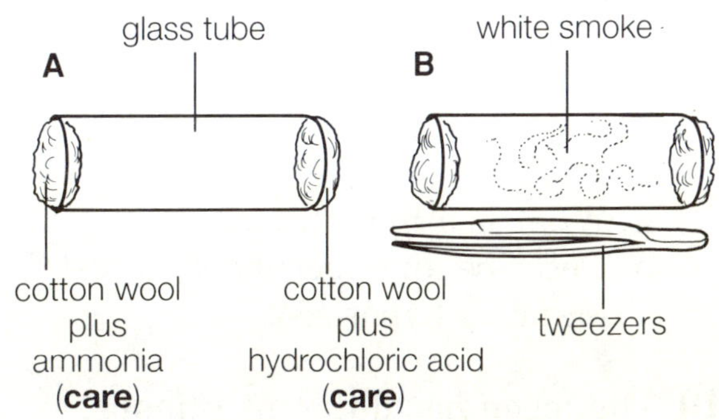

a From the first diagram describe the method of the experiment.

continued ▶

b From the second diagram describe the result of the experiment.

c What must the particles of ammonia and hydrochloric acid be able to do to give this result?

7 Use your ideas about particles to explain why

a a balloon goes down after a few days

b smoke seems to jiggle around if it is looked at under a microscope

c the scent from a flower can be smelt all over the room

d dye can spread through a whole load of white washing.

8 Sandy was asked to draw a diagram which showed the particles in oxygen gas. Here is his drawing.

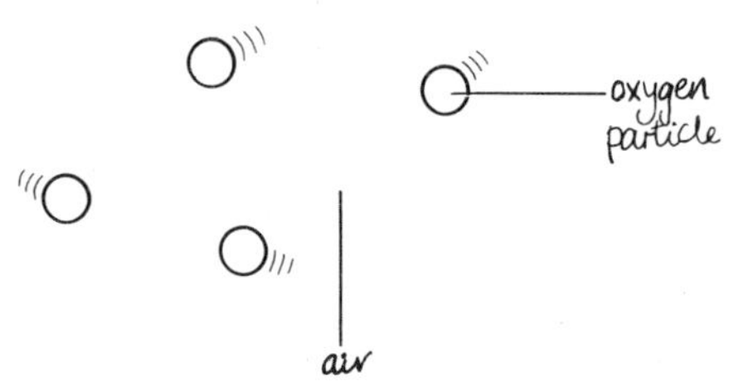

Do you think Sandy's drawing is good or bad?
Explain your answer.

9 Mandy was interested in chocolate. She wondered why some chocolate bars melted more quickly than others. She finally thought up this hypothesis.

A chocolate bar will melt at a higher temperature if it contains raisins or nuts.

a What is a hypothesis?

b Describe an experiment to test Mandy's hypothesis.

10 The moon has different **phases**.

a What does the expression 'phases of the moon' mean?

b Explain why the appearance of the moon changes regularly.

11 Scientists examine their results and think of a hypothesis to explain them. They then use the hypothesis to predict the results of future experiments. In each of the following tales of scientific work, write down the letter of the sentence which describes

(i) the hypothesis

(ii) the result of an experiment.

a A In the 19th Century a scientist called Pouchet thought that microbes could be created by the action of oxygen on soup

B Louis Pasteur was interested in Pouchet's work. He put gravy in a flask and then bent the flask's neck.

C If Pouchet was right then the gravy would begin to grow microbes.

D The microbes didn't grow.

b A Isaac Newton graduated from Cambridge University in 1665.

B He spent part of the next two years at home because of the plague.

C He worked at home using mathematics.

D He thought about gravity.

E He suggested a mathematical link between the force of gravity and distance.

F Using this link he calculated that the period of the moon should be 27.25 days.

G This figure is very close to the modern measured value.

12 A scientist thinks of a hypothesis and uses it to predict the results of future experiments. In the following tale describe what the hypothesis was and the prediction the scientist made using the hypothesis.

Dmitri Mendeleev was a Russian genius. He thought that there was a pattern in the behaviour of the elements. He arranged the known elements into a pattern. In this early periodic table he left a gap if there was no element which fitted the pattern. Mendeleev guessed what the elements in the gaps would look like by using his table. Many years later his descriptions of unknown elements like titanium were shown to be correct.

continued ▶

13 a Write down the names of a solid, a liquid and a gas that you could find in your home.

b Look at these drawings. They represent the arrangement of particles in a solid, a liquid and a gas.

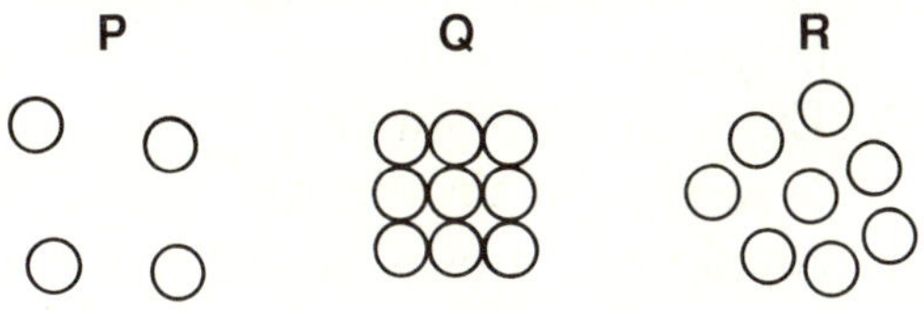

(i) Identify which drawing is the solid, which is the liquid and which is the gas.
(ii) Which drawing shows the substance whose particles are probably moving fastest?
(iii) Which drawing shows the substance which should be easiest to push together?

14 Look at the drawing of a metal pipe.

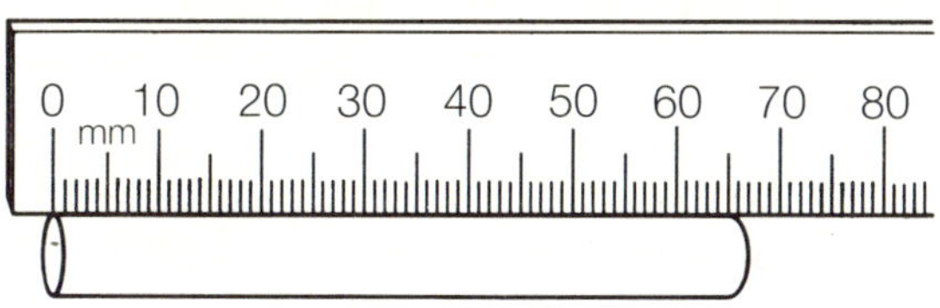

a The pipe is heated strongly. Estimate its new length.
b The pipe is cooled and then put into icy water. Estimate its new length.

15 You can open a glass jam jar more easily if you gently heat the metal lid first.

Explain why this method works, using your ideas about particles.

16 Give an account of what Copernicus and Galileo thought about the position of the Earth. You can use your notes about topic 5.12 to help you remember some of the facts.

17 You have completed many small experiments in this unit which are explained by using the ideas about particles. Pick **one** of these experiments and answer the following questions about it.
a What would be a suitable title of the experiment that you have chosen?
b What was the method used in the experiment?
c What was the result of the experiment?
d Explain this result using your ideas about particles.
e Why did you choose this particular experiment?

18 Use your ideas about particles to predict what will happen next in each of the following situations.
a A tight wire is heated up on a summer's day.

continued ▶

b A coloured solution is boiled until all the water disappears into the atmosphere.

c Too much air is put into a cold tyre. The tyre begins to heat up.

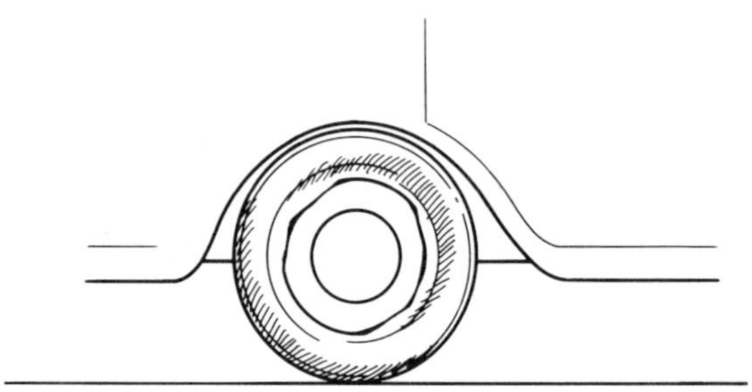

Extension questions

19 Fred thought that his rabbit might get cold when she was outside. He measured the rabbit's temperature in four different places. The results are shown in the table.

Place	Temperature of place/°C	Rabbit's temperature/°C
Living room	22	34
Greenhouse	29	34
Inside hutch	19	34
On lawn	17	34

a Write a suitable title for Fred's experiment.
b What pattern is there in the results of the experiment?
c Write a likely explanation for the pattern that you spot.

20 Sodium chromate is yellow.
Potassium chromate is yellow.
Sodium chloride is white.
Ammonium chloride is white.
a What colour would you expect ammonium chromate to be? Explain your answer.
b What colour would you expect potassium chloride to be? Explain your answer.
c You cannot predict the colour of copper chromate from these results. Explain why not.

21 A molecule of water contains two atoms of hydrogen and one atom of oxygen. The formula for this is H_2O.
a What is an atom?
b What is a molecule?
c Carbon tetrachloride contains one carbon atom and four chlorine atoms in every molecule. How would you write the symbol for this molecule?
d Draw a molecule of water and a molecule of carbon tetrachloride.

22 **a** What does the word *diffusion* mean?
b Write a sentence about the result of an experiment which includes the word *diffusion*.

23 The solar system contains the sun and its planets. You should know the names of these planets.
Use the first letters of the names of the members of the solar system to make up a word. (For example use the letter **E** for **E**arth.) You can only use each member once. Your word should be as long as possible.

continued ▶

24 A cold solid is put into a balloon and the balloon is tied tightly. Five minutes later the balloon is fully inflated. Write a likely explanation for this observation.

25 Emma has written down some statements. She wants to know which statements are about solids, which are about liquids and which are about gases.

A It changes its shape if its container is tipped.
B It is difficult to push into a smaller space.
C It expands when heated.
D It contracts when cooled.
E It spreads out to fill a room.
F It can be melted with heat.

a Write the letters of the statements which describe a solid.
b Write the letters of those which describe a liquid.
c Write the letters of those which describe a gas.
(*Note:* Statements can be used more than once, once or not at all)

26 Imagine that you are a particle in a solid. Describe what happens to you when some person begins to heat the solid.
Use the words *particles, expand, energy, spaces, liquid* and *melt.*

27 Explain how you could use a sundial to tell the time.

True or False 5

Unit 5 Tiny ideas

Name ______________________

Put a tick after the statements which are true. Put a cross after the statements which are false.

1 **a** Volume means the same as weight. ☐
b The volume of an object increases when it is heated. ☐
c The weight of an object increases when it is heated. ☐

2 **a** A solid melts when its particles gain enough energy. ☐
b A gas condenses when its particles gain energy. ☐
c Particles must move faster to cause a liquid to evaporate. ☐

3 **a** A solid changes into a liquid when the particles get more energy. ☐
b Particles are closer together in a solid than in a gas. ☐
c When a substance dissolves the particles disappear. ☐
d Particles in a liquid move as fast as in a gas. ☐
e This is a drawing of particles in a solid. ☐

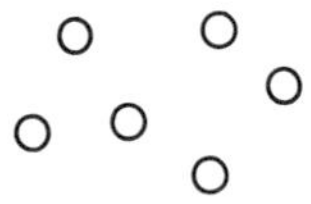

f Dye spreads in water because the dye particles get bigger. ☐

4 **a** A solid expands when heated. ☐
b A liquid contracts when heated. ☐
c Particles move more when heated. ☐
d The spaces between particles change as the energy of the particles changes. ☐

5 **a** A sundial will not work on a cloudy day. ☐
b You need to move part of a sundial to read the time. ☐

6 **a** The phases of the moon are linked to the seasons of the year. ☐
b The phases of the moon change regularly. ☐
c If there is a full moon tonight then there will be no moon in four days' time. ☐

7 **a** Copernicus was a good family friend of Galileo. ☐
b Copernicus had ideas that were popular with the authorities. ☐
c Galileo designed his own telescope to make observations. ☐

8 **a** Experiments are supposed to work; if nothing happens you've made a mistake. ☐
b It is valuable to discuss ideas with others. ☐
c You should test ideas by doing experiments. ☐
d A likely explanation is one which seems to be true to others. ☐

9 **a** An hypothesis is a likely explanation for an observation. ☐
b There is only one possible explanation for an observation. ☐
c An hypothesis is always true. ☐
d Different scientists have different ideas about the same thing. ☐

10 **a** A prediction is the same as a guess. ☐
b A hypothesis can be used to make predictions. ☐
c Predictions should be tested by experiments. ☐

continued ▶

Name ______________________

11 **a** Copernicus believed that the planets went round the earth. ☐
b Galileo made observations of the movement of the planets. ☐
c Galileo thought that the earth went round the sun. ☐
d Galileo worked out a new hypothesis on his own. ☐

Extensions

12 **a** Solids are heavier than liquids. ☐
b Liquids are runnier than solids. ☐
c Gases flow better than liquids. ☐
d Gases keep their shape better than solids. ☐
e Solids stay in one place whereas liquids do not. ☐

13 **a** Everything is made up of small particles called atoms. ☐
b Everything is made up of small particles called molecules. ☐
c An atom is likely to be smaller than a molecule. ☐

14 **a** The solar system is made up of the sun and the planets. ☐
b There are four planets plus the earth. ☐
c It is about 93 thousand miles from the sun to the earth. ☐
d The planets and the sun go round the earth. ☐

15 **a** The sun is a star. ☐
b A star is a hot solid. ☐

Unit 5 Tiny ideas

Name ______________________

Complete each sentence. Put the correct word(s) in each blank space.

1 It is sometimes useful to find a ________________ in observations. A pattern helps you to find a likely ________________ for something that you observe. You are making a ________________ when you think of a likely explanation.

2 Tea tastes sweet because the sugar has ________________. It has broken up into lots of tiny ________________.

Everything is made of tiny ________________.

3 A smell spreads because the particles can ________________ from place to place. In fact particles are always on the ________________.

4 As particles move, they spread out. They have ________________ between them. This hypothesis about particles can be used to make ________________ about what will happen in the future.

5 The following diagrams predict the arrangement of particles in

Solid **Liquid** **Gas**

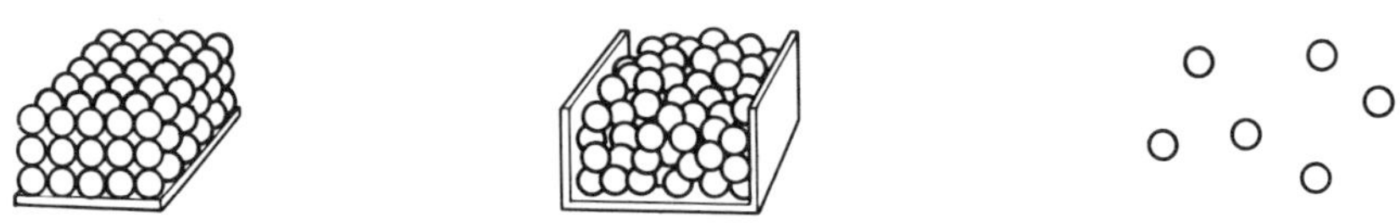

	Solid	Liquid	Gas
Movement	____________	medium	____________
Spacing	____________	close	____________

6 Two examples of solids are ________________ and ________________.

Two examples of liquids are ________________ and ________________.

Two examples of gases are ________________ and ________________.

7 The arrangement of particles in a ________________ should be easiest to push together.

8 When you heat the particles in a solid they will move more. This will cause the solid to expand which means that it gets ________________.

When the solid is cooled the particles will move ________________ and the solid will ________________ which means it gets smaller.

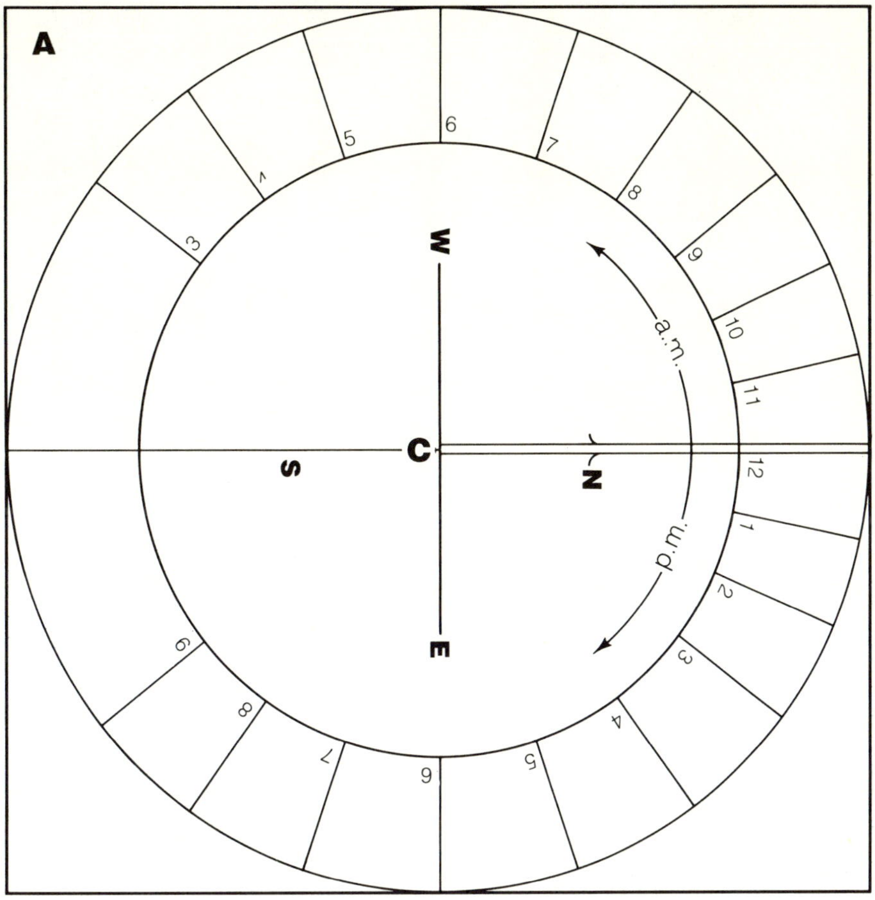

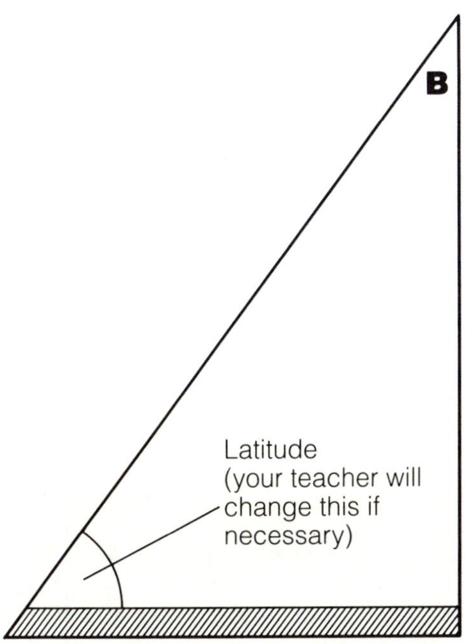

Build a sundial

Instructions

1 Cut out the square (A).
Cut out the triangle (B).

2 Stick the square onto a polystyrene tile.
Stick the triangle onto thin card.

3 With a sharp knife carefully cut a slot into the polystyrene tile along line C–D.

4 Put the triangle into the slot as shown on the diagram on page 80 of the textbook.

5 To use the instrument, take it outside on a sunny day. Point the N line to north. The edge of the triangle's shadow touches the time.

Report on activity 1

Name of activity: ***Crack an egg***

Method

Stand an egg on its pointed end.
Put masses on top of it.
Find out how much weight the egg can hold.

Also look at the diagram on page 80.

Observations

Ideas

Report on activity 2

Name of activity: ***Dry ice***

Method

Using gloves put dry ice on the table.
Wait a few minutes.
Then put dry ice in a little water.

Also look at the diagram on page 80.

Observations

Ideas

Report on activity 3

Name of activity: *Can opener*

Method

Your teacher will put a small amount of water in the can and put the lid on.
Wear safety glasses.
Your teacher will now heat the water in the can until it boils.
Also look at the diagram on page 80.

Observations

Ideas

Report on activity 4

Name of activity: *Squash it*

Method

Try to push in the plunger of each syringe.

Also look at the diagram on page 81.

Observations

Ideas

Report on activity 5

Name of activity: *Hot stuff*

Method

Heat the three solids on top of a tin lid.

Also look at the diagram on page 81.

Observations

Ideas

Report on activity 6

Name of activity: *Toasted sandwich*

Method

Heat the metal strip in a bunsen flame.

Also look at the diagram on page 81.

Observations

Ideas

Report on activity 7

Name of activity: *Airless can*

Method

Switch on the pump.
Take the air out of the can.

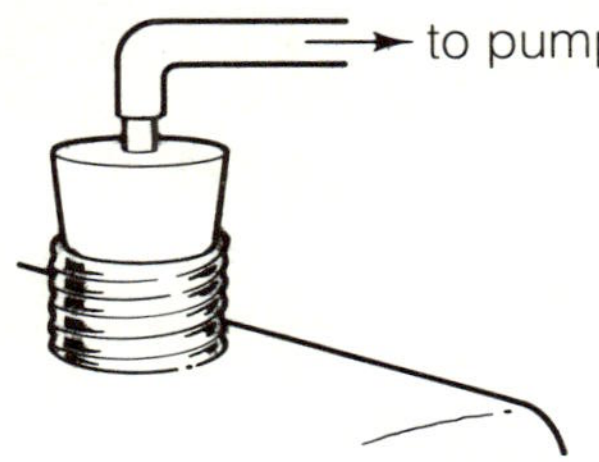

Observations

Ideas

Report on activity 8

Name of activity: *Floating steel*

Method

Place the blade gently onto the water surface.

Observations

Ideas

Fingerprint halves

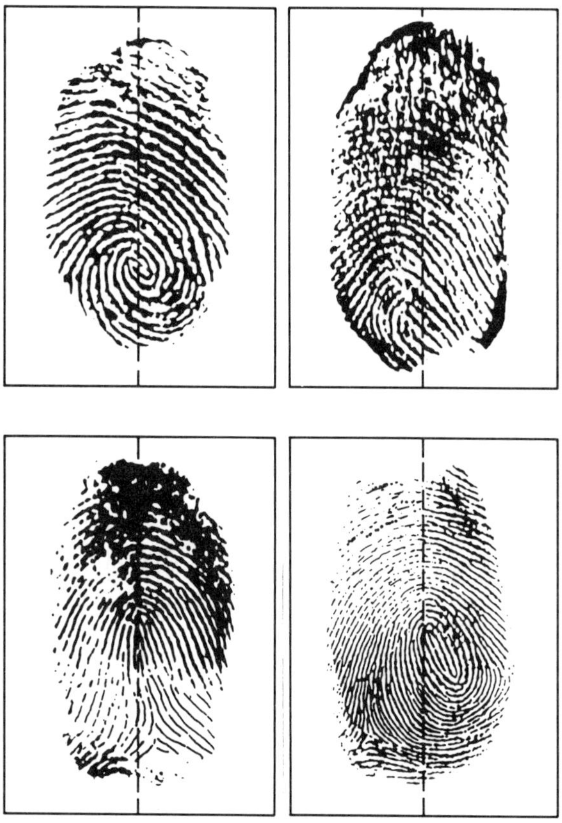

Fingerprint halves

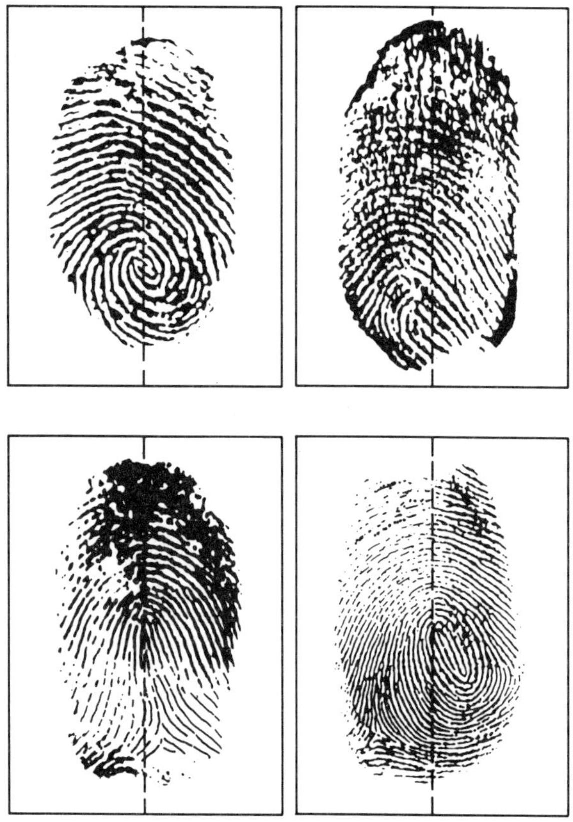

Fingerprint halves

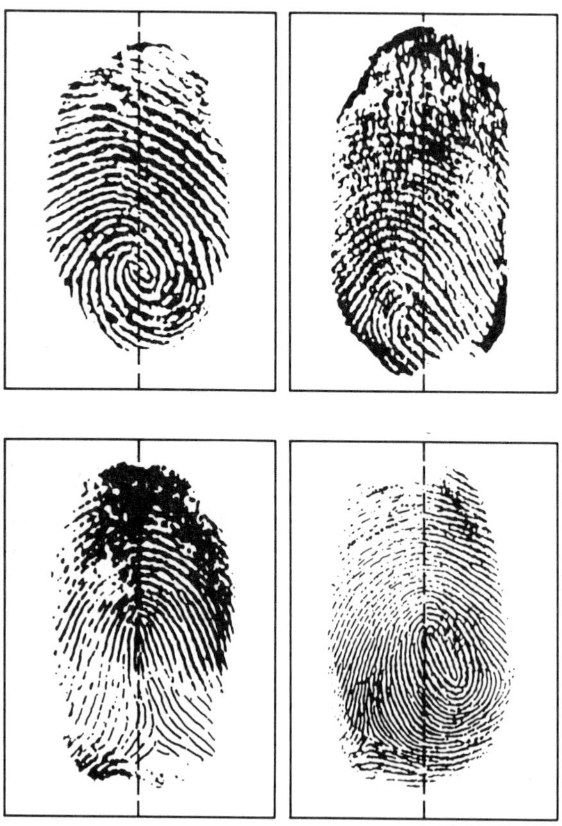

Fingerprint halves

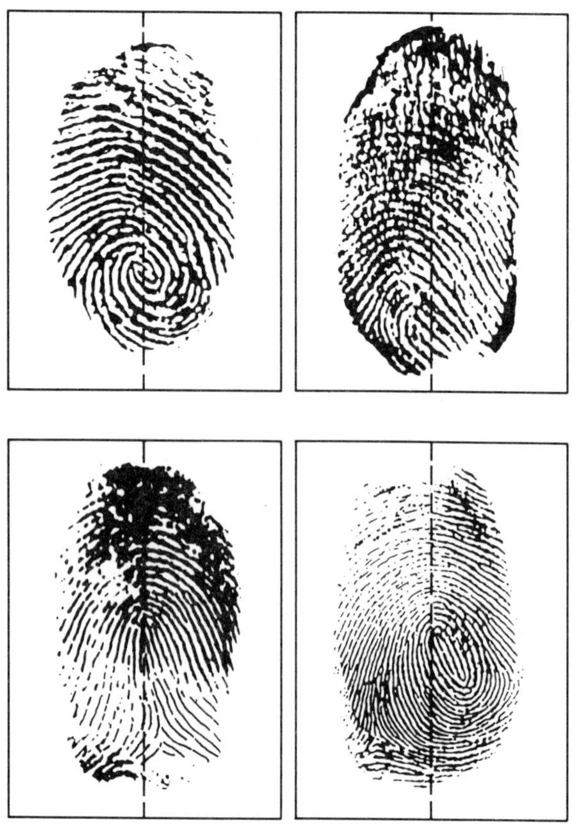

1. Six animals live on the farm. One was found murdered at 2.00 a.m.	**2.** Billy Goat went outside with his gun because he heard a prowler at 1.30 a.m.	**3.** The police are still looking for two large animals.
4. Matt the Cat was hit by a stone at 1.45 a.m. when he was singing in the rain.	**5.** The victim had been dead for about 20 minutes.	**6.** Porky Pig was very fond of fried chicken.
7. Dimwit Sheep always wore a very valuable sheepskin coat.	**8.** The police found a large spade with a dent in it.	**9.** Billy Goat was going to fire his gardener next day.
10. Matt the Cat was known in the area as a poacher.	**11.** The victim had a small bullet wound and a huge lump on the head.	**12.** Horsey Morceaux was the French gardener.
13. Casserola Chicken was in love with Matt the Cat, but Matt hated chickens.	**14.** The farmer heard Dimwit Sheep arguing violently with someone at 1.15 a.m.	**15.** Casserola Chicken was seen leaving the henhouse at 1.25 a.m.
16. All the male animals had handgun licences.	**17.** Porky Pig was grazed by a bullet at about 1.30 a.m.	**18.** The body was found on top of dry hay.
19. There was a pool of blood in the wet yard.	**20.** The milkmaid heard a horse galloping away just after 2.00 a.m.	**21.** Dimwit Sheep used to work backstage at the theatre.
22. Billy Goat was a crackshot.	**23.** Porky Pig had been a captain in the SAS.	**24.** Casserola Chicken was a discus champion.
25. Casserola Chicken was married to Dimwit Sheep.	**26.** Matt the Cat told police that he saw Porky Pig following Casserola Chicken at 1.20 a.m.	**27.** The farmer threw a brick into the yard when he heard a chicken squawking at about 1.35 a.m.

Particle summary

We now have some hypotheses about particles.

- ____________________ is made of particles.

- Particles are ____________________.

- Particles are ____________________.

- Particles are ____________________ out.

Clue card 1

Set up a circuit with the bell and the bimetallic strip in series.

Clue card 2

The circuit should have a gap in it. The gap will be closed when there is heat nearby.

Clue card 3

What does the bimetallic strip do when it is heated? Think of a way of using the strip to close the gap in your circuit.

Clue card 4

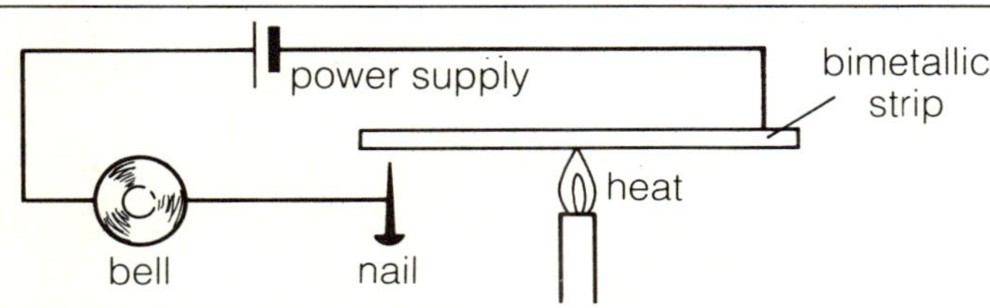

Clue card 1

Set up a circuit with the bell and the bimetallic strip in series.

Clue card 2

The circuit should have a gap in it. The gap will be closed when there is heat nearby.

Clue card 3

What does the bimetallic strip do when it is heated? Think of a way of using the strip to close the gap in your circuit.

Clue card 4

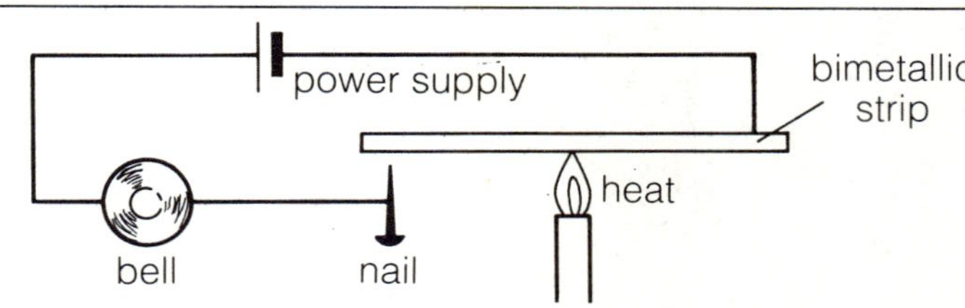

Puzzling things

Explain the following things using your ideas about particles. The words in *italics* will give you some hints. You can also use the books available in the classroom to look up anything that you are finding difficult.

1 Where does sugar go to when it dissolves?

- *particles*
- *tiny*
- *spaces*
- *invisible*
- *taste*

2 Why does a tyre feel harder on a hot day?

- *trapped*
- *particles*
- *heat energy*
- *move*
- *pressure*

3 How does this thermometer work?

- *particles*
- *energy*
- *move*
- *spaces*
- *expand*

4 How does this thermostat work?

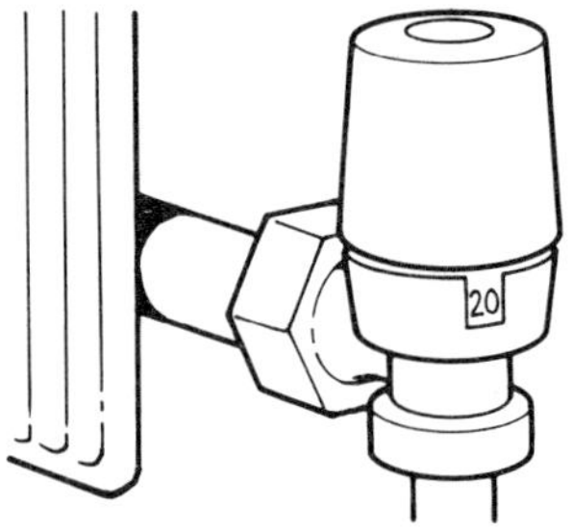

- *bimetallic*
- *heat*
- *expand*
- *bend*
- *circuit*

5 What is there in between particles?

6 Why does a hot air balloon rise through the air?

- *particles*
- *energy*
- *move*
- *spaces*
- *lighter*

1 of 3

Thinking things through

At the beginning of the unit you wrote down your ideas for explaining some activities. It may be interesting to do the same thing using our theory of particles to help with the thinking.

Our theory

You have a **problem** → You do some **thinking** → You work out an **explanation** → Now you can take **action**

Collect

What you need for any **one** activity

Do some or all of the following activities. The instructions are given in the diagram. For each activity describe what you see. Then think of a likely explanation which uses your ideas about particles. (If you need help read over Topic 5.7B.)

1 Smells

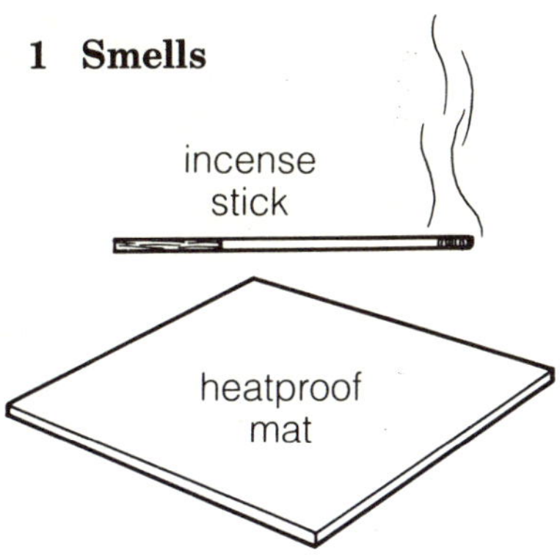

Burn the incense stick over a heatproof mat.

2 Hot air

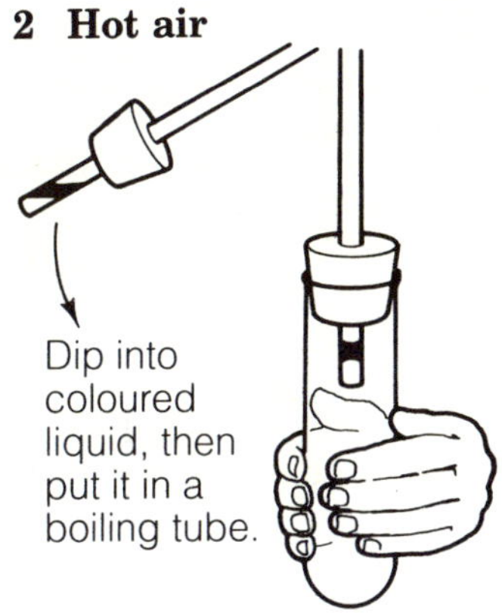

Warm the tube with your hands and watch the drop.

3 Blocks

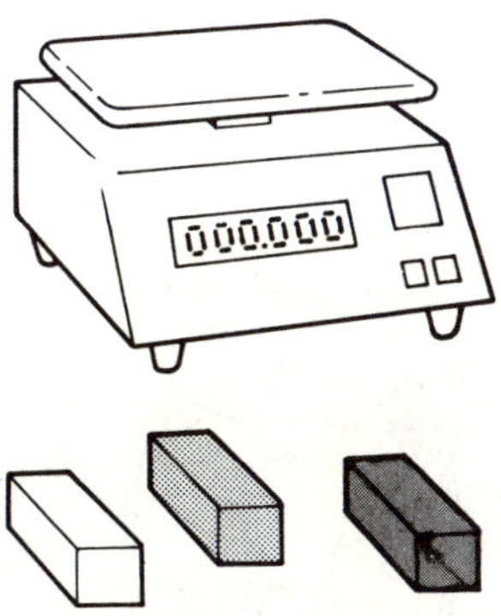

The three blocks are exactly the same size. Weigh each one.

4 Squash it

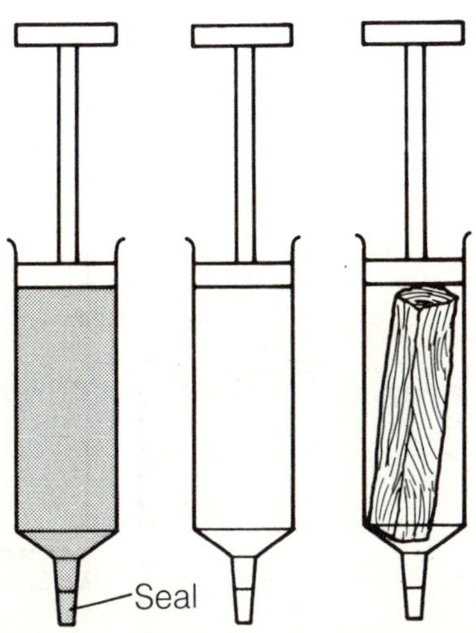

2 of 3

5 Hot stuff

6 Colour all

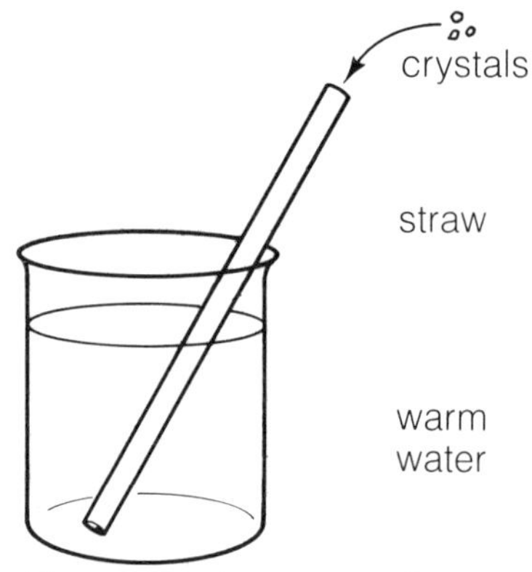

Put two or three crystals of potassium permanganate into the water through the straw. Watch what happens.

Write a short report about each activity. Include your observations and your ideas for explaining what happened.

Collect
Poster paper
Coloured pencils

Your group has to make a poster to explain one of the activities. You have 30 minutes to make the poster.

What to do

1 Each person in the group will read their **observations** aloud. There should be no comment from the other members of the group while this is done. Everyone in the group then agrees which observation to show on the poster.
2 Each person then reads their **ideas** for explaining the observation aloud.
3 The group now has 10 minutes to talk about and then to agree on the best ideas. Write these ideas onto the poster.
4 The class produced posters in Topic 5.1. You have now produced new posters. Discuss the differences between the two sets of posters with your teacher.

Finding out about technology

The first seven topics present information about some uses of scientific knowledge in technology. Pupils use the written passages to practise some of the reading and writing skills that were first introduced in the skills sheets of *Understanding Science 1*. Thus they skim and scan the information and reorganise it into tables and flow diagrams. Work with computers is also encouraged. The accompanying classroom activities and experiments develop high-level practical and investigative skills. The final three topics comprise an investigation, an exercise which requires the preparation and delivery of a short talk, and a short reading exercise. In addition to meeting the general demands of Attainment Target 1, this unit deals specifically with AT 1, levels 4c, 4d, 5a, 5b, 5c.

Core and Reinforcement

6.1 Introducing technology

Identify the problem that is solved by the object in an illustration.
Design and build a clock to time a race.
page 102

Deduce the intended function of an object from its design.
Apply knowledge in an imaginative way.
Devise and build an apparatus which solves a given problem.

6.2 Electronics *AT 12–3a,b,c, 4a,b, 5a*

Extract and present information (using a word processor if possible) from a passage about electronics.
Use a variety of electronic detectors to measure environmental variables. *page 104*

Extract relevant information from a passage.
Translate information from written form to a table.
Translate information from words to a diagram.
Communicate using a word processor.
Reorganise written information using a word processor.

6.3 Telecommunications *AT 12–3b,c, 4a, 6b*

Extract and present information from a passage about telecommunication.
Extract information from a database using a microcomputer. *page 108*

Extract relevant information from a passage, a picture and from self-sought sources.
Extract relevant information from a computer database.

Extension

6.1

Design a solution for four given problems.
page 165

Apply knowledge in an imaginative way.
Devise an apparatus which solves a given problem.

6.2 *AT 12–5b, 6a*

Construct digital circuits and use them to complete/compile truth tables.
page 166

Translate from a circuit diagram to a working circuit.
Translate from experimental data to truth tables.
Devise a truth table to summarise experimental data.

6.3

Identify some components of a radio receiver.
Design an experiment to discover if radio waves can pass through selected solids.
page 167

Follow instructions.
Devise and build a fair experiment where several variables are identified and controlled.

Core and Reinforcement

Extension

6.4 Food science *AT 7–5b; AT 8–6c*

Extract and present information from a passage about the use of microbes in food production.
Use microbes to make yogurt and/or alcohol. *page 110*

Extract relevant information from a passage, a diagram and a table.
Translate information from a table to a flow diagram.
Translate information from a sequence of diagrams to a flow diagram.
Follow instructions.

Extension

Set up a continuous process which uses yeast to change sucrose into glucose. *page 169*

Follow instructions.
Translate information from a diagram to a written passage.

6.5 Chemicals from microbes *AT 7–5b*

Extract and present information from a passage about penicillin and insulin.
Build a batch fermenter and observe the effect of changing three variables on the growth of the microbe. *page 114*

Extract relevant information from a passage and a diagram.
Translate information from a sequence of diagrams to a flow diagram.
Form hypotheses in an unfamiliar context.

Extension

Compare the effect of four household cleaners on the growth of yeast cells in agar. *page 171*

Follow instructions.
Draw conclusions from experimental data.
Communicate in structured written form.

6.6 Materials *AT 6–3a,b, 4a,b; AT 7–4b*

Extract and present information from a passage about materials.
Make some synthetic materials. *page 116*

Extract information from a passage and a pie chart.
Follow instructions.
Communicate in structured written form.
Translate information from a pie chart to a bar graph.

Extension *AT 5–4a, 5b*

Classify items from a simulated rubbish bag as recyclable, biodegradable or other. *page 172*

Extract information from a passage.
Translate from data collected to a bar graph.

6.7 Fuels *AT 7–5c; AT 13–4b, 5a,b*

Extract and present information from a passage about fuels.
Watch a demonstration of how well a fuel can burn.
Separate some alcohol from a batch fermenter. *page 120*

Extract relevant information from a passage, a diagram and a picture.
Translate information from a table to a flow diagram.
Apply knowledge in an imaginative way.

Extension

Identify the use of microbes in given situations. *page 173*

Recognise examples of given categories.

Core and Reinforcement

6.8 Problem—Biological washing powders

> Design a fair experiment to compare the effect of four biological washing powders on protein. *page 123*

Devise and carry out an experiment which is a fair comparison.
Identify variables.
Communicate in structured written form.
Recognise and explain the variability in experimental results.

6.9 Talkabout—Technology

> Prepare and deliver a short talk about one of the topics in the unit.
> *page 124*

Extract information from given and self-sought sources.
Communicate factual material logically and concisely.

6.10—Readabout—Robot surgeon

> Read a short passage about new technology in medicine.
> Answer questions on the passage. *page 125*

Extract information from a given passage.
Discuss the implications of new technology.

Extension

Equipment
required for each pupil group

6.1—Introducing technology

Access to materials useful for building a clock, e.g. yogurt pots, squeezy bottles, paper, sand, water, etc.

6.2—Electronics

- Access to word processor
- Instructions on use of word processor
- Wide variety of sensors (some with digital displays); examples given in the text

Extension

- 3 switches
- 2 batteries
- 9 connecting wires
- 2 bulbs

Notes

Solutions
1 clothes peg, **2** pencil sharpener, **3** smoke sensor, **4** bottle opener for tight lids.
The pupils could be restricted to building a water or a sand clock.

Demonstrate use of the word processor.
Use a networked system if possible (in computing department maybe).
Interface one of the sensors with a computer, and display measurement if possible.

Pupils can build their own sensors if they have time, using the circuit diagrams below:

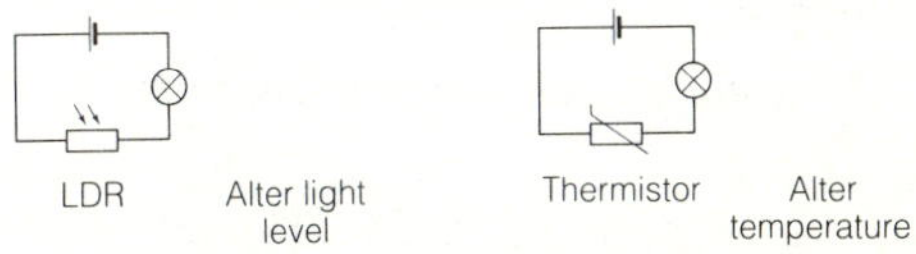

Equipment
required for each pupil group

Notes

6.3—Telecommunication

- Teletext TV (or TV attached to computer with a teletext adaptor)
- Access to Prestel, Campus 2000 or Neris, if available.

Ask computing department for information/help.

Extension

- Working radio receiver with back removed.
- Tuning capacitor, aerial and a loudspeaker
- Aluminium (cooking) foil
- Flat squares of cardboard, steel, thin wood (about 20 cm × 20 cm)

Label these with sticky labels.

6.4—Food science

- Small thermos flask
- Small tin of evaporated milk
- Live natural yogurt
- Teaspoon
- Boiling water from a kettle
- Access to balance
- Brewers' yeast
- Glucose powder
- Limewater
- Bubble trap (used for home winemaking)
- Boiling tube

Pupils can bring their own thermos flask to take the yogurt home after the lesson.

Extension

- Equipment tray containing filter funnel, 100 cm^3 measuring cylinder, yeast, sodium alginate solution, stirring rod, 250 cm^3 0.1 M calcium chloride solution, teat dropper, filter paper, Clinistix, beakers, stand and clamp
- Access to balance

The cells are immobilised in beads of alginate gel which enables continuous production of glucose. 2 g of sodium alginate solution in 50 cm^3 water. Clinistix tests for glucose. Colour chart on the bottle.

6.5—Chemicals from microbes

- Large container (capacity about 500 cm^3) (or 250 cm^3 conical flask)
- Yeast (about 2 g per group)
- Nutrient mixture
- Glucose powder
- Access to boiled water
- Access to warm water (less than 40°C)
- Bubble trap
- Limewater

Nutrient mixture: Ammonium sulphate and potassium dihydrogen phosphate.

Access to boiled water: Boil water for a long time. Store in stoppered container.

Extension

- Yeast agar plate
- Cork borer
- Tweezers
- 4 household disinfectants/cleaners

Prepare agar plate by adding dispersed live yeast cells to warm agar solution (3 g agar in 100 cm^3 water) just prior to use. Diffusion will result in a halo of no growth around each well. Other parts of the plate will have a white covering of yeast.

Equipment
required for each pupil group

Notes

6.6—Materials

- Metal samples (copper foil, iron nail)
- Ceramic tile
- Glass slide
- Fibre samples (wool, nylon etc.)
- Plastic samples (polythene sheet, perspex sheet)

Testing strength

- Rubber stopper with large nail
- 0.5–1 m plastic plumbing pipe
- Plastic tray

Testing flexibility

- Mass hanger with 10 g and 100 g masses
- Wire
- G-clamp
- Ruler

Testing hardness

- Nail
- Binocular microscope

- New material cards **(R6.6)**
- Safety glasses

Pupils must wear **safety glasses** throughout **all** activities.

Making nylon

Demonstrate this experiment in a fume cupboard.

- Small beaker
- 1,6-diaminohexane solution
- Sebacoyl chloride solution
- Glass stirring rod
- Tweezers

Care: sebacoyl chloride is usually sold as a solution in carbon tetrachloride. Both solutions are available commercially at the correct concentrations.

New material 1

- Plastic mixing bowl
- Scoop (as used with baby milk)
- Stirrer (wooden stick)
- Egg box or similar mould
- Cement
- Fine grain sand

New material 2

- Bunsen burner and heatproof mat
- Tongs
- Small piece of potter's clay

New material 3

- Commercial filler for car bodywork
- Tin lid
- Wooden spill
- Protective gloves

Equipment
required for each pupil group

Notes

New material 4

- Latex solution
- Small beaker
- Test tube
- Vinegar
- Dropper

New material 5

- Perspex monomer (methyl methacrylate)
- Releasing oil and small brush
- Tin lid with lip (e.g. syrup tin)
- Wooden spill
- Catalyst—lauryl peroxide
- Oven

Care: use a fume cupboard.
The monomer may have to be cleaned by shaking with a little 4M sodium hydroxide prior to use.
Oven should be set at 75°C.

New material 6

- Commercial epoxy resin glue
- Tin lid
- Wooden spill
- Broken plastic item

Extension

- Black rubbish bag containing sanitised rubbish e.g. tins (no lids), bottle, potato peelings or other vegetable matter, paper (various), plastic items, wooden object

The number of items must be small enough to be recorded on a bar graph.

6.7—Fuels

- Apparatus described in **R6.7** (or other)
- Petrol or pentane

A spectacular and safe demonstration of the burning of a fuel is described by **R6.7** (adapted with permission from *Standard Grade Practical Guides Volume 1* published by Scottish Schools Equipment Research Centre, 1988).
Caution: Flammable fuels—danger of fire/explosion. Keep fuel container closed when not in use and well away from any naked flame. Use only small dispensing containers to minimise fire risk. Do not pump the oxygen syringe back and forth as there is potential for the non-return valve to fill with an explosive mixture of oxygen and fuel. Do not use an oxygen cylinder without a needle reducing valve. Clamp cylinder to bench or trolley. Remember to use the two safety screens—one between the teacher and the experiment and the other between the experiment and the pupils.

- Yeast fermenters
- Distillation apparatus comprising RB flask, stillhead and thermometer, condenser, collecting vessel, anti-bumping granules
- Bunsen burner and heatproof mat

Set up fermenters at the beginning of the unit so that by this point they will have produced enough alcohol to be distilled and burned.
Use Quickfit distillation apparatus if possible.
Burn a little of the distillate on the heatproof mat. Compare with the original liquid from the fermenter.

Extension

- Copy of Microbe picture quiz cartoons **(R6.7E)**

Equipment

required for each pupil group

Notes

6.8—Problem—Biological washing powders

- Bunsen burner and heatproof mat
- Labels
- Four teat pipettes
- Small beakers
- Cork borer
- 2 biological washing powders
- 2 non-biological washing powders
- 2 milk agar petri dishes

Biological washing powders generally contain protease enzymes derived from bacteria. These break down protein. In milk agar this causes the milkiness to clear. The clear zone indicates where the enzyme was active and its area how active the enzyme is.
Prepare milk agar by boiling plain agar (3 g agar per 100 cm^3 water) and skimmed milk separately. Mix after boiling to give plain agar plus 10% vol/vol skimmed milk.

6.9—Talkabout—Technology

- Access to reference books containing information about the suggested topics. The books should have the relevant words in the index. Otherwise prepare a short list of key words for each topic

It may be preferable to encourage each pupil to give his/her talk to a small group. Each group then votes for one talk that will be given to the whole class.

6.10—Readabout—Robot surgeon

No equipment required

Assessment 6

The questions are designed to assess the skills and knowledge developed in the unit, as shown in the table. A selection of questions would be appropriate for a unit test.

Topic	*Core*	*Extension*
6.1	1	20
6.2	2, 3, 4, 5, 27	21, 22
6.3	6, 7	—
6.4	8, 28	—
6.5	—	23, 30
6.6	9-14, 16	24, 25
6.7	15, 17, 18, 19	26, 29

Answers

1 a (i) Hunt/forage, **(ii)** grow/process.
b (i) Clothes/fire, **(ii)** produce energy.
c (i) Talk, **(ii)** telephones etc.
d (i) Natural remedies,
(ii) medicines/doctors/NHS.
2 a Chapter 1; **b** chapter 4; **c** chapter 2;
d any suitable use.
3 Any suitable device (see pupils' text, page 104).
4 A—3, B—2, C—1
5 a Input—typing, output—printed document.
b Input—heat, output—displayed number.
c Input—liquid, output—displayed number.
d Input—noise, output—siren sound.
6 a Transmitter, carrier, receiver.
b Any three (see pupils' text, page 108).
c Identify transmitter, carrier, receiver.
7 'a Stored information, sometimes on disc to be used by a computer.
b Description of the use of numbers to find specific pages from a menu choice.
c More information stored, easily updated, information can be found more quickly (*any one*).
8 a Uses of alcohol.
b Check meanings in the dictionary available.
c

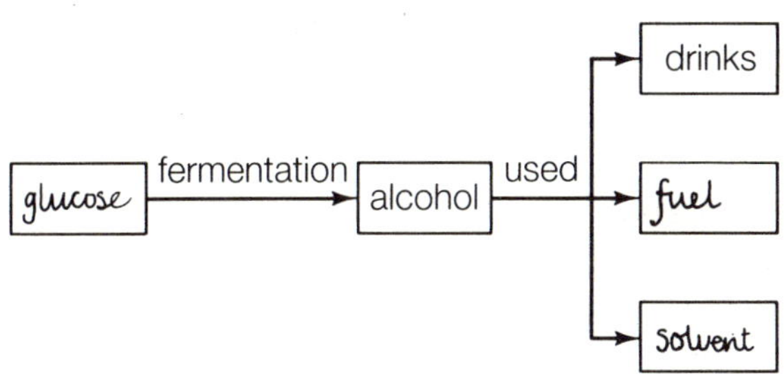

9 a Cotton, wool, leather, silk (*any two*).
b Nylon, polystyrene, PVC, polyester (*any two*).
10 a C; **b** D.
11 a Metals; **b** plastics; **c** fibres; **d** plastics.
12 a strength; **b** flexibility; **c** solubility;
d flexibility
13 a See through, insulator; **b** conductor;
c strong; **d** strong, non-poisonous;
e heat-resistant.
14 a Doesn't break; **b** Doesn't corrode;
c cheap/strong.
15 a Chapter 3; **b** chapter 5; **c** chapter 4;
d chapter 7; **e** e.g. uranium

16 a A steel ball, B clear plastic tube, C ruler, D metal, E hard plastic.
b height of ball, thickness of metal, weight and size of ball, type of hard plastic.
17 a See pupils' text, page 120
b **(i)** removes source of heat; **(ii)** removes oxygen.
18 a When a substance burns it joins with *oxygen* from the air to make *oxides*. This process releases *heat* and *light* energy. It is called *combustion*. Another process called *respiration* also uses the same part of the air. In this case living things . . .
b . . . Use oxygen to produce heat energy from food (or similar)
19 Coal, wood, food, petrol.
20 Problem should have been clearly understood. Solution will give an indication of how well it was analysed.
21 a A; two analogue devices given in pupils' text, page 166.
b Digital; two digital devices given in pupils' text, page 166.
22

A	B	Bulb
0	0	0
0	1	0
1	0	1
1	1	1

23 Explanation should refer to the diagrams making the connection between them clear. To make the experiment fair, certain variables should be kept constant; e.g. concentration of antibiotic, volume used, incubation temperature, agar recipe, time elapsed, light level.

24 a 72 items.
b Plastic.
c Paper/fabric (natural)/vegetable.
d Paper/metal/glass/as much of 'others' as possible.
25 a Non biodegradable/doesn't corrode.
b Strong.
c Flexible, strong.
d Ceramic/metal—strong, easily shaped at first.
e Flexible, strong, light.
26 a Materials; **b** fuel/materials;
c telecommunications/electronics;
d food (microbes); **e** materials.
27 a Voyager II visits Neptune.
b **(i)** The distance of Neptune from the earth; **(ii)** why Voyager II will have been worthwhile.
c Search for knowledge.
d 1613.
e Six (Neptune, Jupiter, Pluto, Earth, Mercury, Venus)
f An outstanding success.
g Makes people realise that there is a limit to the mess that can be made of the planet before life becomes impossible.
28 a Food poisoning by microbes.
b **(i)** Contamination of pâté by Listeria; **(ii)** Salmonella survives cooking in poultry.
c Pâté, eggs, poultry.
d Listeria, Salmonella.
e Cannot uniformly heat foods.
29 Coal, oil, gas, tar sand, oil shale (*any three*). These fuels are non-renewable. Can make them last longer by using them sparingly and by using renewable fuels as much as possible.
30 *Plastics:* PVC, perspex, polyethene
Fibres: Beech, oak
Metals: aluminium, copper

True/false 6

Each statement is marked as either true or false by the pupil. This gives a rapid assessment of a pupil's grasp of the Attainment Targets covered in the unit. The following list gives the Attainment Targets covered by each set of statements.

1	AT 4–5a	13	AT 12–4a
2	AT 6–3a	14	AT 12–4b
3	AT 6–3b	15	AT 12–6b
4	AT 6–4a	16	AT 13–4b
5	AT 6–4b	17	AT 13–5a
6	AT 7–4b	18	AT 13–5b
7	AT 7–5b	19	AT 2–4b
8	AT 7–5c	20	AT 5–4a
9	AT 8–6c	21	AT 5–5b
10	AT 12–3a	22	AT 12–5a
11	AT 12–3b	23	AT 12–5b
12	AT 12–3c	24	AT 12–6a

Unit 6 Science in use

Test 6

1 People long ago had very simple technology to solve problems. People now have different ways of solving problems. For example, faced with the problem of finding a home
- *people long ago* used a cave
- *people now* make bricks and build a house.

For each of these problems, write down
(i) a solution used by people long ago
(ii) a solution used by people now.

a food
b warmth
c communication
d health.

2 Here is the contents page of a book about microelectronics.

a Which chapter would you read to find out about electrons?
b Which chapter is likely to mention detectors?
c Which chapter would you read to discover the symbol for a resistor?
d Name one topic that might be included in chapter 5.

3 Microelectronic devices can be used for
- detection
- measurement
- control.

Name **one** type of device in each group.

4 Match the symbol of the electrical component with the correct job description. Name each component.

Symbol

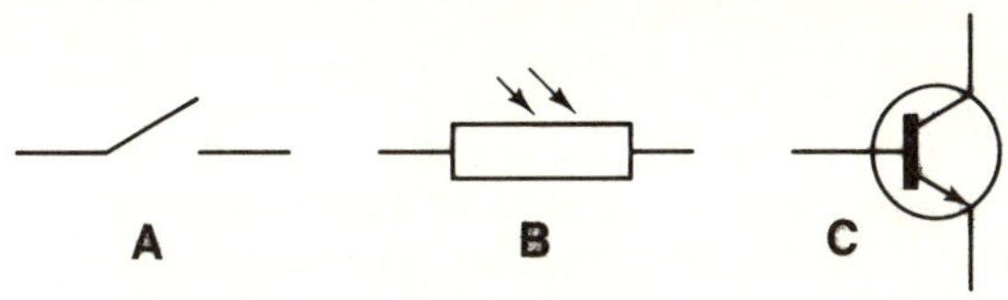

Job description
1 Fast acting, sensitive switch
2 Resistance is changed by light
3 Stops and starts the current

5 An electronic system has three parts:
- the input
- the processor
- the output.

Describe the input and the output of
a a word processor
b a digital thermometer
c a pH meter
d a burglar alarm.

6 A telecommunication system has three parts. The diagram shows a television system.

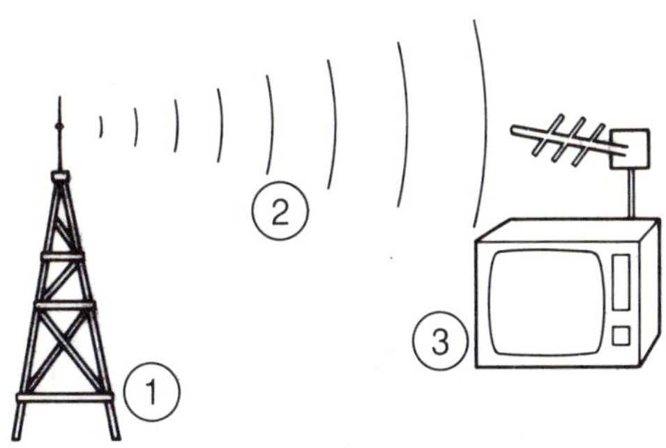

a Name the three parts of a telecommunication system.
b Name three other telecommunication devices (apart from a TV).
c Choose one of your named devices and describe the three parts of the system.

continued ▶

7 You have used a teletext database in school.

a What is a *database*?

b Describe how you would search the database for information.

c Name one advantage that a database system has over a newspaper.

8 Fermentation is used to change glucose into alcohol. Drinks like wine and beer are made by fermentation. However, alcohol is not only used in drinks. It is also a good fuel and is used as an alternative to petrol in some parts of South America. It is also a very good solvent.

a What might be a good title for this passage?

b Use a dictionary to find the scientific meanings for the following words: *fermentation, fuel, solvent.*

c Copy and complete the flow diagram to present the information in the passage.

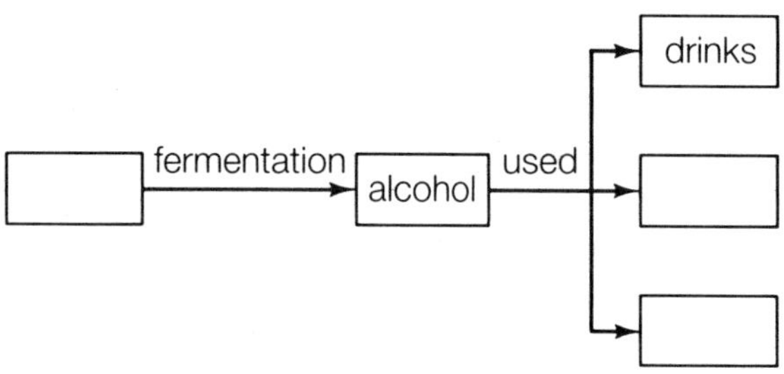

9 Look at the following list of materials.

- cotton
- wool
- nylon
- polystyrene
- PVC
- leather
- silk
- polyester

a Name two natural materials from the list.

b Name two synthetic (man-made) materials from the list.

10 a Which diagram shows metal being used because it is flexible?

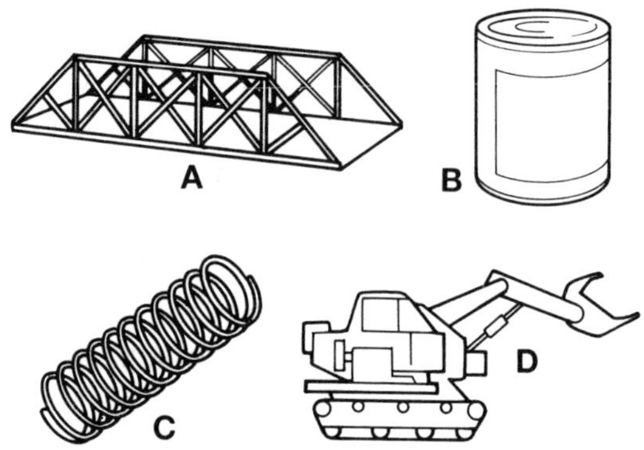

b Which diagram shows plastic being used because it is strong?

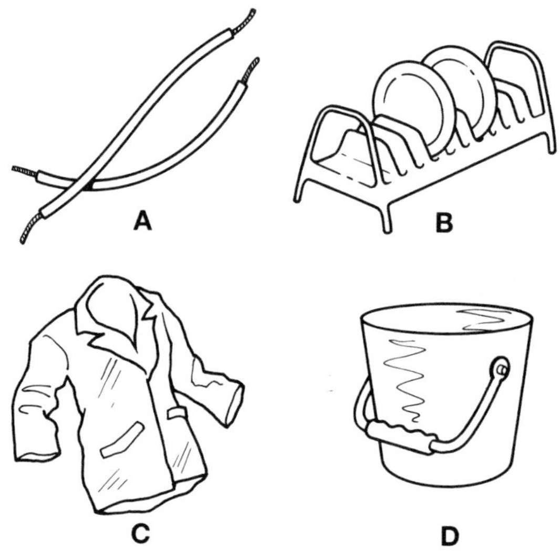

11 The main sets of materials are

- metals
- ceramics
- plastics
- glass
- fibres

What is the correct set name for each of the following groups of substances?

a

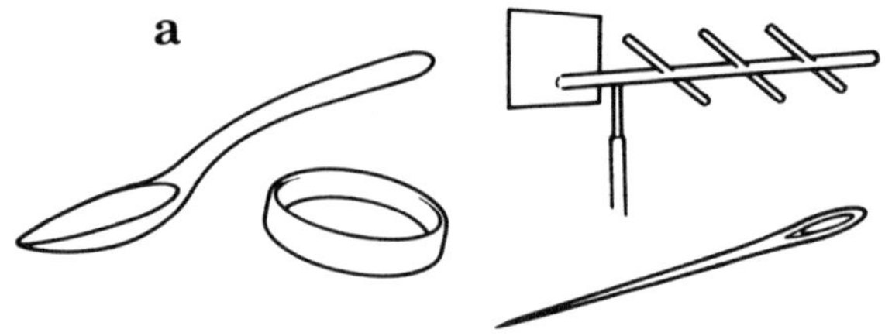

continued ▶

b

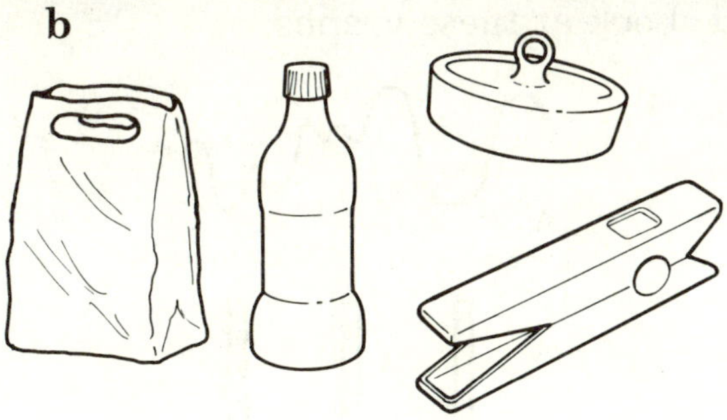

c Cotton, wool, silk, nylon.

d Perspex, PVC, polythene, polystyrene.

12 Look at this list of different properties.

- flexibility
- strength
- hardness
- solubility

Which **one** property is each of the following sentences about?

a The chassis of a motor vehicle must be able to support a heavy weight.

b Rulers are designed to bend easily without breaking.

c Statues shouldn't be damaged by rain.

d A trampoline mat gives you a safe landing.

13 Give **one** reason for choosing the material used in each of these situations.

a Glass for windows.

b Copper in electrical wiring.

c Steel to build cars.

d Plastic to make food containers.

e Ceramic tiles on the outside of the space shuttle.

14 Explain the following uses of materials.

a Some laboratory chemicals are now supplied in plastic bottles instead of glass bottles.

b Gold is expensive yet it is used to make rings.

c Car bodies are made of iron and yet iron rusts.

15 Here is the contents page of a book about oil.

Chapter 1 Introduction
Chapter 2 The origin of oil
Chapter 3 The properties of oil
Chapter 4 Oil and the environment
Chapter 5 Separating chemicals from oil
Chapter 6 Making plastics
Chapter 7 Other fossil fuels
Chapter 8 Alternative energy

a What chapter would you look in to find out whether oil was soluble?

b What chapter would you look in to find out about making petrol?

c Which chapter is likely to contain information about pollution problems?

d Which chapter title suggests that oil was made from tiny creatures that died?

e Name one substance that would probably be mentioned in chapter 8.

16 The following description is about an experiment.

To find out the hardness of metal, put a piece of metal on top of a piece of hard plastic. Drop a steel ball down a clear plastic tube so that it falls onto the metal. The ball will bounce. Measure the height that the ball bounces to with a ruler.

a The diagram shows the apparatus for this experiment. What should the labels be?

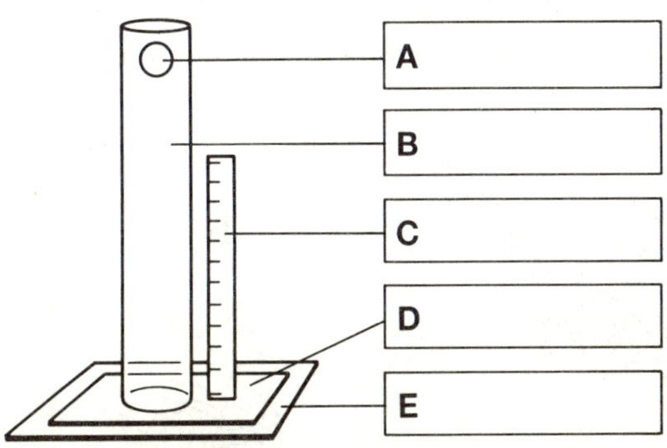

b If you used this apparatus to compare the hardness of two metals, what things would you have to keep the same to make the comparison fair?

continued ▶

17 If a chip pan full of oil catches fire then you should
(i) switch the electricity off
(ii) cover the pan with a damp cloth.
a Draw the fire triangle.
b Explain the two actions to put out the chip-pan fire.
Mention the fire triangle in your answers.

18 a Copy the passage and complete it using words from the list (not all the words will be used).
b Finish the last sentence in your own words.

- oxygen
- heat
- respiration
- nitrogen
- stored
- hydrogen
- oxides
- light
- combustion
- electrical

When a substance burns, it joins with ____ from the air to make ____. This process releases ____ and ____ energy. It is called ____. Another process called ____ also uses the same part of the air. In this case living things . . .

19 Which of these substances are fuels?

- water
- coal
- wood
- sunlight
- food
- heat
- petrol

Extension questions

20 Draw and describe a design which would solve **one** of these problems.

a

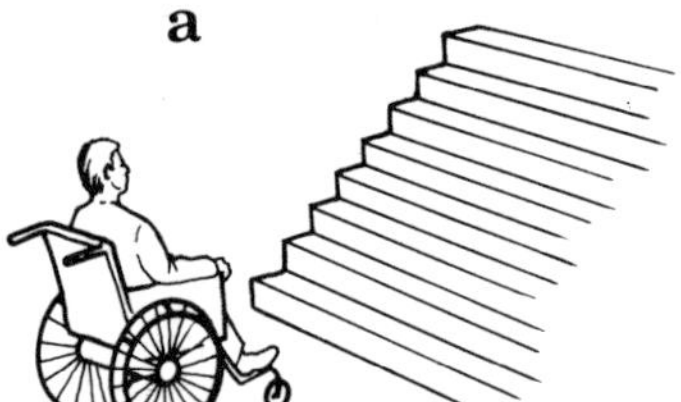

b

c

21 Look at these graphs.

A

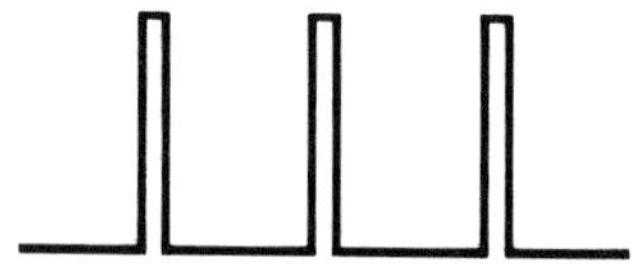

B

a Which graph shows analogue information?
Name two devices which use analogue information.
b What kind of information does the other graph show?
Name two devices which use this type of information.

22 Construct a truth table for this circuit.

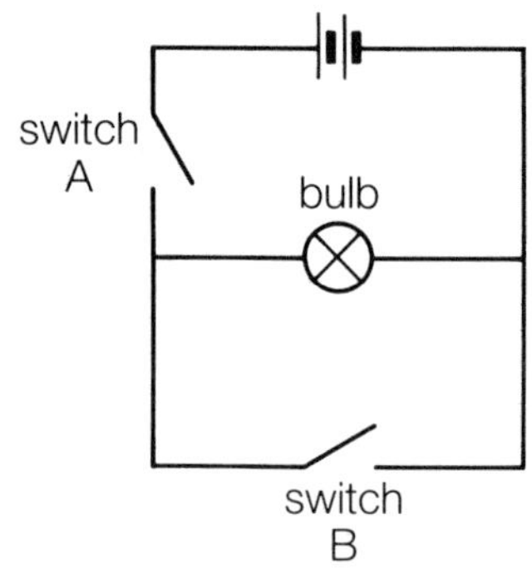

23 The diagram shows an experiment to compare the effect of a liquid on the growth of microbes.

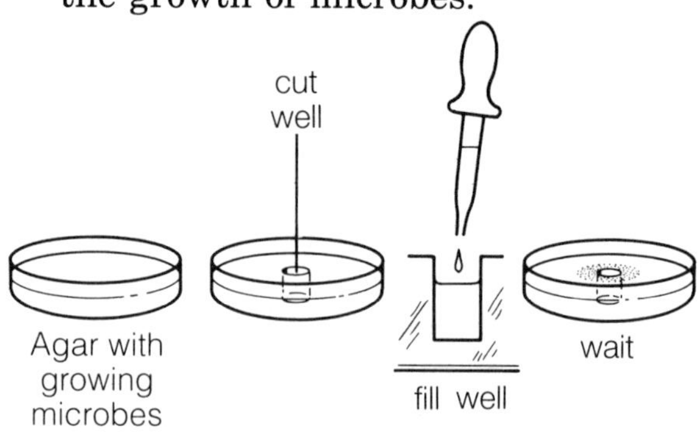

Explain in your own words how you would use this experiment to compare the effects of two antibiotics.
Mention how you would ensure that the comparison was fair.

continued ▶

24 The bar graph shows the amount and type of rubbish collected from a house in one week.

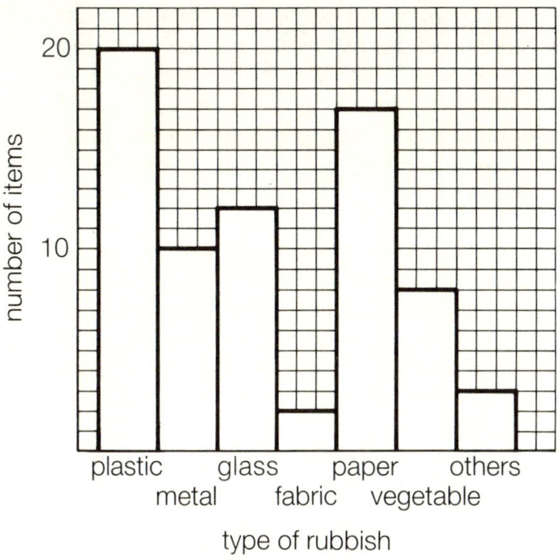

a How many items were collected altogether?
b What is the most common type of rubbish?
c What type(s) of rubbish is/are biodegradable?
d What type(s) of rubbish should be recycled?

25 The diagram shows some parts of the body that doctors can now replace with artificial materials.

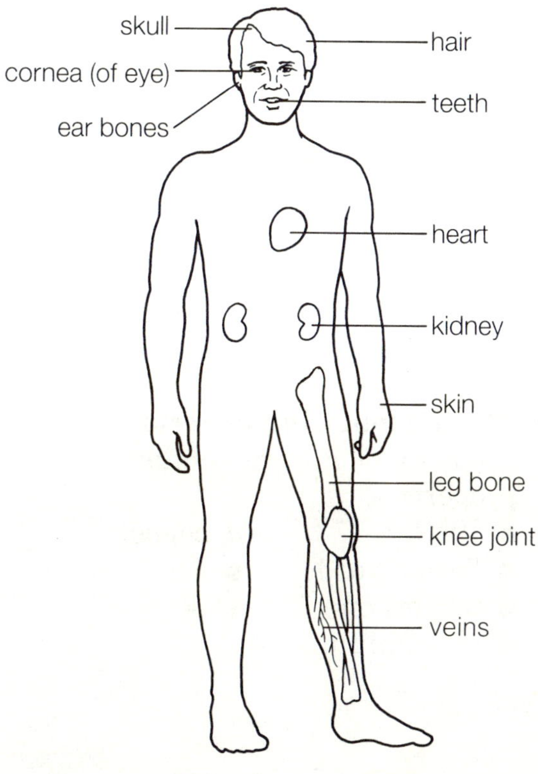

a Why is plastic used for heart valves?
b Why are metal parts used for the bones and the skull?
c What properties must the material used for the veins have?
d What kind of material is found in tooth fillings?
Why do you think this kind of material is used?
e What kind of material would you use to replace the skin?
Why did you pick this material?
Give **two** reasons.

26 Look at the following drawing. Describe the uses that are being made of technology in it.

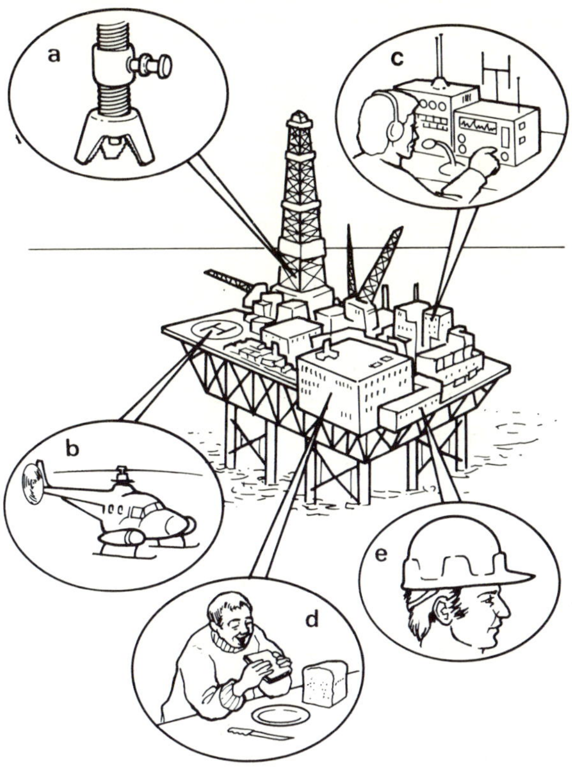

27 Read the following passage

Neptune is so faint and so distant that its surface and atmosphere can be explored only by a spacecraft. Voyager II has done this.

A Neptune is the most distant of the four giant planets in the Solar System—so far from Earth that it is dimly lit by the Sun. It can be seen only by telescope, and then you need to know where to look.

Galileo saw it by chance in 1613, when it happened to be close to Jupiter, but thought it might be another of Jupiter's moons. It was not discovered and recognised as a planet until 150 years ago.

continued ▶

The Grand Tour of the planets which Voyager has now completed, is the culmination of 30 years of spacecraft research of the Solar System. Only Pluto, a comparatively tiny planet, remains to be visited, but a mission is not planned.

There are no planets beyond and if anything remains undiscovered in this Solar System it must be minor. The Grand Tour is unique and will not be repeated in a lifetime.

Voyager II is an outstanding success. Now is the time to take stock of what has been learned.

The motive for Voyager was the search for knowledge, but the first gain has been the acceptance of the view long held by experts that the Solar System holds no place other than Earth where life can exist.

The more that is seen of the planets, their moons and their atmospheres, the more it is realised that conditions on Earth are special and precarious. We live within a thin skin on the surface of one of the smaller planets, balanced between the searing heat of Mercury and Venus and the freezing cold of the outer planets. Only Earth has an atmosphere which can sustain life.

Voyager II will have been worthwhile if it does nothing more than make people realise that there is a limit to the mess that can be made of this planet before life becomes impossible.

(From *The Guardian*, 26th August 1989)

a Skim the passage.
Write down a suitable title for the passage.

b Skim the passage again.
(i) What is the main idea in paragraph **A**?
(ii) What is the main idea in the last paragraph of the passage?

c Scan the passage to find out what the *motive for Voyager* was.

d Scan the passage to find out when Neptune was discovered.

e Scan the passage to discover how many planets are mentioned.

f What is Voyager II?

g Why has Voyager II been worthwhile?

28 Read the following passage.

One sample in ten of pâtés, which are cooked in central kitchens and then chilled for weeks before sale, were found to be contaminated with Listeria, the bacterium that can cause still-births and death to infected newborn and others, like the elderly and ill, with weakened immune systems. Listeria bacteria have the unusual ability to multiply and even grow more virulent at refrigerated temperatures as low as 4°C.

Poor old pâté has had a bad press, and like eggs after the Salmonella outbreak, its sales could plummet. The truth is that many foods are now contaminated with food-poisoning organisms, and putting them into a microwave is a recipe for illness because the machines cannot uniformly heat foods of uneven density and water content.

Researchers have also found that Salmonella in fresh poultry is infrequently killed even when the birds are cooked to manufacturers' instructions, according to a report in The Food Magazine of the London Food Commission.

(From *The Guardian*, 26th August 1989)

a Skim the passage.
Write a suitable title for the passage.

b Skim the passage again.
(i) What is the main idea of the first paragraph?
(ii) What is the main idea of the last paragraph?

c Scan the passage to discover which foods are mentioned.

d Scan the passage to discover the names of two microbes which cause food poisoning.

e Why might some microwave ovens not prevent food poisoning?

29 Name three types of natural fuel. Explain why these fuels will not last forever and how we can help make them last longer.

30 Put the following materials into groups which have similar properties:

- PVC
- beech wood
- polyethene
- aluminium
- copper
- oak
- perspex

Unit 6 Science in use

True or False 6

Name ____________________

Put a tick after the statements which are true. Put a cross after the statements which are false.

1 a Your genes will pass on information to your children. ☐
b You can have an operation to change your genes. ☐
c Different cells in the same body can have different genes. ☐

2 a All materials are found naturally. ☐
b Synthetic means that the substance is made by humans. ☐
c Nylon is natural. ☐
d A cotton shirt is made of synthetic material. ☐
e A raw material is a substance that can be changed into something more useful. ☐
f The following are examples of raw materials: air, water, coal, oil. ☐

3 a Materials used for clothing are similar because they are non-poisonous, soft, can be cut and stitched. ☐
b Materials used for building are similar because they are strong, can be shaped, can be joined together in structures. ☐
c Materials used for clothing are similar to materials used for building. ☐

4 a These materials are given in order of increasing strength: cotton, wood, brick, steel. ☐
b These materials are given in order of increasing hardness: talc, chalk, diamond, granite. ☐
c These materials are given in order of increasing flexibility: concrete, plastic, cloth. ☐
d These materials are given in order of increasing solubility: salt, sugar, glass, sand. ☐

5 a A strong material would be good for building houses. ☐
b A hard material would be good for building cars. ☐
c A flexible material would be good for building banks. ☐
d A soluble material would be good for building statues. ☐

6 a Raw materials are manufactured from useful materials by humans. ☐
b Humans can use chemical reactions to change raw materials into useful ones. ☐
c A product of a reaction is a substance which is made in the chemical reaction. ☐
d Polymers are made by joining little molecules together. ☐

7 a Fermentation is used to convert sugar into alcohol. ☐
b Yeast can ferment glucose. ☐
c Some microbes make useful enzymes which change raw materials into useful products. ☐
d Enzymes are found in microbes and nowhere else. ☐
e Microbes make enzymes when we need them. ☐

8 a A microbe uses oxygen to undergo daily combustion. ☐
b When something undergoes combustion, it makes compounds called oxides. ☐
c Respiration uses up the gas called nitrogen from the air. ☐
d Many microbes produce useful substances when they are respiring. ☐

9 a The word equation for fermentation is glucose $\xrightarrow{\text{yeast}}$ carbon dioxide + alcohol. ☐
b The word equation for burning petrol is petrol $\longrightarrow$ oxygen + oxides. ☐

continued ▶

Name ____________________

c The word equation for making a plastic is polymer + polymer ⟶ monomer. ☐

10 **a** A tape recorder and a digital watch store information. ☐
b A TV and a record player transmit information. ☐
c A stereo radio and a TV receive information. ☐

11 **a** Information can be stored electronically. ☐
b Facts can only be stored in the form of words. ☐
c Electronic information can be output as sound and as pictures. ☐

12 **a** A word processor is just an electronic dictionary. ☐
b A word processor is quicker to use than a typewriter. ☐
c A word processor is more efficient than a typewriter. ☐

13 **a** Microelectronic devices are too small to see. ☐
b A TV, a video camera and a computer are all microelectronic devices. ☐
c A radio telescope is a microelectronic device. ☐

14 **a** A pH meter measures the sourness of a liquid. ☐
b A digital thermometer is one which can be held on your finger. ☐
c Some electronic detectors can measure the level of a variable in the environment. ☐

15 **a** Telecommunication devices can be used to communicate over long distances. ☐
b The following are all telecommunication devices: telephones, radios, satellite TV. ☐
c The following are all telecommunication devices: video recorders, video cameras, tape recorders. ☐

16 **a** A fuel is a substance that releases energy when burned. ☐
b Oil is the main fuel. ☐
c The following are all fuels: petrol, wind, waves, sun. ☐
d The following are all fuels: alcohol, diesel, wood, coal. ☐

17 **a** The world's supply of oil will last for thousands of years. ☐
b One source of fuel can always be replaced by another. ☐
c We should be careful not to waste fuel. ☐
d Coal and oil are not important if everyone has gas or electricity. ☐

18 **a** A resource is a source which is being saved. ☐
b Fossil fuels are fuels such as coal, oil and natural gas. ☐
c Fossil fuels are made all the time as living things die. ☐
d Fossil fuels may run out if animals begin to live longer. ☐
e The world has a limited supply of energy resources. ☐

Extensions

19 **a** All substances decay within a few years. ☐
b Microbes are needed to remove biodegradable material. ☐
c A compost heap must be warm and moist before it decays properly. ☐

continued ▶

Name ____________________

20 a Recycling is not a good thing because it is expensive. ☐

b The following materials are all worth recycling: glass, paper, aluminium. ☐

c The following materials are all worth recycling: plastic, rust, wood. ☐

21 a Biodegradable means that the substance can be broken down if it is thrown away. ☐

b The following substances are all biodegradable: meat, lettuce, wool, granite. ☐

c The following objects are all biodegradable: your Sunday lunch, the walls of the school, the TV in your house. ☐

22 a A switch changes the amount of electric current. ☐

b A switch starts and stops electron flow. ☐

c A small switch lowers the value of the current by a small amount. ☐

23 a A truth table is constructed by asking a scientist questions. ☐

b Truth tables are true/false tables, like these statements. ☐

24 a This is an analogue trace. ☐

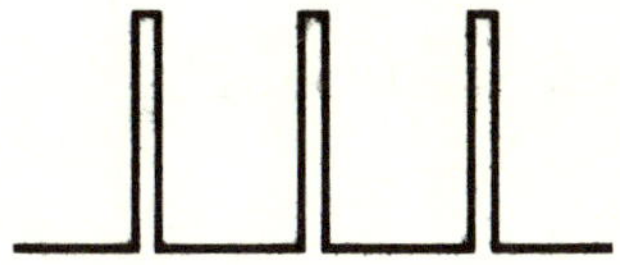

b This is an analogue trace. ☐

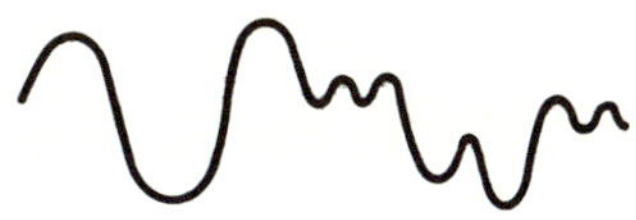

c Digital signals use the two bits of information, **on** and **off.** ☐

d A computer uses analogue information. ☐

e An analogue receiver will capture information on a carrier wave. ☐

Unit 6 Science in use

Name ____________________

Complete each sentence. Put the correct word(s) in each blank space.

1 Scientific ideas and knowledge are used in ________________ to make and test the ________________ solution for problems.

2 Technology is used to make electronic devices. These contain microelectronic ________________. The circuits are built from parts called ________________. Two important components and their symbols are

- ________________: **symbol–**
- ________________: **symbol–**

Very small circuits containing all the necessary components can now be built on a piece of ________________. These are called ________________ circuits. Separate electronic circuits can be joined to make an electronic ________________. An electronic system has three parts:

- the ________________ is what you must put into the system
- the ________________ is what does the work
- the ________________ is the job that the system is to do.

Three examples of things which use electronic technology are ________________, ________________ and ________________.

3 Technology has solved communication problems. Satellite TV and telephones are examples of ________________ devices. Two other examples are ________________ and ________________. Many telecommunication devices use electronics in either the transmitter or the ________________.

continued ▶

Name ____________________

4 Technology has solved some food problems. Many foods are now made with the help of small ____________. Two examples are ____________ and ____________. Often the way of making food depends on the process the microbe uses to get energy from its food. (This process is called ____________.) Some microbes also produce useful chemicals called ____________ which help control chemical reactions.

5 Other complicated chemicals have been extracted from living things. Two examples are ____________ which is an antibiotic and ____________ which controls the sugar level in our blood.

6 Technology has solved material problems. The five main groups of materials are

- ____________
- ____________
- ____________
- ____________
- ____________.

Many materials are natural (like ____________ and ____________), but some can be made by humans (like ____________ and ____________) and are therefore called ____________. Plastics are synthetic. Many plastics are made of little molecules all joined together to form a big molecule called a ____________. Two examples of these are ____________ and ____________.

7 Technology has also helped us to make fuels. We already have natural fuels like ____________ and ____________. However, they are used up by burning in oxygen in a reaction called ____________. Fire can only occur if three things are present:

- ____________
- ____________
- ____________.

Fossil fuels are being used up. New fuels like ____________ will become more important in the future.

New material 1: *Mortar*

Cement is made from natural materials: limestone and clay.

Collect
- Plastic mixing bowl
- Scoop
- Stirring stick
- Egg box or similar
- Cement
- Sand
- Safety glasses

1 Put **three** scoops of sand and **four** scoops of cement into the bowl.

2 Mix with the stick.

3 Add a little water and keep mixing.

4 Add enough water to get a smooth paste. Pour this into the egg box.

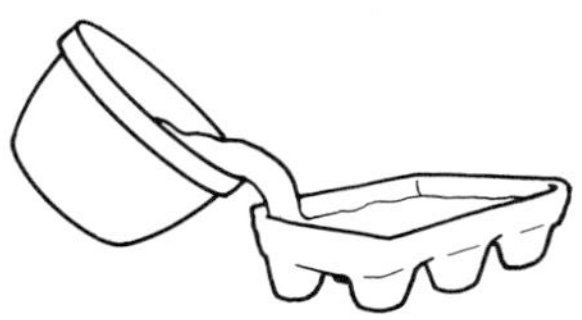

New material 2: *Brick*

Clay is dug up from the ground.

Collect
- Bunsen burner
- Heatproof mat
- Tongs
- Safety glasses
- **Small** piece of clay

1 Heat the piece of clay gently at first.

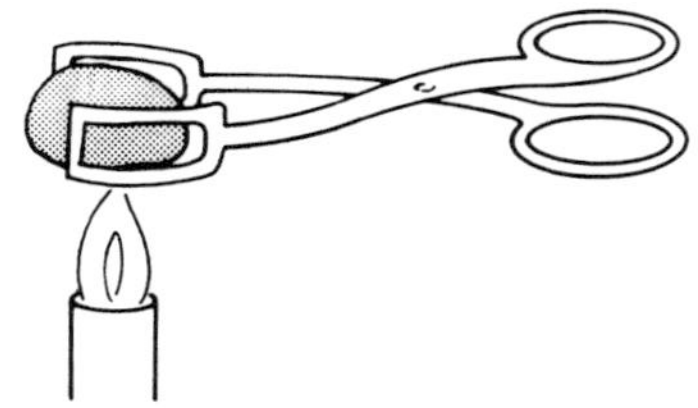

2 Increase the heat until the clay is red hot.

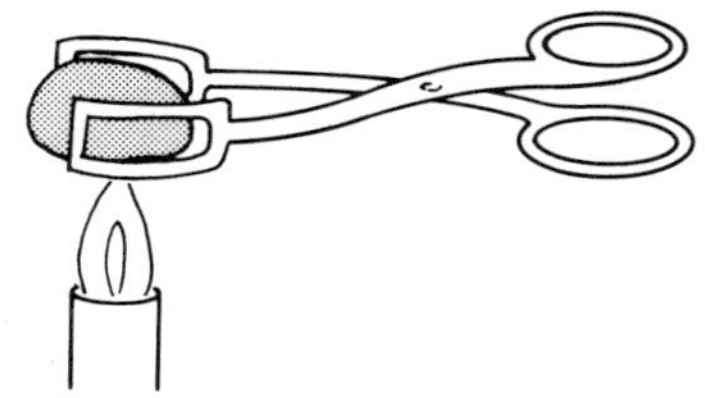

3 Leave the material on the heatproof mat to cool.

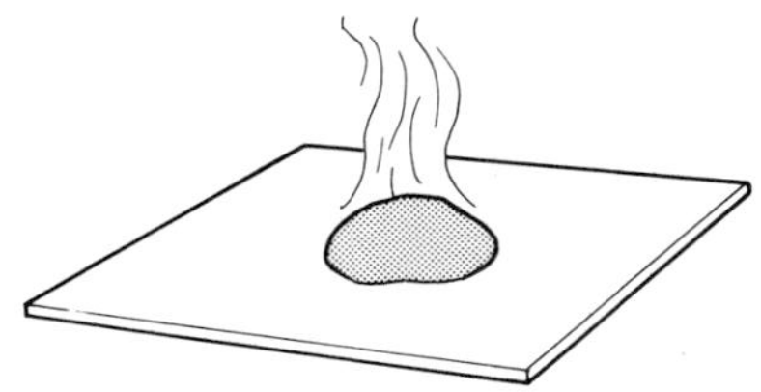

New material 3: *Filler paste*

Most filler pastes are polymers.

Collect
Tube of filler paste
Tube of hardener
Tin lid
Wooden splint
Protective gloves
Safety glasses

1 Read the instructions on the paste tube very carefully.

2 Add a small amount of paste to the tin lid.

3 Add a **small** amount of hardener and mix with the wooden spill.

4 Work the paste into a pleasant shape and leave it to set. Wear gloves if necessary.

New material 4: *Rubber*

Trees produce a liquid called sap when the trunk is cut. The sap of the rubber tree is called latex.

Collect
About 10 cm^3 latex solution in a small beaker
Small test tube
Vinegar
Dropper
Safety glasses

1 Add a dropper full of vinegar to the latex solution.

2 Stir with the test tube.

3 Allow the layer of rubber on the test tube to dry then roll it off to make a rubber band.

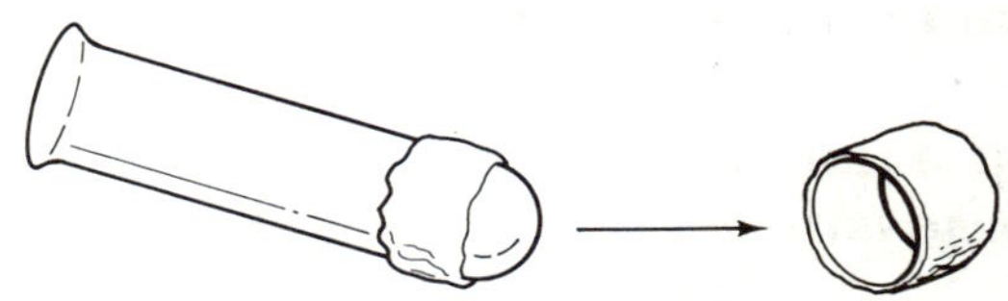

New material 5: *Perspex*

Perspex is made from a flammable monomer. Do this experiment in a fume cupboard.

Collect
Releasing oil and paintbrush
Small tin or tin lid with lip
Perspex monomer
Wooden splint
Safety glasses

1 Coat the tin with a layer of releasing oil.

2 Add about 5 cm^3 of Perspex monomer.

3 Ask your teacher to add a little hardener.
Stir with the wooden spill.

4 Put the tin in an oven or on a hot plate for about half an hour.
Knock out the hard Perspex.

New material 6: *Resin glue*

Many modern glues are *polymers;*
***Solvent glues* contain the polymer dissolved in a solvent. The solvent evaporates to leave the polymer behind.**
***Resin glues* are formed from two monomers. The polymer is made when the monomers join together.**

Collect
Packet of epoxy resin glue
Tin lid
Wooden splint
Broken pen or similar object
Safety glasses

1 Read the instructions on the packet very carefully.

2 Add a small amount of the glue to the tin lid.

3 Add a **small** amount of hardener and mix with the wooden spill.

4 Stand the broken pen in the glue and leave to set.

Petrol/oxygen explosion

Apparatus

- Syringe—plastic (20 cm^3, without plunger, with hole cut out to take lighter nozzle)
- Lighter—gas (piezoelectric or spark generated across the gap of a spark plug)
- Syringe—plastic (20 cm^3 with plastic tube for collecting oxygen)
- Gas—oxygen (cylinder with needle reducing valve) or generator (electrolysis or $H_2O_2 + MnO_2$)
- Fuel—petrol or lighter (alternative: petroleum ether, boiling range 40–60 °C)
- Dropper—glass
- 2 safety screens
- Non-return valve
- Safety goggles

Procedure—*Teacher demonstration only*

Attach the tube of the syringe with plunger to the oxygen cylinder outlet (needle reducing) valve or generator alternative. With the plunger of the syringe initially pressed fully in, adjust the valve very slowly till the plunger moves out to the 20 cm^3 mark. Shut off the valve completely.

Fix the tubing to the non-return valve of the adapted 20 cm^3 syringe body. Using the dropper, put one drop of petrol into this syringe, inject about 10 cm^3 of oxygen and create a spark using the piezoelectric sparker. After the explosion inject a further 10 cm^3 of oxygen and repeat. One drop of fuel may provide about 4–5 explosion attempts.

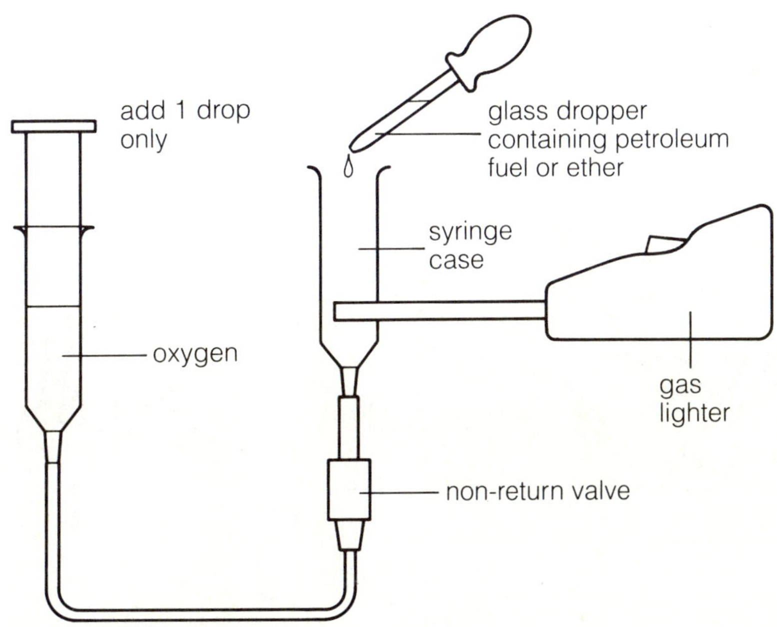

Microbe Picture Quiz

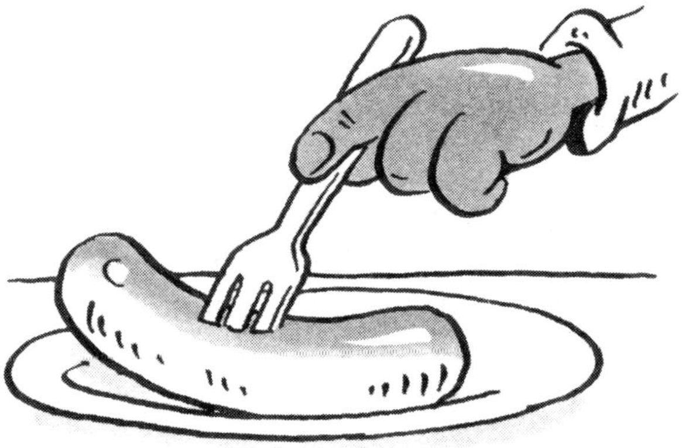

Skills sheets

The following 45 exercises are intended to:

- make pupils aware of essential skills in science
- give pupils practice in specific skills
- provide targeted extension material that supports very worthwhile objectives
- provide material that is largely self-corrected

Organisation

The sheets cover several categories of skills. These are:

- reading skills
- writing skills
- number skills
- revision skills
- experimental design skills

The skills are developed in the context of science and technology and attempt to extend the pupils' awareness of science in society.

The exercises are arranged in a linear sequence. This logical order develops the more complex skill areas slowly. However the exercises can stand alone and so offer a valuable resource bank that can be used in a variety of ways:

- *As additional extension material:* the sheets would be arranged in booklet form in the order suggested. Each individual pupil can then work through the booklet during those odd free times during, or at the end of, a lesson. Questions are answered at the back of the pupil's notebook and work can be self-marked from a prepared marked copy of the sheets.
- *As targeted extension material for specific lessons:* scale work, number work, specific reading tasks and so on.
- *As the central material for a lesson where the aim is to develop reading or other skills*.
- *As homework*.

These sheets also provide a model that could be used to generate additional material. They are reusable.

Experience suggests that the majority of exercises will take about 10–15 minutes to complete.

Sheet	Skill	Notes
1	Reading—Using a dictionary	Finding scientific and non-scientific meanings for words
2	Writing—Using fewer words in sentences	Identifying relevant details in a scientific note
3	Writing—Making notes from short passages	Skimming a passage to find the main ideas
4	Number—Multiplying whole numbers	Finding the product of up to three whole numbers
5	Experimental Design—Spotting the variables 1	Identifying constant and changing variables
6	Writing—Using fewer words in reports	Crossing out unnecessary details in experimental reports
7	Number—Adding decimal numbers	Adding numbers with one or two decimal places
8	Writing—Writing an experimental report	Including a title, method, results and conclusions sections
9	Experimental Design—Spotting the variables 2	Identifying constant and changing variables
10	Writing—Making notes from longer passages	Skimming a longer passage to find the main ideas
11	Reading—Finding information 1	Skimming and scanning two passages to select the most useful one
12	Reading—Remembering what you read 1	Remembering factual information
13	Writing—Recording facts in notes 1	Skimming and scanning a passage and recording details
14	Writing—Using diagrams in notes 1	Summarising a short passage in note or diagrammatic form
15	Number—Averages	Finding the (decimal) average of a series of numbers
16	Reading—Spotting correct conclusions	Identifying valid conclusions from an experimental description
17	Experimental Design—Fair tests 1	Controlling variables in an experimental design
18	Revision—Organising revision	Making a revision timetable

Sheet	Skill	Notes
19	Reading—Reading line graphs 1	Describing the relationship between the two variables on a line graph
20	Reading—Finding information 2	Skimming and scanning a passage and recording details in a table
21	Writing—Using diagrams in notes 2	Summarising details from a passage in diagrammatic form
22	Number—Subtracting decimal numbers	Finding the difference between two decimal scale readings
23	Writing—Recording facts in notes 2	Scanning a passage and recording details
24	Reading—Reading line graphs 2	Describing the relationship between the two variables on a line graph
25	Writing—Making conclusions 1	Describing valid conclusions from an experimental description
26	Experimental Design—Fair tests 2	Identifying constant and changing variables
27	Reading—Remembering what you read 2	Remembering factual information
28	Number—Multiplying decimal numbers 2	Multiplying numbers with one or two decimal places
29	Reading—Reading line graphs 3	Interpreting line graphs with more than one line
30	Writing—Using diagrams to shorten notes 1	Making spider diagrams to describe main ideas
31	Writing—Making flow diagrams	Completing a flow diagram with guidance
32	Revision—Making a revision summary 1	Skimming and scanning a passage and recording important details
33	Experimental Design—Fair tests 3	Identifying constant and changing variables
34	Reading—Finding information 3	Skimming and scanning a passage and recording details in a table
35	Writing—Making conclusions 2	Describing valid conclusions from an experimental report
36	Number—Multiplying decimal numbers 2	Multiplying numbers with one or two decimal places
37	Reading—Understanding flow diagrams	Describing flow diagrams in words
38	Writing—Using diagrams to shorten notes 2	Making spider diagrams to describe main ideas
39	Reading—Finding information 4	Scanning a passage and recording details
40	Revision—Making a revision summary 2	Skimming and scanning a passage and summarising it
41	Writing—Using a flow diagram in notes	Organising written information into a flow diagram
42	Reading—Reading line graphs 4	Using a graph to change from Celsius to Fahrenheit
43	Reading—Recognising fact and opinion	Categorising sentences as either fact or opinion
44	Reading—Collating information	Finding information using two tables
45	Revision—Making a revision summary 3	Skimming and scanning a passage and summarising it

Skills sheet 1

Reading skills—Using a dictionary

You probably know how to use a dictionary. For example, if you want to look up the meaning of the word **silly,** then you search for

S
then **Si**
then **Sil**

There are guide words at the top of each page to help you. For example, the page with **silly** on it may have **sil**ent at the top. Eventually you will find an entry something like this:

> **silly** *adj.* (sillier, silliest) **1.** lacking good sense, foolish, unwise. **2.** feeble-minded. **3.** (of a fieldsman's position in cricket) close to the batsman, *silly mid-on.* *—n. (in-formal) a foolish person.*
> From *The Oxford Senior Dictionary* (OUP 1982)

Silly has at least three meanings. Many scientific words have a **scientific use** and other uses. For example, a dictionary will give the following meanings for the word **cell:**

> **cell** a very small room *(non-scientific use)*
> a compartment in a honeycomb *(non-scientific use)*
> a device for producing electric current (**scientific** *use)*
> a microscopic unit of living matter (**scientific** *use)*
> a small group of people *(non-scientific use)*

Use a dictionary to find one scientific and one non-scientific use for each of the following words.
Copy and complete the table.

Word	Scientific use	Non-Scientific use
current		
heat		
energy		
key		
dissolve		
solution		
potential		
scale		
circuit		
static		

Skills sheet 2

Writing Skills—Using fewer words in sentences

Good notes use as few words as possible. For example, the following sentence is very long. It contains words which are not needed in a **scientific** note.

Some of the acid was added to the powdered chalk while I was standing at the bench and the whole mixture fizzed up and bubbles and froth showed.

The important words are underlined. The sentence could be rewritten as

Acid was added to the powdered chalk and the mixture fizzed.

An even shorter version would be

Acid + powdered chalk gives fizz.

Rewrite the following sentences using as few words as possible. Try to keep the scientific facts and miss out the rest.

a We watched the lion while we were eating our ice cream and it spent most of the time resting, almost as if it was watching TV.

b Fine sand is used to dry flowers because it absorbs moisture and it can be collected when the tide in the bay is out.

c To make the cement that you see in cement bags you need to mix powdered limestone and shale and heat the mixture in a kiln to 800°C, which is as hot as a bunsen-burner flame.

d Small bits of gold are swept from rocks into the water of the stream and they fall and mix with the mud on the bottom. The gold is heavy and it can be separated from other substances by swirling the mud with some water in a large pan.

Skills sheet 3

Writing skills—Making notes from short passages

A written passage often has a lot of unnecessary details. You should read it to find the main ideas. These main ideas can then form the starting point of your notes about the passage.

What are the main ideas in each of the passages?

a

> HOSPITAL STATION by James White does not deal with the galaxy wars, or science gone mad. Its heroes are not space-men or technicians. It is the story of a vast, galactic hospital—where everyone—and everything in the universe can be treated. The heroes are doctors and nurses—who have eight legs . . . or none; who breathe methane—or water. Each patient is a fantastic and challenging problem—such as getting close to an invalid whose 'food' is radiation; caring for a baby, who weighs half a ton . . .
>
> *Back-cover description* (Corgi 1967)

b

> Hal had been trained for this mission as thoroughly as his human colleagues—and at many times their rate of input, for in addition to his intrinsic speed, he never slept. His prime task was to monitor the life—support systems, continually checking oxygen pressure, temperature, hull leakage, radiation and all the other interlocking factors upon which the lives of the fragile human cargo depended. He could carry out the intricate navigational corrections, and execute the necessary flight manoeuvres when it was time to change course. And he could watch over the hibernators, making any necessary adjustments to their environment, and doling out the minute quantities of intravenous fluids that kept them alive.
>
> From *2001: A Space Odyssey*, A.C. Clarke (Hutchinson 1973)

Skills sheet 4

Number skills—Multiplying whole numbers

In many science experiments you measure something. The results are written down as numbers. To make sense of the numbers you must have good arithmetic skills.

1 Write down the answers to the following multiplications:
a $2 \times 4 \times 8 =$
b $16 \times 3 \times 7 =$
c $25 \times 10 \times 4 =$

2 In a class of 19 pupils the teacher gave each pupil two batteries, five connecting wires and three bulbs to make a circuit.
How many pieces of electrical apparatus did the teacher hand out altogether?

3 A solar powered car can move non-stop at an average speed of 16 kilometres per hour.
The distance it can travel can be found by multiplying the time it is travelling for by its speed.
How far will the car travel in:
a 1 hour
b 1 day
c 1 week
d 1 year
e 10 years?

Skills sheet 5

Experimental design skills—Spotting the variables 1

In science it is important to be able to trust the results of experiments. Experiments must be **fair**. You must think about all of the things that might affect the result. These things are called **variables**. When you give a description of something you are describing the variables.

Spot the variables in the three situations given below.

a Comparing coins

Look for variables that stay the same and for variables that change.

Copy and complete the table below for another three variables.

Variable	Stays the same	Changes
colour of coin	✓	

b More coins

Look for variables that stay the same and for variables that change.

Make a table like the one above to show five variables.

c Comparing faces

Look for variables that stay the same and for variables that change.

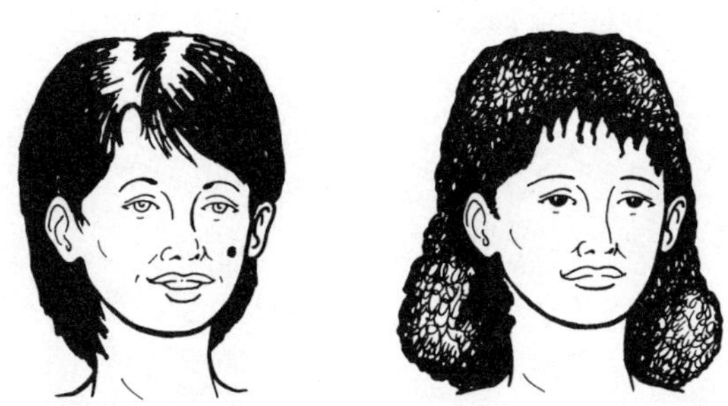

Make a table to show five variables.

Skills sheet 6

Writing skills—Using fewer words in reports

Pupils often use too many words in written work. For example, an experimental report should be as short as possible. The following report includes a lot of unnecessary details. These have been crossed out.

> "Mixing two ~~pretty~~ chemicals
>
> ~~Lisa was my partner. She collected the two bottles of chemicals and I put the stools under the desk~~. One chemical was called cobalt chloride solution. It was pink ~~and it was in a 500 cm³ bottle~~. The other chemical was called copper sulphate solution. ~~It was also in a 500 cm³ bottle and~~ it was blue ~~like our school blazer. We collected a test tube and rack. I poured the first chemical into the test tube and Lisa added the second~~. When the two mixed it went all cloudy and lumpy and purple ~~like my Gran's custard~~."

The report is now a lot shorter. It will be easier to read and remember.

1 **Collect** a copy of some experimental reports.
Read each report.
Re-read each report and cross out anything that you think is unnecessary.

2 Look through your own book.
Find a long experimental report.
Count the number of words that you could cross out without changing the sense of the report.

Skills sheet 6

Worksheet

Experimental reports

a

colin and I collected two small test tubes. They were in the box near the window. We added a little blue liquid called copper sulphate solution to one test tube. Colin then opened the ammonia solution bottle. Powee: what a pong. He told me to hold his nose while he poured some into the second test tube. When we mixed these solutions the colour changed from light blue to dark blue. There were lots of lumps in the mixture.

b

I took five wires. Each wire was a different colour. I put the wires on the table and picked out one. It was yellow. I put the yellow one next to the continuity tester and connected it. The bulb on the tester lit. This shows that the wire was unbroken. I repeated this test with the other wires. The green one was the only one which didn't light the bulb so it must have been broken. The red, orange, black and yellow wires lit the bulb.

c

I planted a bean seed on the first Wednesday in March (3rd March). the pot with my bean was put on the window ledge next to the first year worksheets. I measured its size each month for 4 months. During the fifth month it withered because of lack of water. My bean had been and gone.

Skills sheet 7

Number skills—adding decimal numbers

In many science experiments you measure something. The results are written down as numbers. To make sense of the numbers you have to have good arithmetic skills.

Adding decimal numbers is not difficult. Every time you buy more than one item in a shop you add decimals to find out how much you must pay.

1 Find the total (sum) of the following:

a	**b**	**c**
8.2	11.21	25 + 2.23 + 4.76 + 9.99 =
9.1	12.09	
4.4	23.23	
6.2	18.09	
3.7	12.56	
___	_____	

2 An experiment was carried out to compare how far three wind-up cars would travel. Each car carried a microcomputer, which measured the distance travelled each second. Here are the results.

	Distance travelled in each second/cm		
	Car 1	**Car 2**	**Car 3**
1st second	4.6	8.71	1.9
2nd second	4.1	7.94	1.4
3rd second	3.3	6.46	0.7
4th second	2.3	4.33	0.1
5th second	0.3	1.12	0.0

How far did each car travel in the first five seconds?

3 Three pieces of wood are shown below.

What will their total length be if they are joined together?

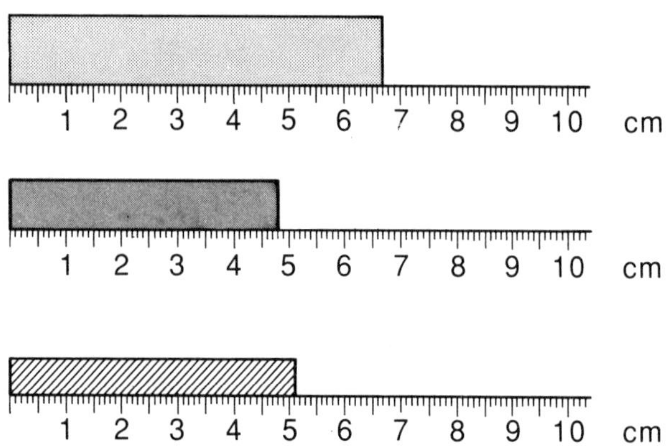

Skills sheet 8

Writing skills—Writing an experimental report

You will often write reports about experiments. A report is often made up of four sections. Other people will understand your report more quickly if it has these sections:

Title: *What was the purpose of the experiment? (Why did you do it?)*

Method: *What did you do? (Include a labelled diagram if it will help). Another person should be able to do the experiment by following your method section.*

Results: *What happened? Include observations, measurements and graphs.*

Conclusions: *What do you think the results mean?*

1 Look through your own book. Find three reports about experiments.
Mark each report out of 4. Give 1 mark for each of the important sections that you included.

2 Write an imaginary report about **one** of these experiments.

a An experiment to discover whether fresh grass burns.

b An experiment to compare the eating habits of snails and slugs.

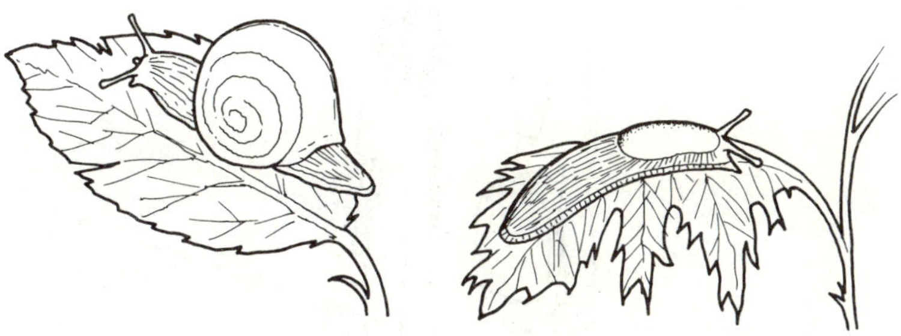

Skills sheet 9

Experimental design skills—Spotting the variables 2

In science it is important to be able to trust the results of experiments. Experiments must be **fair**. You must think about all of the things that might affect the results. These things are called **variables**.

1 Look for variables that stay the same and for variables that change in these two examples.

Find as many variables as you can.

Record your answers in a table with three columns.

The headings are *Variable, Stays the same,* and *Changes.*

a Stamps

b Team strips

2 Race You!
Two girls decide to have a race to the nearest tree. It's not going to be a fair race. What variables should be made the same to make it fair?

Skills sheet 10

Writing skills—Making notes from longer passages

A written passage often has a lot of unnecessary details. You should read it to find the main ideas. These main ideas can then form the starting point of your notes about the passage.

What are the main ideas in each of these passages?

a

In 1967 a Kiev film company produced a costly professional film about a middle-aged Leningrad housewife. She is shown sitting at a table in a physiology laboratory after being medically examined and X-rayed to ensure that nothing is hidden on or in her body. She puts out her hands, with the fingers spread, about six inches above a compass in the centre of the table and tenses her muscles. She stares intently at the compass, lines etched deeply in her face showing the strain of a body under acute tension. Minutes pass and sweat breaks out on her brow as she continues the struggle, and then, slowly, the compass needle quivers and moves to point in a new direction. She starts to move her hand in a circular motion and the needle turns with them, until it is rotating like the second hand of a watch. The field produced by the body can, under certain conditions, it seems, be stronger even than the field of earth itself.

From *Supernature*, L. Watson (Hodder & Stoughton 1973)

b

Fresh southwesterly winds were yesterday breaking up a vast blanket of orange algae off the Cornish coast which swimmers had been warned could cause skin irritation.

The algae bloom, measured from the air at one stage as four miles long, revived a fierce controversy over sewage outfalls and tourism in Mount's Bay, near Penzance.

South West Water yesterday confirmed the algae species involved was Gyrodinium aurellum, which had been reported in previous years in the resort area bounded by Newlyn and St Michael's Mount.

On Monday Penwith District Council put out a statement warning bathers they could suffer a slight skin irritation, and advised people not to eat local shellfish. No signs were visible on the beaches.

The day before, holiday-makers had found the sea cloudy with yellow-orange algae, and lines of dead sea urchins on the shore. Some reported seeing lugworms coming out of the sand and exploding on contact with the algae.

High temperatures, bright sunshine, low neap tides and several months of calm seas, have all been suggested as necessary preconditions for the algae growth, but many locals blamed the alleged toxicity of the bloom on the large number of short sewage outfalls which pour out extra weight at the height of the tourist season.

From *The Guardian*, 9th August 1989

Reading skills—Finding information 1

You often have to read to find answers to a question or a problem. You may also have to collect information for a project. When you find a passage you should **skim** it quickly to see if it has the information that you want. You can then **scan** the passage to select details.

Skim and **scan** both passages below to find three disadvantages of collecting and cooking with wild mushrooms.

Passage A

Blewits *Tricholoma saevum*

Not uncommon in grassy pastures, October to December. The cap is flattish with an incurving marginal edge, two to five inches across, dry to touch but slightly jellyish and translucent, pale brown to greyish in colour. Gills: crowded, white to greyish pink. Stem: stout, tinged with blue and occasionally swollen at the base. No ring. Flesh white and firm.

Blewits (named after the bluish violet tinge of their stems) were one of the few fungi sold commercially in Britain. The trade was especially strong in the Midlands, and it is from there that the traditional way of cooking blewits as tripe comes.

Blewits often grow in large rings, and it is easy to overlook them in the late autumn for their flat irregular caps look like dead leaves scattered over the field. Pick them on a dry day (they are very porous), clean, and chop off their stems. Then cut up the stems finely with an equal amount of onions and pack round the caps with a little chopped sage and bacon fat. Just cover the blewits with milk and simmer for half an hour. Pour off the liquid, thicken with flour and butter and seasoning and pour back over the fungi mixture. Simmer for another quarter of an hour, and then serve the whole mixture inside a ring of mashed potatoes, with toast and apple sauce.

This way of cooking the fungi is probably not entirely fortuitous, for their aromatic taste with jellyish texture are indeed reminiscent of tripe, though they are considerably more digestible.

From *Food for Free*, R. Mabey (Collins 1972)

Passage B

Friends think you must be suicidal to hunt, never mind eat wild fungi. If you protest that mushrooms are hunted in every European country, they will counter with the annual death toll of Italians who ate the wrong ones.

None of my family will eat the Puffballs, Blewits and stranger things I bring in each year, and the way they watch me with interest for an hour or two after I've done so can be unnerving.

Identification by book is not always easy; identification can take so long that dinner has come and gone before you've satisfied yourself exactly which boletus you have.

There is another, less alarming disadvantage to wild mushrooms. They can be maggoty. You can be sitting picking them over in front of the telly when suddenly an army of the little flies hatched by the heat, will emerge. I've proudly presented my restaurant chef with trays of wonderful parasol mushrooms, only to find that the heat of the kitchen made a home for a colony of mushroom flies.

You cannot easily tell without cutting them open. Do that, and discard all the ones with innocent looking holes in them— they are home to these unwelcome guests.

But, for all that, looking for mushrooms is marvellous. Even if you don't consciously set out mushrooming, at least give the ones you find by accident a second thought. You wouldn't pass up a tree laden with walnuts would you? Or a hedge heavy with damsons?

Adapted from article by Pru Leith in *The Guardian*, 18th August 1989

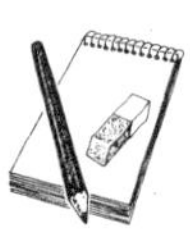

1 Which passage contains the information you want?

2 Read the useful passage again. Write down three disadvantages of collecting and cooking with wild mushrooms.

Skills sheet 12

Reading skills—Reading and remembering what you read

Some science books are designed to give you information. There are many ways to help you remember information that you read. Your memory will be better if you do something when you read; for example if you make notes or answer questions.

To help you remember facts

- first skim the passage
- then read the passage slowly.

Read the following passage. Then read the questions about it on the next page. Re-read the passage then answer the questions **without looking again** at the passage.

During the 1960s the satellites became more and more like rocketships. They weren't simply put into orbit. They could be manoeuvred by the people aboard. Two satellites could join each other, and people could travel from one to the other. They could put on space suits, leave the ship for a space walk, and return.

The Americans began to take a longer and longer lead over the Soviet Union in such experiments. They began to plan to reach the Moon before 1970, making use of *Apollo* Rockets.

The attempt did not proceed without tragedy. On 27 January 1967, three American astronauts died in a fire while testing an Apollo capsule on the ground. The effort to reach the Moon was delayed while rocket designs were changed to limit the danger of fire.

The Soviets suffered tragedy, too. In April 1967, a Soviet cosmonaut died while his rocketship was returning to Earth.

But the American effort was not stopped. In December 1968 an Apollo rocketship went out to the Moon, circled it 10 times at a height of about 112 kilometres above its surface, then returned safely to Earth.

Other close approaches were made, and then the rocketship *Apollo 11* was sent out to the Moon in July 1969 with the three men on board. One man stayed in orbit around the Moon, while the other two went down to the surface with part of the ship. On 20 July 1969, Neil Armstrong became the first human being ever to set foot on the surface of another world. As his foot moved down to touch the Moon, he said, "That's one small step for man, one giant leap for mankind."

From *Outer Space*, I. Asimov (Longman 1982)

continued ▶

▶ *continued*

Questions

1 In the 1960s which country began to take the lead in Satellite experiments?

2 What were the rockets called?

3 What happened on the 27th January 1967?

4 What happened in April 1967?

5 In 1968 a spaceship circled the moon. How many times did it do this?

6 How many people were on the mission which finally landed on the moon?

7 How many people went to the surface?

8 Who was the first human to set foot on the surface of another world?

9 What famous sentence did this person say?

10 What was the date of this landing?

Skills sheet 13

Writing skills—Recording facts in notes 1

Many science books contain good ideas and lots of interesting facts. You might want to understand the ideas. You might also want to remember some of the facts.

To record facts properly:

- Skim the passage.
- Write down the main ideas from the passage (only two or three at any one time).
  Leave several lines between each main idea.
- Read the passage again.
  Write each fact that you want to remember underneath the correct main idea.

Read the passage below. It has two main ideas:
- the first computers
- how computers have changed.

Write these headings in your book leaving four lines between each one.

Read the passage again and write three interesting facts underneath each of the correct main ideas.

> Charles Babbage was an English mathematician. He was born in 1791 and died in 1871. Amazingly he designed the first true computer—nearly 200 years ago! Babbage realised that if he could make a machine that could remember numbers and could recognise simple arithmetic instructions it would be able to carry out complicated calculations automatically. He called the first calculating machine he invented the 'difference engine'. With this he could produce quite complicated tables of numbers. The machine did not have a memory. His next invention was never built. It was named the 'Analytic engine'. Sadly for Babbage the engineers of his time were not able to produce a working model of his design which was full of moving parts.
>
> What would Babbage have thought of one of the first computers to work? It was made in the USA in 1946. It filled a room and had about 18 000 radio valves! What could this fantastic machine do? It could store 20 numbers in its memory! Babbage would have been impressed. Since then the valves have been replaced by integrated circuits. These are much smaller and more reliable. Computers are becoming ever more powerful. There are new developments almost daily. Today just about anyone can afford to buy a computer that is thousands of times more powerful than the computer imagined by Charles Babbage.

Skills sheet 14

Writing skills—Using diagrams in notes 1

A written passage often has a lot of unnecessary details. You should read it to find the main ideas. These main ideas then form the starting point of your notes about the passage. You can note the main ideas in different ways.

> There he lay, a vast red-golden dragon, fast asleep; a thrumming came from his jaws and nostrils, and wisps of smoke, but his fires were low in slumber. Beneath him, under his limbs and his huge coiled tail, and about him on all sides stretching away across the unseen floors, lay countless piles of precious things, gold wrought and unwrought, gems and jewels, and silver red-stained in the ruddy light.
>
> Smaug lay, with wings folded like an immeasurable bat, turned partly on one side, so that the hobbit could see his underparts and his long pale belly crusted with gems and fragments of gold from his long lying on his costly bed.
>
> From *The Hobbit*, J.R.R. Tolkien (Allen & Unwin 1966)

You might describe the main ideas

- in writing

Big dragon, asleep, wisps of smoke, huge coiled tail, wings folded, lying on piles of precious things.

- or as a diagram

Read the following passage and write a note to describe the main ideas in it.
Read it again and draw a labelled diagram to describe the main ideas.

> What is a hobbit? I suppose hobbits need some description nowadays, since they have become rare and shy of the Big People, as they call us. They are (or were) a little people, about half our height, and smaller than the bearded Dwarves. Hobbits have no beards. There is little or no magic about them, except the ordinary everyday sort which helps them to disappear quietly and quickly when large stupid folk like you and me come blundering along, making a noise like elephants which they can hear a mile off. They are inclined to be fat in the stomach; they dress in bright colours (chiefly green and yellow); wear no shoes, because their feet grow natural leathery soles and thick warm brown hair like the stuff on their heads (which is curly); have long clever brown fingers, good-natured faces, and laugh deep fruity laughs (especially after dinner, which they have twice a day when they can get it). Now you know enough to go on with.
>
> From *The Hobbit*, J.R.R. Tolkien (Allen & Unwin 1966)

Skills sheet 15

Number skills—averages

A scientist often repeats an experiment or takes several measurements of the same thing. This is to make sure that the results can be trusted. If you have several sets of results they are unlikely to be all the same. Rather than choose a result it is fair to take an average of the set of results.

It is not difficult to work out an average. There are two steps:

step one — add up all the numbers in the set of results to get a total

step two — divide this total by the number of measurements or results in the set.

Here is an example.

Find the average of this set of numbers: 12, 18, 42, 32, 19, 15:

step one — *the total is 138*

step two — *there are 6 numbers in the set so divide the total by 6, which gives 138 ÷ 6 = 23*

The average is 23

1 Find the average of the following sets of numbers:

a 14, 26, 16, 24

b 11, 27, 14, 21, 19

c 36, 47, 24, 33, 50

d 1.5, 2.8, 2.2, 1.7, 3.6

2 A survey was carried out to find the number of fillings in a class. The results are shown below.

Number of fillings per pupil	0	1	2	3	4	5	6
Number of pupils	3	8	7	2	5	4	2
Total number of fillings	0	8	14				

a What is the total number of fillings in the class? (This calculation has been started in the last row of the table.)

b How many pupils are there in the class?

c What is the average number of fillings per pupil?

	Time taken to fall/seconds		
	Ball	**Cube**	**Tear drop**
1st experiment	11.6	16.4	10.9
2nd experiment	12.1	17.2	9.8
3rd experiment	11.4	16.9	10.1

3 An experiment was done to find out how quickly three different shapes would fall through a cylinder of water. The experiment was done three times. What was the average time each shape took to fall?

Skills sheet 16

Reading skills—Spotting correct conclusions

There are several sections in most experimental reports. These are

Title: *What is the purpose of the experiment?*
Method: *What did you do?*
Results: *What happened?*
Conclusion: *What do you think the results mean?*

Read the following report.

Testing a shark's acoustic sense organ

Hans Hass once made a dangerous experiment in the Caribbean. He had been wondering why, a few seconds after he had harpooned a fish, a shark previously invisible would nearly always come darting along to contest his catch. How did the shark know there was something to be had there? It could not see, for it was outside sighting distance. Nor could it have smelt blood, because odours do not spread with lightning speed. Could it have heard something?

Dr. Hass caught a large bass, but this time with a sling. The fish at once started struggling wildly, and as he had hoped, a shark turned up in a matter of seconds. The same moment he loosened the sling, so that the bass calmed down and swam off as if nothing had happened. Thereupon the shark merely looked a bit puzzled, and without molesting the bass swam around a few times and disappeared.

From *The Magic of the Senses,*
V. B. Droscher (W. H. Allen 1969)

1 Which of the following conclusions might be correct for this experiment?

A The shark was not hungry. If it was it would have darted upwards to take the fish by surprise.
B The shark had come to the spot because of the noise of the struggling bass.
C The shark came to the fish but did not like the look of the bass which was large.
D If a shark is around you should keep perfectly still.
E Sharks are not dangerous if they are a bit puzzled.

2 Explain your choices.

Skills sheet 17

Experimental design skills—Fair tests 1

Experiments must be **fair**. In fair experiments only one variable should be changed. All the others must stay the same.

To design a fair experiment:

- first decide what variables might affect the result of the experiment
- then decide which variable to **change** and which variables to **keep the same**.

Imagine that you are given this problem to solve:

Find out what type of bunsen flame will bring water to the boil most quickly.
Equipment: bunsen burner, tripod, mat, beaker, water.

1 What variables could affect the time taken for the water to boil? (Look at the labels on the diagram)

2 What one variable should be changed?

3 Three groups tried to solve the problem as shown below. One pupil in each group has made a mistake.

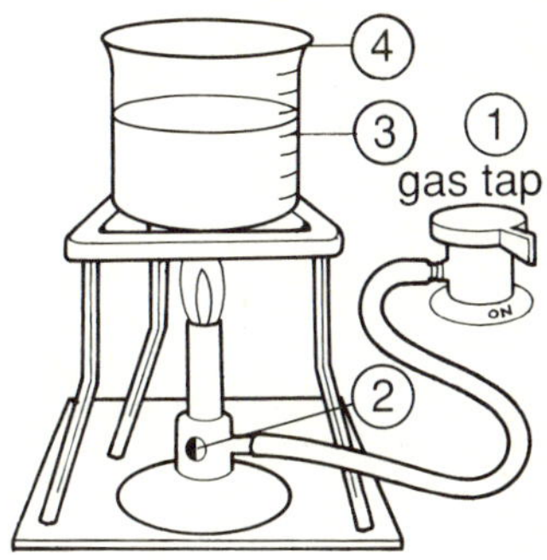

Group 1

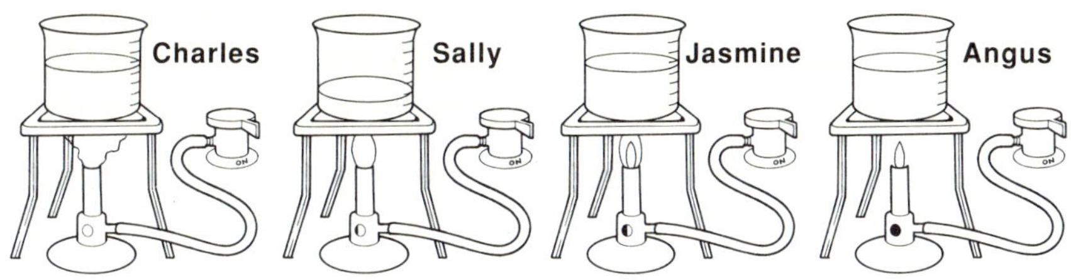

Group 2

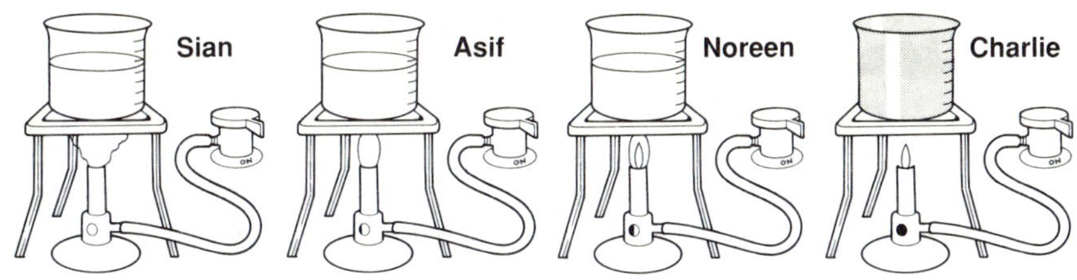

Group 3

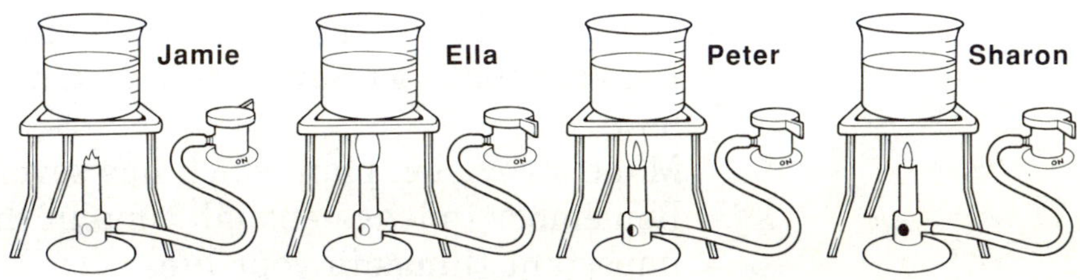

For each group write down

a the name of the pupil who set the experiment up incorrectly

b which variable has not been kept the same.

Skills sheet 18

Revision skills—Organising revision

Revision is easier if you plan it carefully.
To revise for a unit test, you should

- look through all the work that you have to revise
- decide how long your revision will take (for example about 2 hours)
- make a revision timetable.

For example, Gina has a science test next week.
She decides that she doesn't know her work very well. She needs 3 hours of revision. She makes out a revision timetable.

	17.00–17.30	17.30–18.00	18.00–18.30	18.30–19.00	19.00–19.30	19.30–20.00	20.00–20.30	20.30–21.00
Monday	French vocab.	Science homew'k	Maths homew'k	Food	Write to pen-pal		Watch T.V	
Tuesday	Badminton		Club	Food	Science revis.	R.E homew'k	Read book	
Wednesday	Watch T.V		Geog. homew'k	Food	Hist. homew'k	?	Read book	
Thursday	Shopping in town		Eng. homew'k	Food	Eng. homew'k	Science revis.	Watch T.V	
Friday	Watch T.V		Science revis.	Food	Phone Gran	Science revis.	Library books	
Saturday	Art and design		Out to pictures with T.H →					
Sunday	Visiting		Science revis.	Food	Maths homew'k	Science revis	T.V	Early night

Gina has been sensible. She has planned to revise in six **short** sessions rather than leave it all to the night before the test. She has also left enough time in her plan for **other** important things in her life.

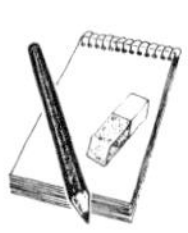

Look over Unit 1 of this year's science course.

1. How well do you know this work?
   (very well, quite well, sort of well, not very well, not at all.)
2. How long do you think you would need to learn this work?
3. Imagine that you have a test on Unit 1 one week from now.
   Make a revision plan which has several short sessions.
   Remember to leave enough time in the week for the other important things in your life.

Skills sheet 19

Reading skills— Reading line graphs 1

A line graph shows how a change in one variable affects a second variable. The names of the variables are always shown on the **axes** of the line graph. The scale reading on the *x*-axis increases as you move to the right. The scale reading on the *y*-axis increases as you move upwards.

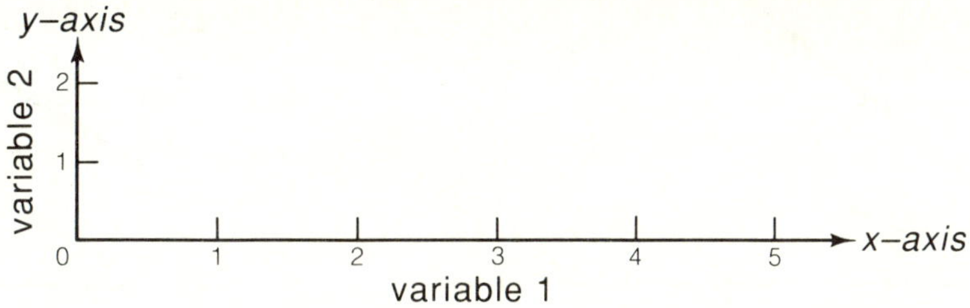

The **shape** of the line on the graph allows you to describe the relationship between the two variables.

Collect a worksheet showing the graphs below.
Complete the statements to describe what each graph shows.

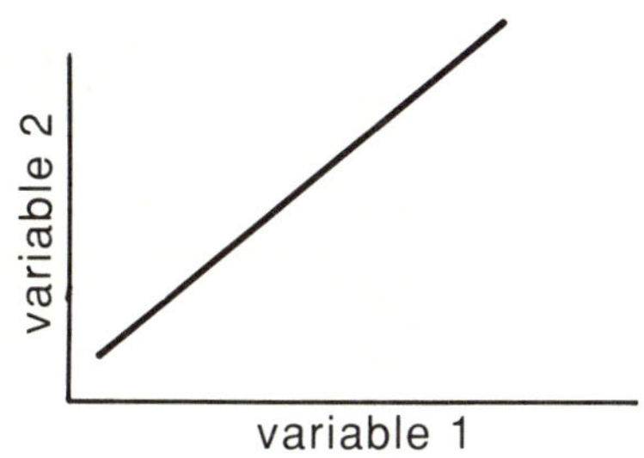

As variable 1 increases variable 2 increases

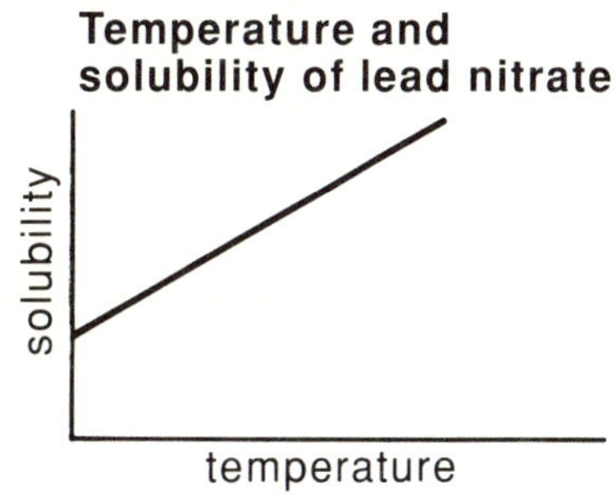

As temperature increases the solubility of ______________
will ______________

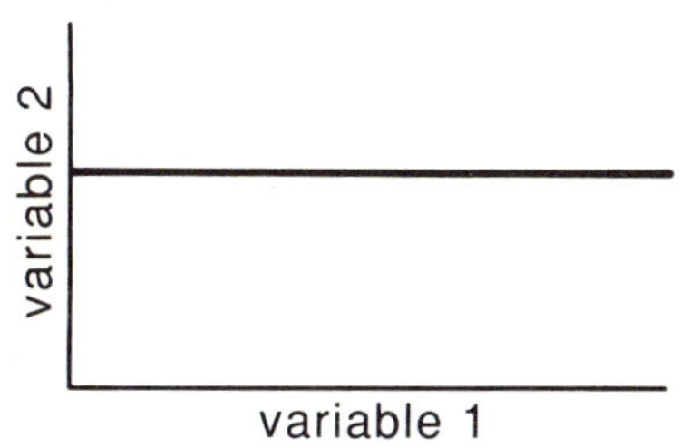

As variable 1 increases variable 2 ______________

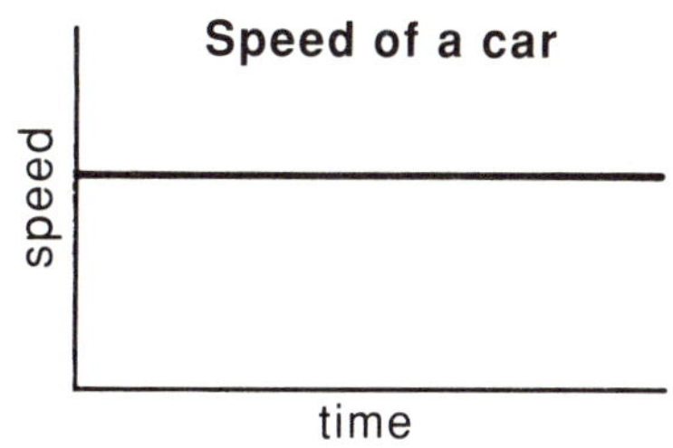

As time increases speed ______________
____

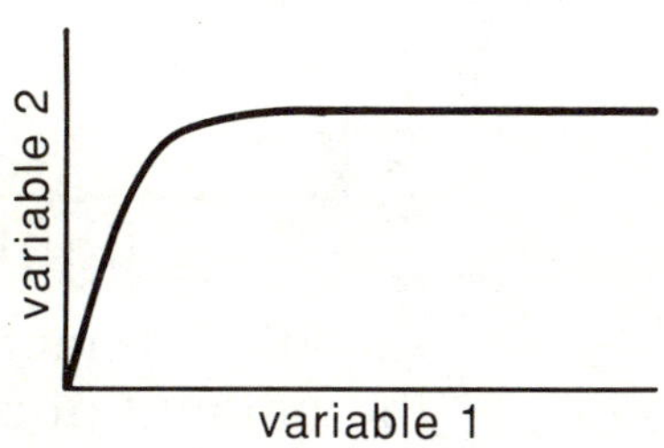

As variable 1 ______________
variable 2 ______________
then ______________

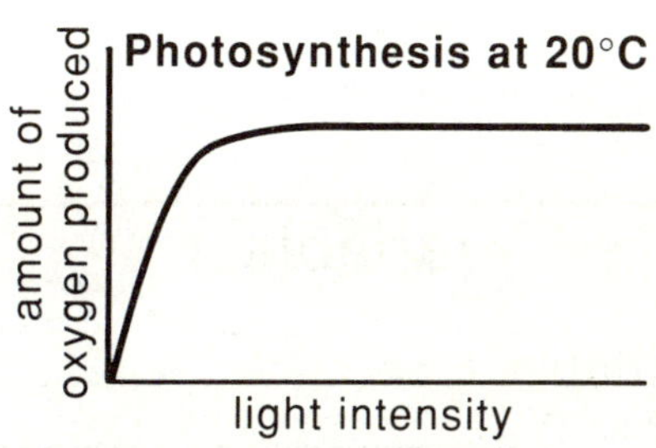

As light intensity ______________
the amount of oxygen produced
____
then ______________

Worksheet

Skills sheet 19

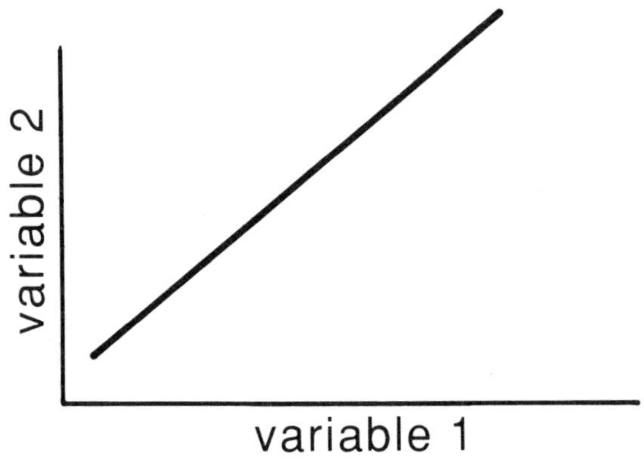

As variable 1 increases variable 2 increases

Temperature and solubility of lead nitrate

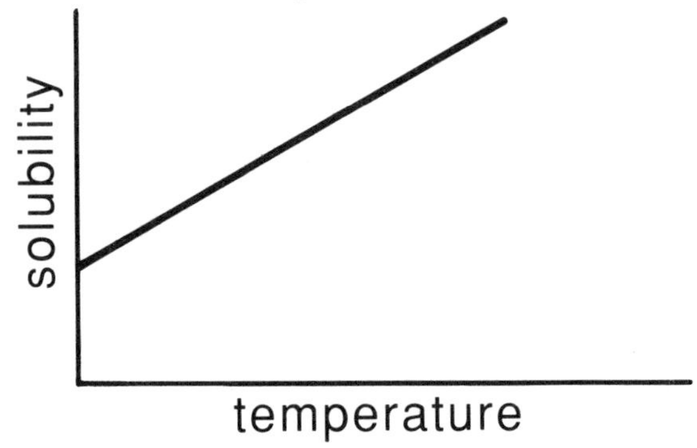

As temperature increases the solubility of ______________
will ______________

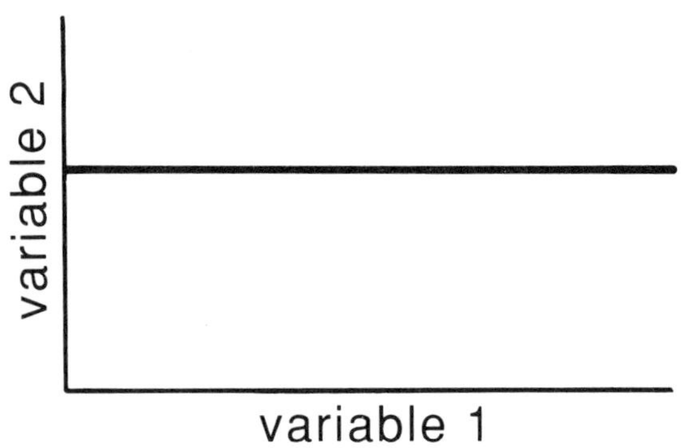

As variable 1 increases variable 2 ______________

Speed of a car

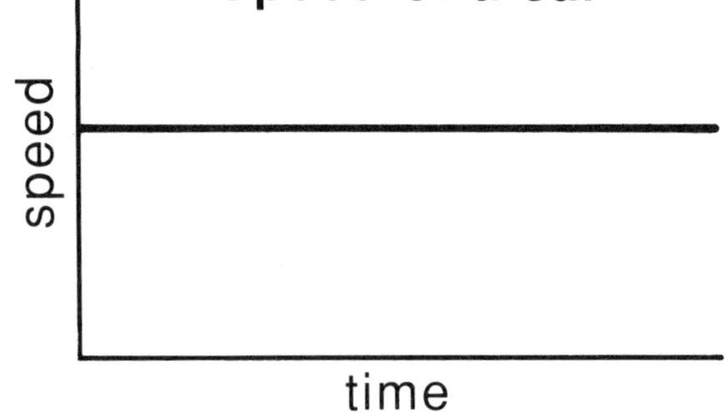

As time increases speed
____
____

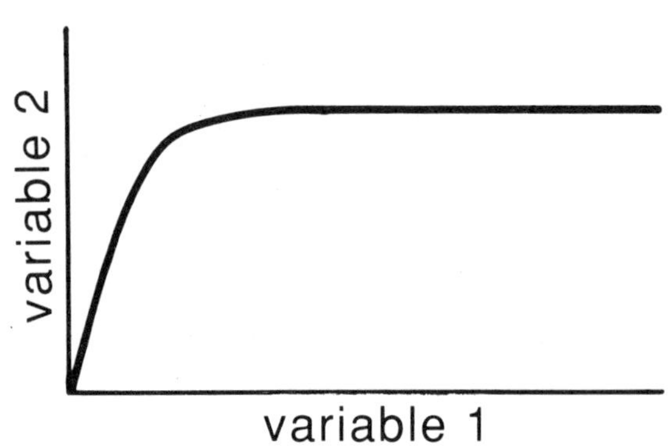

As variable 1 ______________
variable 2 ______________
then ______________

Photosynthesis at 20°C

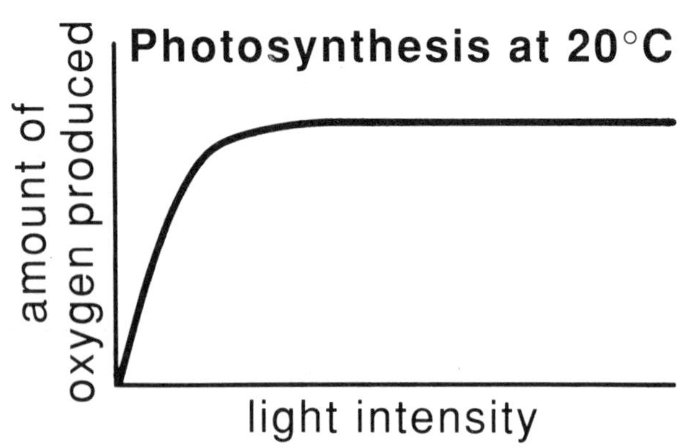

As light intensity ______________
the amount of oxygen produced
____
then ______________

Skills sheet 20

Reading skills—Finding information 2

You often have to read a passage to find information. This might be the starting point for your notes on a topic. A good way of organising the information you find is to make a table. This makes a good summary and lets you see if any information you need is missing. You can then look for this information somewhere else.

Imagine you are making notes for a project on seals. Read the passage below to find out

- the names of different types of seal
- what seals eat
- the size of seals.

1 Copy the table below before you start.
Complete the table after reading the passage.

Type of seal	Food	Size

2 What information would you have still to find?

The Weddell seal regularly makes dives lasting up to a quarter of an hour to depths of 300 metres or more. There, in the blackness, it pursues fish using sonar—emitting high-pitched squeaks and detecting the position of fish by the echoes they cause. It is the most southerly living of all mammals and is not deterred by the ice which covers the seas around the continent in the winter. It breathes either from pockets of air trapped beneath the ice or by maintaining small holes in the ice floes, keeping them open by chewing the edges. The crab-eater seal, the most numerous of all the family in the Antarctic, feeds entirely on krill, and has special cusps on its cheek teeth that act as sieves, keeping the krill in the mouth while the unwanted water is expelled. The leopard seal, growing to a length of 3.5 metres, is slim and sinuous and eats meat of all kinds—fish, krill, young seals of other species and occasionally, penguins.

The biggest of all is the elephant seal. This is a truly monstrous creature which may weigh as much as 4000 kilos. When an angry male rears up at you on a beach, it towers to over double your height. It owes its name not only to its immensity but also to an inflatable trunk on the top of its nose which it can blow up into a huge bladder. The elephant seal also dives to great depths and there feeds on squid. It has the thickest blubber of all. Every year it moults the thin layer of hair that covers its skin. Growing new hair requires an abundant supply of blood close to the surface of the skin and vessels therefore open up through the fat. With their blubber-wrap punctured in this way and blood circulating close to the surface of their body, the animals are no longer efficiently insulated so they have to come out of the water.

From *The Living Planet,* D. Attenborough (BBC/Collins 1984)

Skills sheet 21

Writing skills—Using diagrams in notes 2

Drawing a diagram can be a good way of organising the information in a passage. It helps you to concentrate and to pick out the important points. A diagram also makes a good summary. You may find a diagram easier to remember and learn from than a written passage.

Read the passage below.

'Here, have a look at this,' said Ford. He sat down on one of the mattresses and rummaged about in the satchel. Arthur prodded the mattress nervously and then sat on it himself: in fact he had very little to be nervous about, because all mattresses grown in the swamps of Sqornshellous Zeta are very thoroughly killed and dried before being put to service. Very few have ever come to life again.

Ford handed the book to Arthur.

'What is it?' asked Arthur.

'The Hitch Hiker's Guide to the Galaxy. It's a sort of electronic book. It tells you everything you need to know about anything. That's its job.'

Arthur turned it over nervously in his hands.

'I like the cover,' he said. '*Don't Panic.* It's the first helpful or intelligible thing anybody's said to me all day.'

'I'll show you how it works,' said Ford. He snatched it from Arthur who was still holding it as if it was a two-week-dead lark and pulled it out of its cover.

'You press this button here you see and the screen lights up giving you the index.'

A screen, about three inches by four, lit up and characters began to flicker across the surface.

'You want to know about Vogons, so I enter the name so.' His fingers tapped some more keys. 'And there we are.'

The words *Vogon Constructor Fleets* flared in green across the screen.

Ford pressed a large red button at the bottom of the screen and words began to undulate across it. At the same time, the book began to speak the entry as well in a still quiet measured voice. This is what the book said.

'Vogon Constructor Fleets. Here is what to do if you want to get a lift from a Vogon: forget it. They are one of the most unpleasant races in the Galaxy—not actually evil, but bad tempered, bureaucratic, officious and callous. They wouldn't even lift a finger to save their own grandmothers from the Ravenous Bugblatter Beast of Traal without orders signed in triplicate, sent in, sent back, queried, lost, found, subjected to public inquiry, lost again, and finally buried in soft peat for three months and recycled as firelighters.

'The best way to get a drink out of a Vogon is to stick your finger down his throat, and the best way to irritate him is to feed his grandmother to the Ravenous Bugblatter Beast of Traal.

'On no account allow a Vogon to read poetry at you.'

Arthur blinked at it.

'What a strange book.'

From *The Hitch Hiker's Guide to the Galaxy*, D. Adams (Pan Books 1979)

1 Draw the cover of the book.

2 Draw the book. Label the parts.

Skills sheet 22

Number skills—Subtracting decimal numbers

In many science experiments you measure something. The results are written down as numbers. To make sense of the numbers you must have good arithmetic skills.

Subtracting decimal numbers is easy. You do this every time you buy something in a shop and work out the change you expect to get.

1 What is the change in volume in these two examples?

a

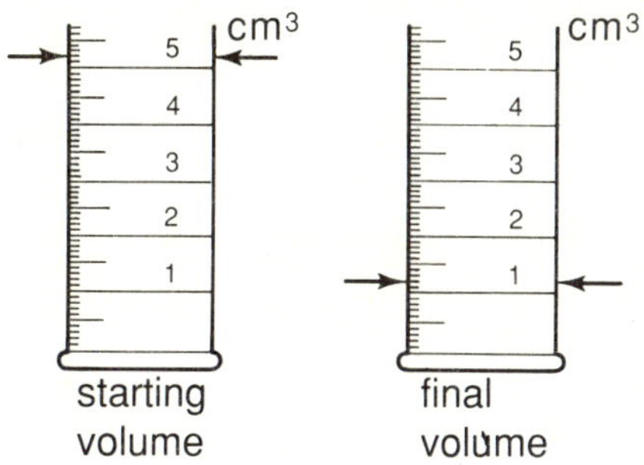

b

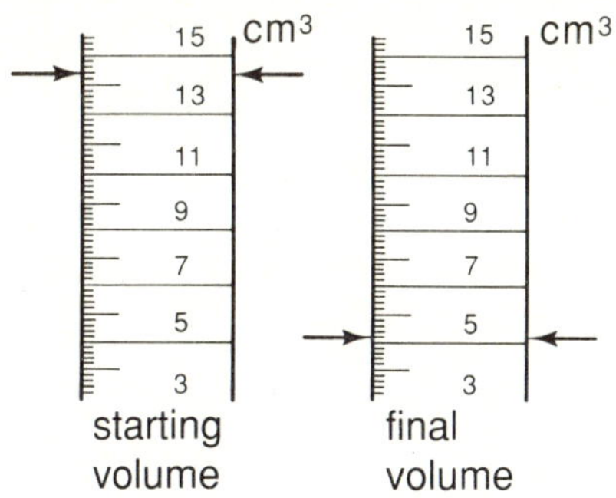

2 What is the change in temperature in these two examples?

a

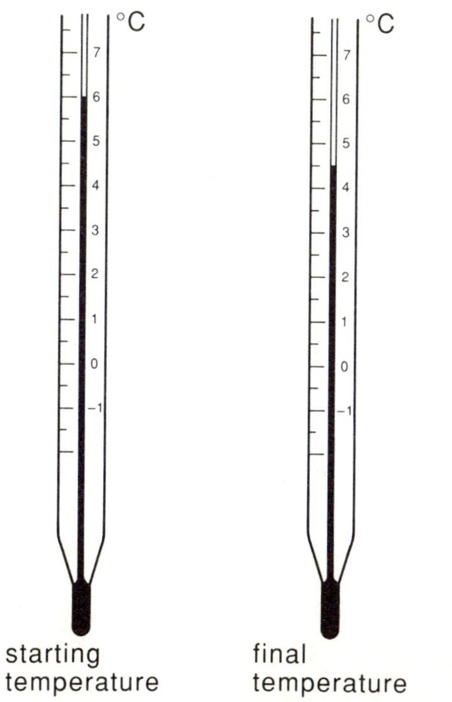

b

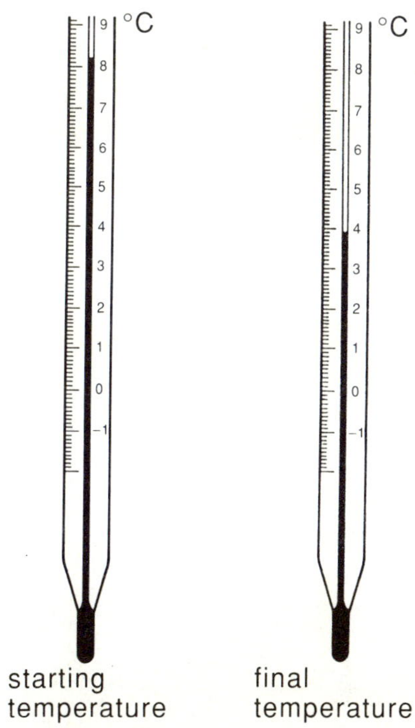

Skills sheet 23

Writing skills—Recording facts in notes 2

Many science books contain good ideas and lots of interesting facts. You might want to understand the ideas. You might also want to remember some of the facts.

To record facts properly

- Skim the passage.
- Write down the main ideas from the passage (only two or three at any one time). Leave several lines between each main idea.
- Read the passage again. Write each fact that you want to remember underneath the correct main idea.

Skim the passage below. It has two main ideas.
Write these in your book leaving 6 lines between each one.
Read the passage again and write the most interesting facts underneath the correct main idea.

Seeing without eyes

At the end of 1962 a strange report was making the rounds of the illustrated papers, daily press, and even scientific journals. It was claimed that a young Russian woman, Rosa Kuleshova, could see with her fingers: that after members of a "testing commission" had blindfolded her, she could still read letters, and recognize drawings and colours, with the tips of the middle and ring finger of her right hand.

She and her testing commission have since been exposed as frauds: the miracle girl had been squinting past her eye bandage. Yet this supposed phenomenon was the subject of debate by reputable neurophysiologists all over the world for two years. They treated the claim seriously because science was familiar from the animal world with many examples of light sensitivity of the skin, a faculty of registering light without eyes.

From *The Magic of the Senses*,
V. B. Droscher (W. H. Allen 1969)

Main ideas

A strange report

claim treated seriously

Skills sheet 24

Reading skills—Reading line graphs 2

A line graph shows how a change in one variable affects a second variable. The names of the variables are always shown on the **axes** of the line graph. The scale reading on the *x*-axis increases as you move to the right. The scale reading on the *y*-axis increases as you move upwards.

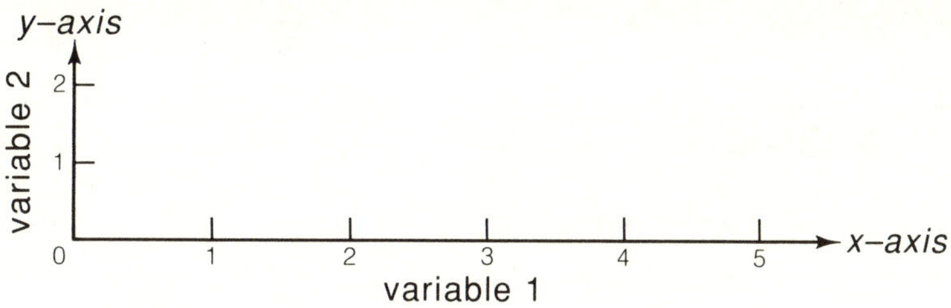

The **shape** of the line on a graph allows you to describe the relationship between the two variables.

Collect a worksheet showing the graphs below.

Complete the statements to describe what each shows.

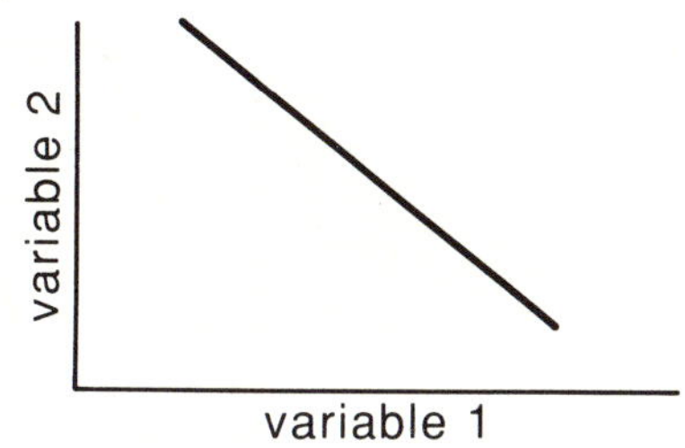

As variable 1 increases variable 2 ____________

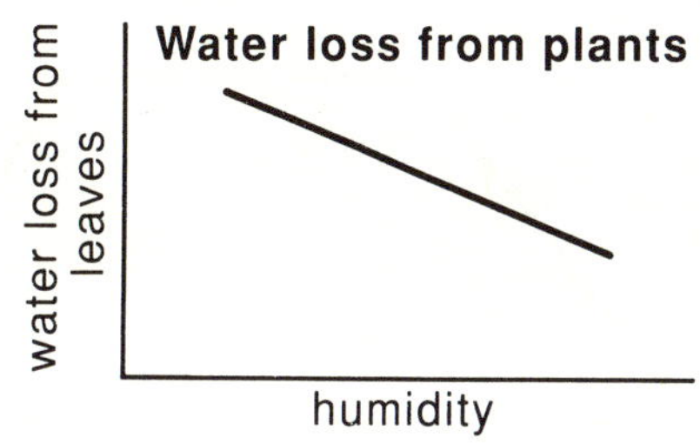

As humidity increases water loss ____________

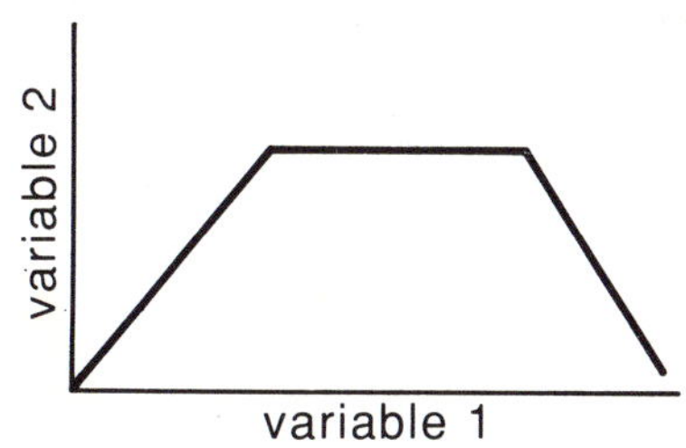

As variable 1 increases
variable 2 increases
then ____________
then ____________

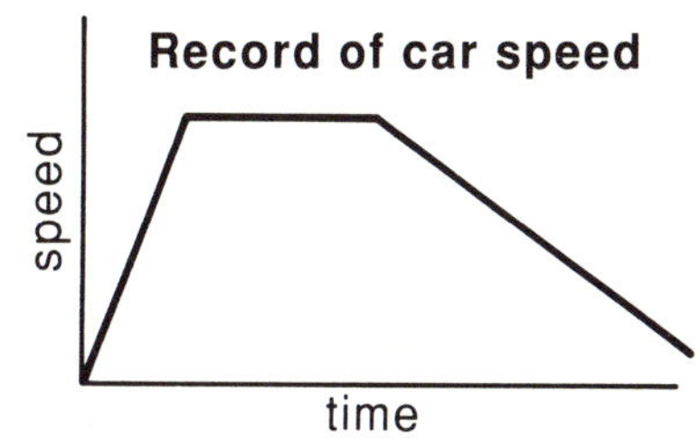

As time increases speed ____________
then ____________
then ____________

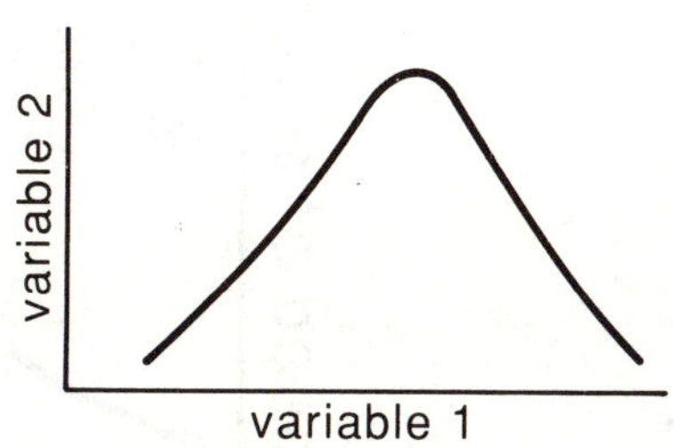

As variable 1 ____________
variable 2 ____________

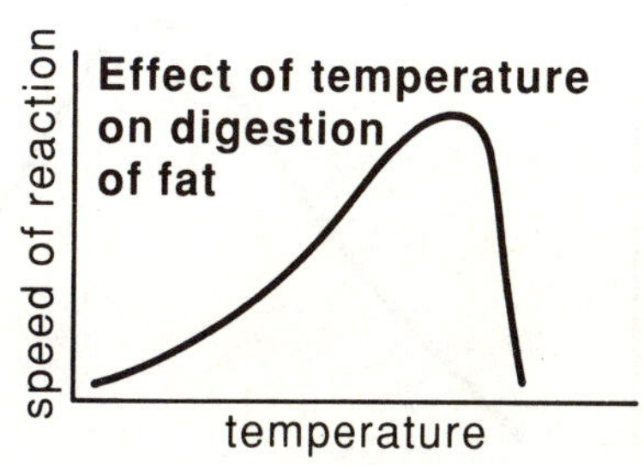

____
____

Worksheet

Skills sheet 24

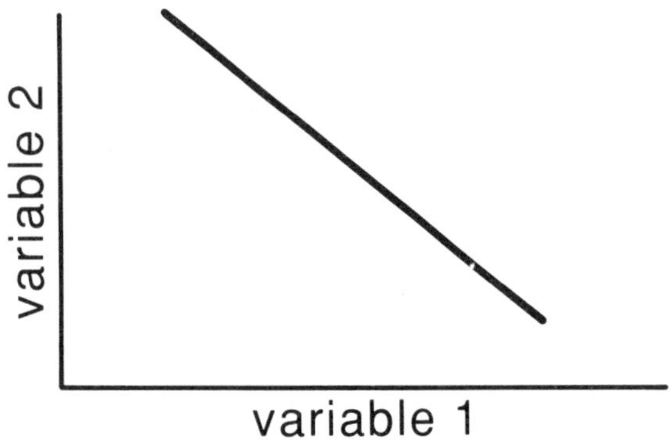

As variable 1 increases variable 2 ____________

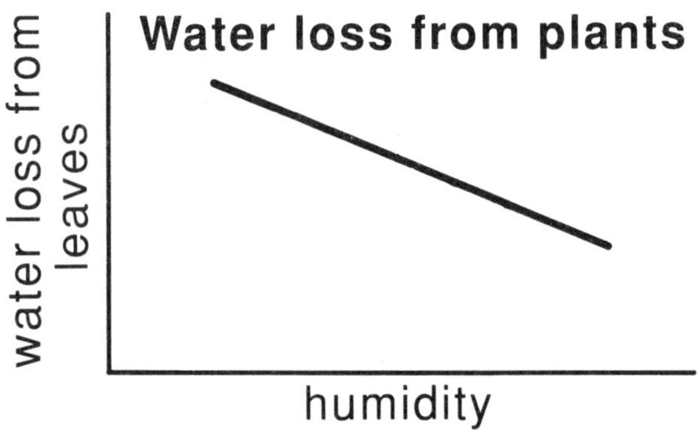

As humidity increases water loss ____________

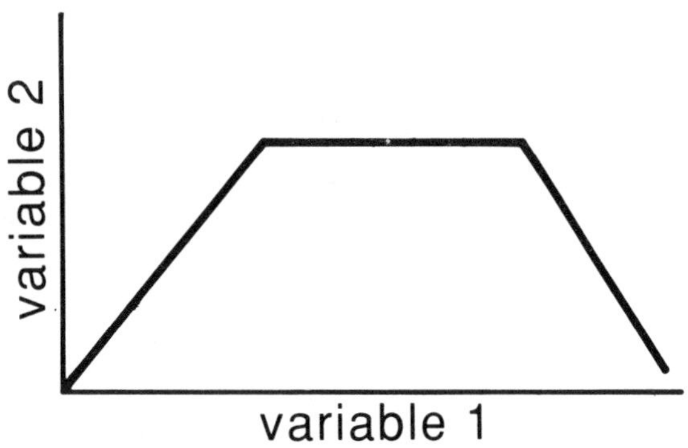

As variable 1 increases
variable 2 increases
then ____________
then ____________

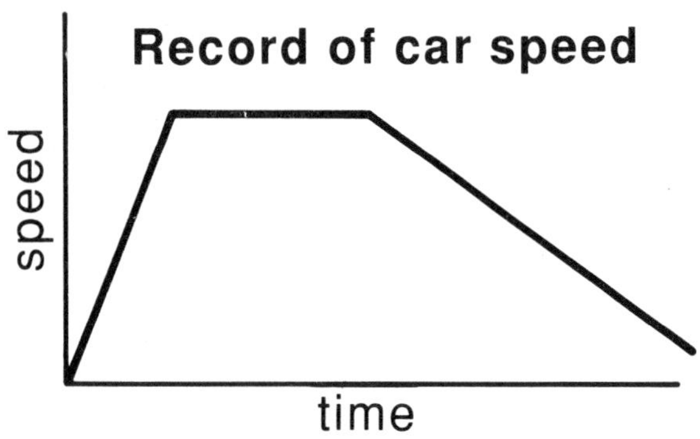

As time increases speed ____________
then ____________
then ____________

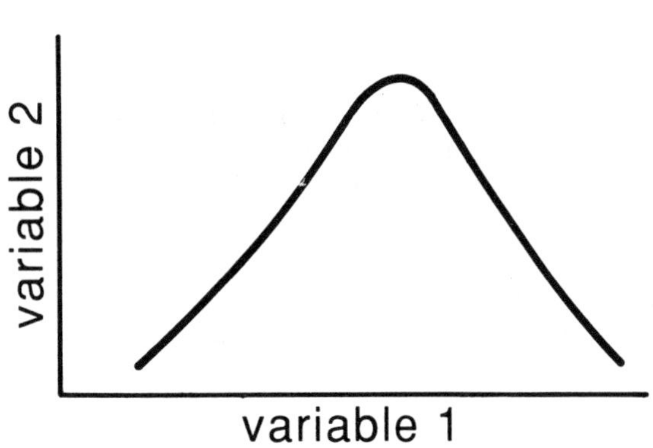

As variable 1 ____________
variable 2 ____________

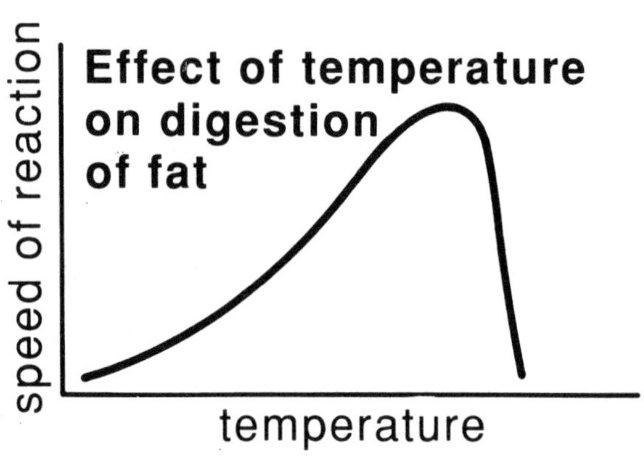

____
____

Skills sheet 25

Writing skills—Making conclusions 1

There are several sections in most experimental reports. These are

Title: *What is the purpose of the experiment?*
Method: *What did you do?*
Results: *What happened?*
Conclusion: *What do you think the results mean?*
The conclusion is often the most difficult section to write.

Read the following report. Look at the results.

> Our class tried to find out where a woodlouse would prefer to live. Forty woodlice were released into a container that contained different habitats. The animals were left for 2 hours to explore their surroundings. We then counted the number of woodlice in each habitat. The bar chart below shows our results.

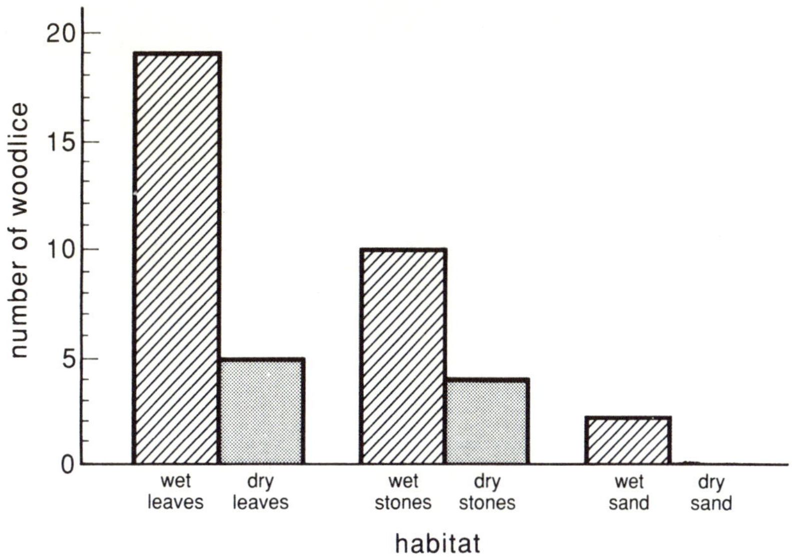

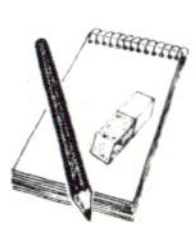

Write down two conclusions from these results.

Skills sheet 26

Experimental design skills—Fair tests 2

Experiments must be **fair**. In fair experiments only one variable should be changed. All the others must be kept constant (stay the same).

To design a fair experiment:

- first decide what variables might affect the result of the experiment
- then decide which variable to **change** and which variables to **keep constant**.

In each of the three examples below write down
- which variable changes
- which variables stay constant.

a Growing seeds

b Swinging pendulum

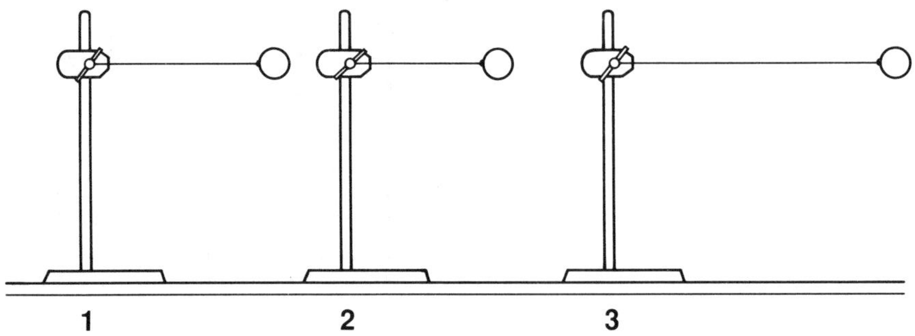

c Strength of ice-lolly sticks

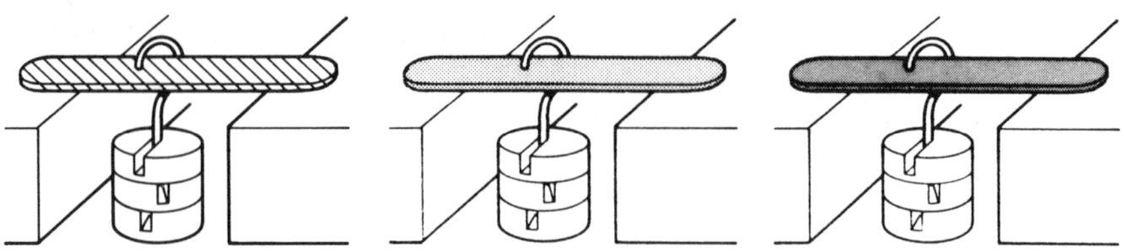

Reading skills—Remembering what you read 2

Some science books are designed to give you information. There are many ways to help you remember information that you read. Your memory will be better if you do something when you read; for example make notes or answer questions.

To help you remember facts:

- first skim the passage
- think of questions that the passage would give an answer to
- read the passage slowly
- answer the questions without looking at the passage.

Read the following passage. Then read the questions on the next page.

Re-read the passage then answer the questions **without looking again** at the passage.

> Gloria was born "in the Cabbage Patch" on 1 November, and of course she has the birth certificate to prove it. Gloria, you see, belongs to that infuriating breed of toy dolls called the Cabbage Patch Kids. Gloria, however, is not just any old kid from the Cabbage Patch. She is a Talking Kid, and this is what makes her so interesting to the researchers from Artificial Intelligence.
>
> Gloria may look as if butter won't melt in her mouth, but don't be fooled by her nauseously cute appearance. Inside she has a heart of pure silicon. A microprocessor synthesises her voice and stores her vocabulary of more than 400 words. She has a collection of touch sensors in her cheeks, hands, head and tummy. Another sensor tells her, and her lucky owner, which way up she is. A magnetic sensor in her lips picks up signals from her "sippy cup" when gulping her favourite drink, and there is a sound sensor to pick up the sound, but not the meaning, of the human voice.
>
> Just for good measure, Gloria and other Talking Kids can communicate behind their owners' backs with the help of radio transmitters and receivers, broadcasting at 49 megahertz. In this way they can decide which songs to sing, and they love to surprise people by singing in unison. You can see when they are singing, and talking for that matter, because tiny motors make their lips move.
>
> Before being bought, Gloria had a rough childhood. The company's quality controllers dropped her four times from a height of 30 inches onto a concrete slab 2·5 inches thick, and applied 35-pound weights to each part of the doll. Their only concern was that "the unit shall remain functional and exhibit no signs of damage".
>
> From *New Scientist*, 24th/31st December 1987

continued ▶

Skills sheet 27

▶ *continued*

1 What is Gloria?

2 What is her heart made of?

3 How many words does she know?

4 Where are her four touch sensors?

5 What does she drink from?

6 How does she communicate?

7 At what frequency in megahertz, does she broadcast?

8 What makes her lips move?

9 How many times was she dropped?

10 What was she dropped onto?

Skills sheet 28

Number skills—Multiplying decimal numbers 1

Scientific results must be accurate. This often means that the results will include decimal numbers. You use decimal numbers every day, when you handle money. If you buy several of the same item you multiply decimal numbers to work out how much you must pay.

The only problem is remembering where to put the decimal point.
This example shows what to do.

Multiply 6.25 × 3.61

- count the numbers to the right of the decimal point. *There are 4.*
- find the answer to the multiplication. Do not worry about the decimal point.
  The answer is 225625
- remember how many places there were to the right of the decimal point to begin with. There **must be** the same number in the answer.
  There were four in this multiplication.
  The answer is 22.5625

1 Find the answers to the following:

a 8.13 × 16

b 27.94 × 11.43

c 15.87 × 9.7

2 Smoking is very expensive.
If a packet of 20 cigarettes cost £1.73, work out the amount of money spent by the two people:

a If John smokes 1 packet every day, how much will he spend on cigarettes every
- week
- month
- year?

b If Sarah smokes one and a half packets every day, how much will she spend every
- week
- month
- year?

Reading skills—Reading line graphs 3

A line graph shows the relationship between two variables. Sometimes there is more than one line on the graph. This allows you to make comparisons.

In this graph the masses of three boys are being compared:

- Joe is greedy; his mass goes up.
- Walter is boring; his mass stays the same.
- Peter feels unwell; his mass falls.

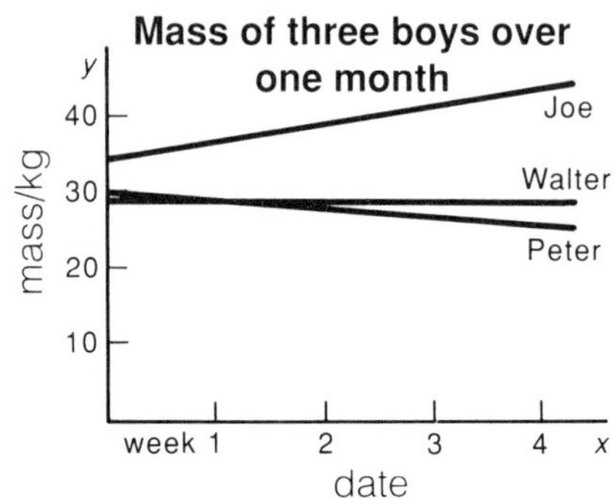

Look at the graphs below and answer the questions.

1 a Which animal's temperature changes most as the air temperature rises?

b Describe the relationship between rise in air temperature and body temperature for the other two animals.

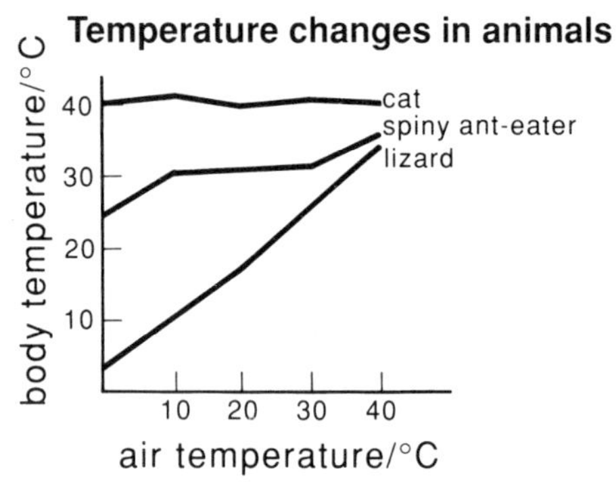

2 a How many substances are being compared on this graph?

b Describe the effect of a rise in temperature on the solubility of each of these substances.

c Which substance is
(i) most soluble at 60°C?
(ii) least soluble at 60°C?

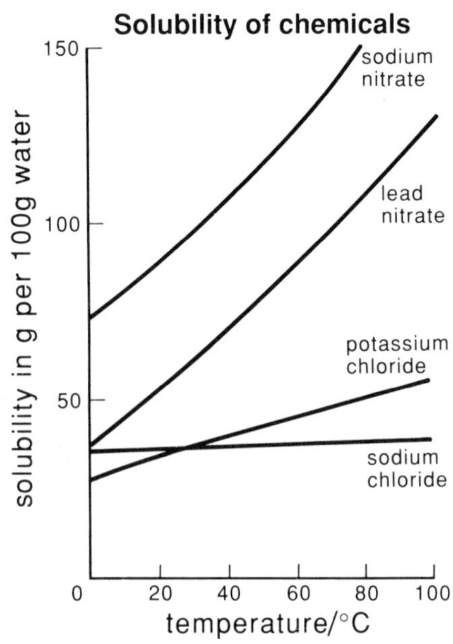

Skills sheet 30

Writing skills—Using diagrams to shorten notes 1

In a well written passage each paragraph tells you about one main idea. The paragraph may also give some

- facts about the main idea
- examples of the main idea
- opinions of the main idea
- explanations of the main idea

A spider diagram is a good way of organising the information you read about. It is a good starting point for making notes.

Read the following passage:

> Although they reproduce by spores, not flowers, seaweeds have seasons of growth like other plants. They produce shoots in the spring, grow quickly and luxuriantly during the summer, and wither in the winter. The best months to gather most seaweeds are May and June.
>
> Seaweeds obtain their food entirely from the surrounding sea water and do not have roots in the conventional sense. However they do have hold-fasts, by which they attach themselves to rocks and stones, and from which the stem-like part, or stipe, grows. The weed itself can regenerate from a cut stipe, provided the cut is not too near the hold-fasts. So if you are cutting seaweed rather than gathering leaves which have been washed free of their moorings, leave plenty of stipe so that the weed can grow again.
>
> Before cooking any seaweed always wash thoroughly in fresh water to remove sand, shells and other shoreline debris which may have stuck to it.
>
> Seaweeds are rich in minerals, particularly iodides, and you may take a little while to get used to their flavours. But do give them a fair chance; they are intriguing foods, and quite undeserving of their freakish, joke-book reputation.
>
> From *Food for Free*, R. Mabey (Collins 1972)

The passage is about seaweed as food. You can show the main ideas in a spider diagram like the one below.

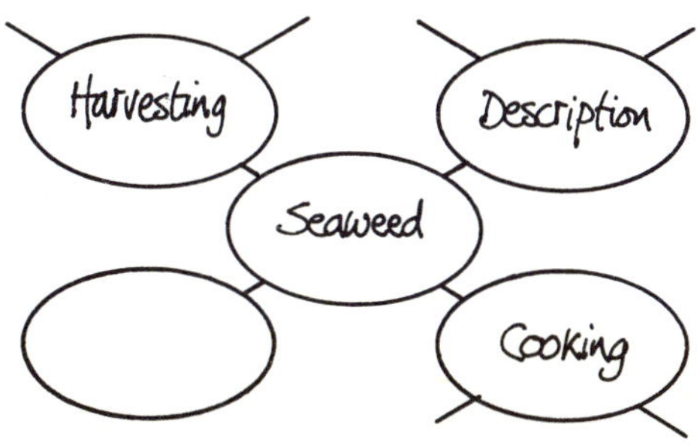

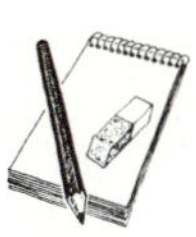

1 Copy the spider diagram.
There is one main idea in each paragraph. Add the final main idea to the diagram.

2 Read the passage again.
Find two details about the main idea in each paragraph. Complete the diagram by adding these details.

Skills sheet 31

Writing skills—Making flow diagrams

A flow diagram summarises a process. It breaks the process into steps. The steps follow on. Each step is linked to the next one by an arrow.

Collect a worksheet with a flow diagram about rubber.
Read the passage below.
Use the passage to complete the flow diagram.
Stick the worksheet in your book.

Rubber
The material that you call rubber can be either natural or synthetic (man-made).

Natural rubber is called latex and it comes from the rubber tree. It is collected as it drips from a cut in the tree trunk. Natural rubber is soft and bouncy and very stretchy. This natural rubber can be changed into a harder, less bouncy and less stretchy material by a process called vulcanisation. In this process small amounts of sulphur (or carbon) are added to the natural rubber.

Synthetic rubber is made from chemicals that are separated from crude oil. Scientists can make different types of synthetic rubber by using different mixtures of these chemicals. For example, they can make very hard rubbers or very elastic rubbers or oil-resistant rubbers.

Skills sheet 31

Worksheet

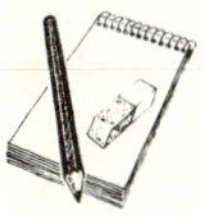

1 There are two types of rubber.
Complete the empty box.

2 Where does each type of rubber come from?

3 What are the properties of natural rubber?

4 Properties can be altered by changing the composition.
Write vulcanisation and mixing chemicals in the correct boxes. Write down what is added to vulcanised rubber.

5 What are the properties of the two types of rubber?

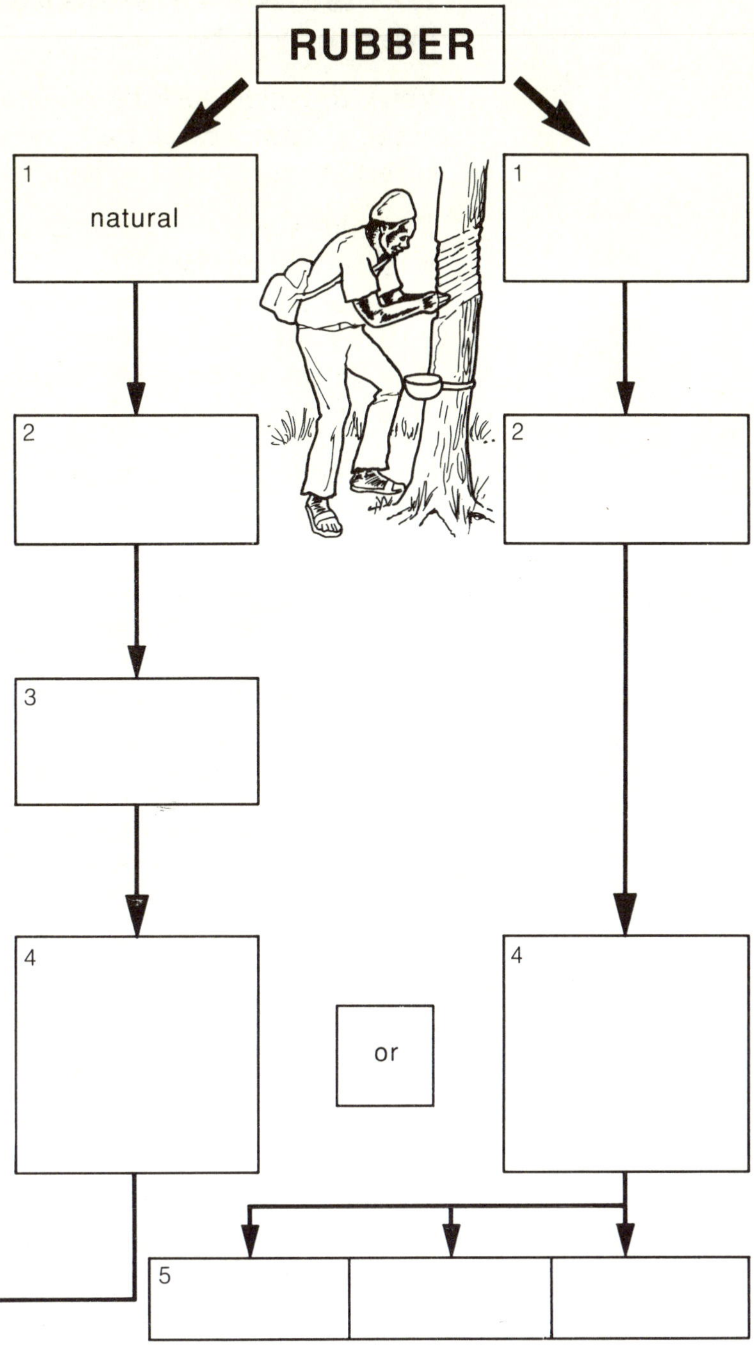

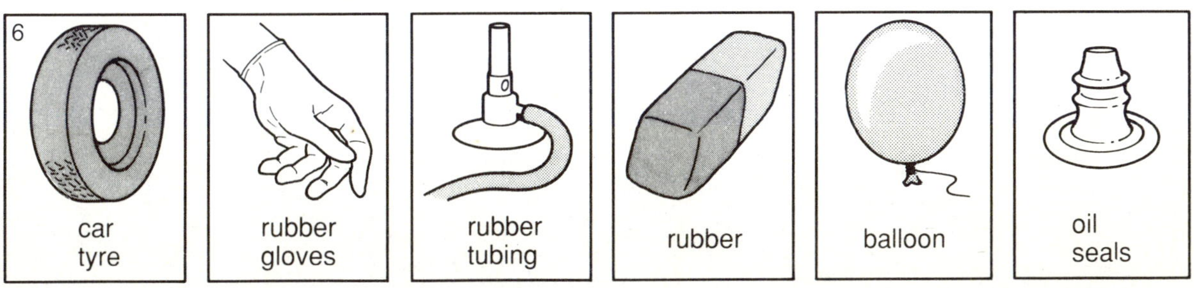

6 Look at these objects. Which type of rubber would you use to make each of these?

Skills sheet 32

Revision skills—Making a revision summary 1

You can learn work by revising in an active way. You could make a summary of your work as you revised. This uses several reading and writing skills.

To make a revision summary you have to
- skim the passage
- write down the main ideas in the passage, leaving several lines between each one
- scan the passage for important facts
- write these facts underneath the correct main idea.

Read the following passage. There are two main ideas in it. Follow the steps above and make a revision summary for the passage.

> It was 1855 in the growing industrial town of Lille, in Northern France. A young chemistry professor turned his mind to a problem that had troubled France's beer and wine industry for many years. Sometimes, no one knew why, the beer and wine would suddenly go bad as it aged. Professor Louis Pasteur began to look at beer and wine down the microscope. He took a close look at the tiny bits of yeast. Yeast is the fungus which turns the sugar in beer and wine into alcohol. The process is called fermentation. Good yeasts were round, like tiny balls. But in bad wine and beer, Pasteur found lots of stick-shaped yeasts. These made sour-tasting lactic acid instead of alcohol. "Heat your beer and wine at an early stage," Pasteur told the brewers and wine-makers, "and you will kill any trace of bad yeast before it does any harm." The wine-makers were horrified! *Heat* their precious wine? But they tried it—and it worked. This way of killing off microbes in drink and food quickly became known as "pasteurisation". We use the same method with milk today.
>
> From *Famous Names in Medicine,* G. De Stevens (Wayland 1979)

Skills sheet 33

Experimental design skills—Fair tests 3

Experiments must be **fair**. In fair experiments only one variable should be changed. All the others must be kept constant (stay the same).

To design a fair experiment:

- first decide what variables might affect the result of the experiment
- then decide which variable to **change** and which variables to **keep constant**.

Imagine you are given these problems to solve.

a Which ball will bounce highest?
Equipment: 3 balls, 1 metre rule

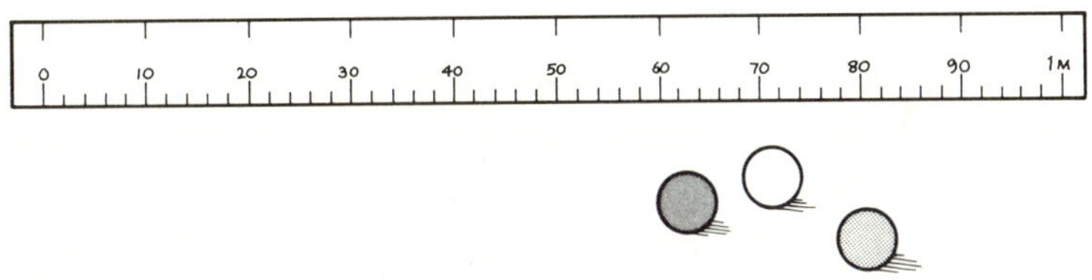

b Which pen will write the most before the ink runs out?
Equipment: 2 pens, paper, ruler

c Will a folded towel dry as quickly as a flattened out towel?
Equipment: 2 dry towels, heater, timer, water

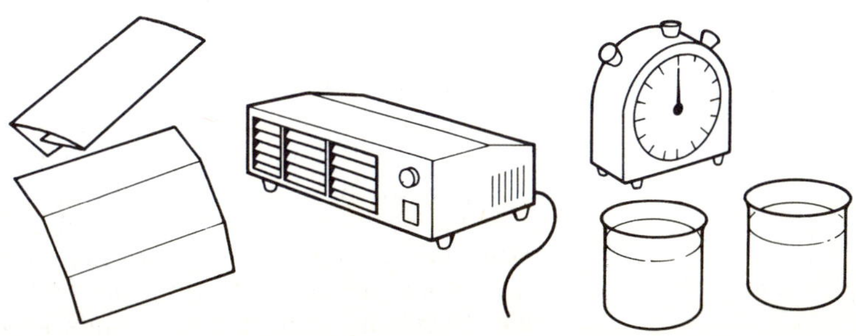

For each of the three problems write down

- what variables might affect the result of the experiment
- which one variable should be changed.

Skills sheet 34

Reading skills—Finding information 3

You often have to read a passage to find information. This might be the starting point for your notes on a topic. A good way of organising the information you find is to make a table. This makes a good summary and lets you see if any of the information you need is missing. You can then look for this information somewhere else.

Imagine you are making notes for a project on small mammals.
Read the passage below to find out

- the names of the five most common small mammals in Britain
- how these mammals can be identified
- what they eat.

1 Make up a table with three headings before you start. Complete the table after reading the passage.

2 What information would you have still to find?

The five commonest species of small mammal to be found in the hedgerow over most parts of Britain are the wood mouse, bank vole, field vole, common shrew and pygmy shrew. The characteristic external appearances are shown opposite, but the main differences between the rodents and the shrews lie in the teeth and fore-feet. Shrews have a continuous row of teeth, but in the mice and voles there is a gap between the front cutting teeth (incisors) and the chewing or cheek teeth (molars), typical of most vegetarian mammals. In addition, shrews have five toes to their fore-paws, and mice and voles have only four. Their small size—the pygmy shrew is our smallest mammal—together with the long, tapering snout and small eyes, should serve to distinguish the shrews from the mice and voles on superficial appearance.

Wood mice are at their most numerous in the early autumn. They are agile climbers and are particularly fond of rose hips, which they collect by gnawing the stalk diagonally across just below the base of the fruit. They are also fond of the kernel of the hawthorn berries, which they extract by gnawing a circular hole in the stone. Hazel-nuts are a favourite food of both wood mice and bank voles, and it is sometimes possible to tell from the empty shells which of the two it is that has been feeding on them. Both hold the nut with the base pressed to the ground with their fore-paws, but the wood mouse leaves a ring of tooth-marks around the outside rim of the hole whereas the vole tends to leave a clean outside edge to the hole. Wood mice are essentially nocturnal animals, their prominent black eyes and large ears being well adapted to such an existence. As their name implies, they are characteristically a woodland animal, but they are also common in hedgerows, fields and gardens and are happy in habitats with less ground cover than the bank vole. They vary their diet with buds, seedlings, various insects and also snails, which they extract by biting through the shell.

In southern England and parts of Wales a second mouse, the yellow-necked mouse, may occur in the same sort of habitats as the wood mouse. It is larger, with a longer tail, and it has a conspicuous yellow band stretching across its chest between its front legs. Like wood mice, they often come into buildings, such as barns and apple lofts, during the winter.

continued ▶

continued ▶

The bank vole is very much an animal of the woodland edge and hedgerow, requiring a great deal more ground cover than the wood mouse, which is hardly surprising as it is far more diurnal in its habits. The rounded muzzle, small ears and short tail at once distinguish the voles from the mice, and the bank vole has a rich chestnut-coloured coat and a tail which is about half the length of the body. It is more vegetarian than the wood mouse and prefers the flesh of the haws to the kernel.

The short-tailed vole is less often found in the hedgerow, being predominantly an animal of rough grassland, but it does resort to the hedge when the surrounding fields are disturbed by cutting or ploughing. It feeds almost wholly on grass and its numbers can fluctuate enormously from year to year. It is browner than the bank vole, has a shorter tail and the small ears are almost completely hidden in its fur.

From *Discovering Hedgerows,* D. Streeter & R. Richardson (BBC 1982)

Skills sheet 35

Writing skills—Making conclusions 2

There are several sections in most experimental reports. These are

Title: *What is the purpose of the experiment?*
Method: *What did you do?*
Results: *What happened?*
Conclusion: *What do you think the results mean?*

The conclusion is often the most difficult section to write.

Read the following report. Look at the results.

How wet can you get?

We tried to find out how much water different types of clothing would hold.
We collected four size 12 hats made of different material. We weighed each hat. We then immersed all the hats in a basin of cold water for 30 minutes. Our results are as follows:

Hat	Weight when dry	Weight when wet
Nylon	200 g	205 g
Cotton	270 g	350 g
Wool	300 g	600 g
P.V.C.	400 g	405 g

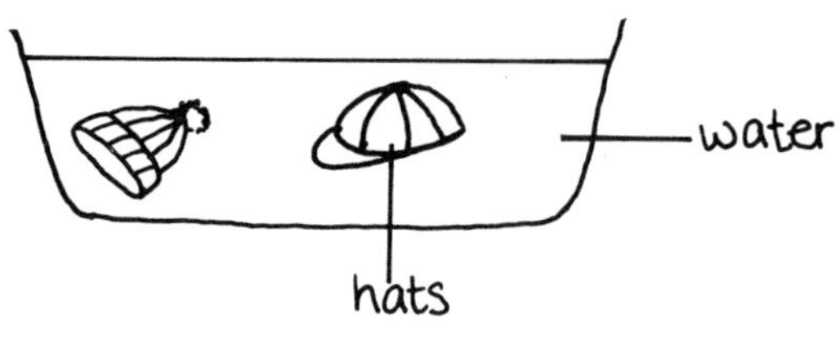

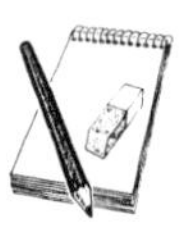

Write down two conclusions from these results.

Skills sheet 36

Number skills—Multiplying decimal numbers 2

Scientific results must be accurate. This often means that the results will include decimal numbers. You use decimal numbers every day, when you handle money. If you buy several of the same item you multiply decimal numbers to work out how much you must pay.

The only problem is remembering where to put the decimal point.

The example below shows what to do.

Multiply 6.25 × 3.61

- Count the numbers to the right of the decimal point.
  There are 4
- Find the answer to the multiplication. Do not worry about the decimal point.
  The answer is 225625
- Remember how many places there were to the right of the decimal point to begin with. There **must be** the same number in the answer. There were 4 in this multiplication.
  The answer is 22.5625

1 Find the answers to the following:
a 6.25 × 5
b 8.12 × 7
c 12.13 × 4.23

2 Part of a catalogue for science equipment is shown below.

BEAKERS, SQUAT FORM, GRADUATED, WITH SPOUT
Borosilicate glass

Capacity cm^3	Each
25	£0.68
50	£0.61
100	£0.63
250	£0.60
400	£0.77
600	£0.97
800	£1.47
1000	£1.59
2000	£2.90
3000	£5.50
5000	£9.32

BEAKERS, POLYPROPYLENE, TRI-POUR
Rigid, polypropylene, graduated. Tri-corner design provides three dripless pouring spouts. Autoclavable to 121°C. Supplied in packs of 10.

Cap. cm^3	Grad. cm^3	Pack
50	5	£1.48
100	10	£1.71
250	10	£2.55
400	20	£3.36
800	50	£3.89
1000	50	£4.29

BELL JAR
Borosilicate glass, with B29 tubule at top.

Height mm	Diam. mm	Each
250	150	£20.10
300	200	£24.50
Stopcock for above		Each £11.30

BELL JAR, STOPPERED
Borosilicate glass.

Height mm	Diam. mm	Each
250	150	£29.52
300	150	£29.94
300	200	£36.34

How much would it cost to buy each of the following?

a three stoppered bell jars (height 300 mm)
b 10 packs of polypropylene beakers (100 cm^3)
c 5 packs of polypropylene beakers (400 cm^3)
d 25 squat form glass beakers (250 cm^3)
e What would be the total cost of this order?

Reading skills—Understanding flow diagrams

Flow diagrams show several steps in a process. You can follow the steps in the correct order if you use the arrows. For example, this flow diagram explains the process of making a pot of tea.

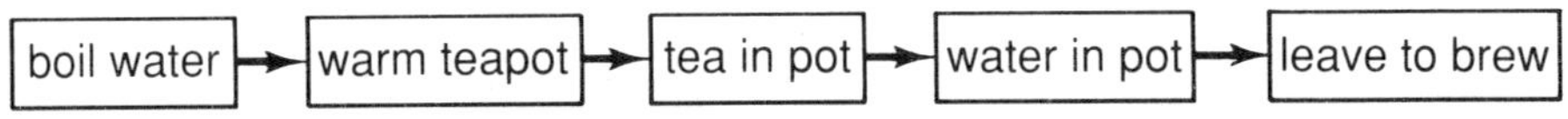

Look at the following flow diagrams and answer the questions about each one.

1 a What do you need to do to chalk to make lime? What other substance is produced?

b Describe how you would make limewater from lime.

c What must be added to limewater to make chalk?

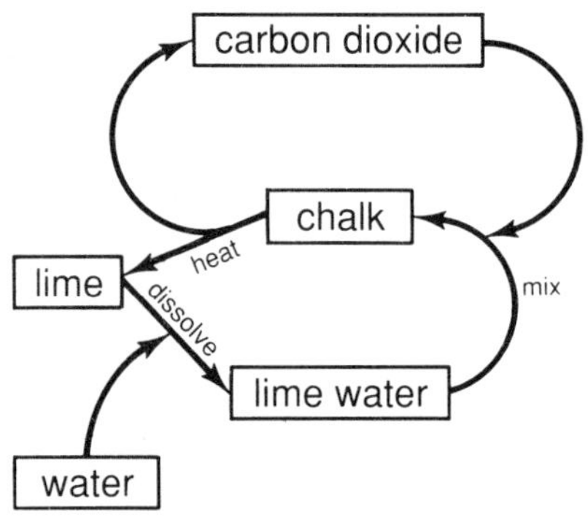

2 a What is the flow diagram describing?

b What do you do if the colour changes?

c What do you do if the colour does not change?

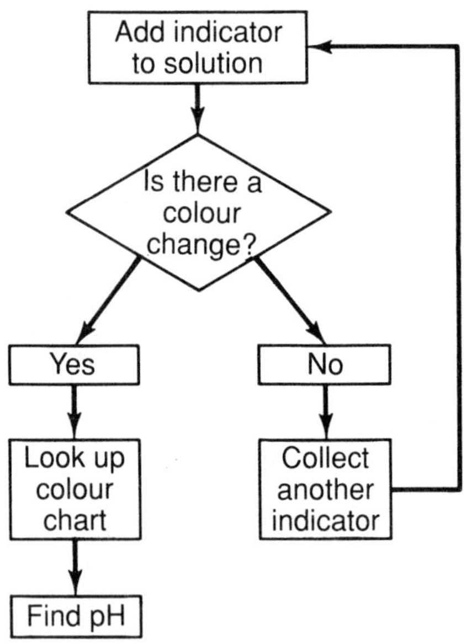

Skills sheet 38

Writing skills—Using diagrams to shorten notes 2

In a well written passage each paragraph tells you about one main idea. The paragraph may also give some

- facts about the main idea
- examples of the main idea
- opinions of the main idea
- explanations of the main idea.

A spider diagram is a good way of organising the information you read about. It makes a good starting point for making notes.

The passage below explains some of the problems of making a human-like robot called an android. Read the passage to find three major problems with designing an android.

> The idea of making a machine that behaves like a human—an android—is fascinating.
>
> A vast amount of work has been done, but at the end of it all we have to admit that compared with Mother Nature, we know very little about either computing or engineering. Let us look at the major problems one at a time.
>
> We need a machine that is capable of moving itself about over rough ground, up stairs, up trees, and even cliffs for several days before its batteries run down. It should be able to pick up the equivalent of its own weight and stagger with it. The same hands and arms must be capable of picking up and threading a needle. We have nothing remotely capable of this sort of performance. A machine using electric motors and batteries would go on the flat, for less than an hour before running down—one flight of stairs would exhaust it. A mechanical arm strong enough to use for a tug-of-war would weigh nearly 100 pounds. Even if we knew how to build walking legs (which we do not yet), they would come out weighing more in the region of tons than tens of pounds.
>
> The human eye has the equivalent of some three million pixels, the best available televisions have 1 million. But even if we had a suitably sensitive mechanical eye, we could not process its information in less than hours—as against the eye and brain's $\frac{1}{25}$ second - and we still do not know how to do more than 1 per cent of the necessary processing.
>
> The human brain contains 10,000 million neurons. Each neuron is attached to many others and has an unknown value in terms of byte storage, but we might assume that it can store 100 bytes. The brain is then equivalent to a million million bytes or the contents of a 100-foot cube full of today's memory chips. And that again assumes that we would know how to organize the memory if we had it. One of today's 16-bit micros would take more than three weeks to search that much memory for one four-letter word.
>
> From *The Joy of Computers*, P. Laurie (Hutchinson 1983)

1 Copy and complete the spider diagram below.

2 Read each paragraph again. Add two explanations for each of the problems to your diagram.

Skills sheet 39

Reading skills—Finding information 4

When you have found a passage that seems to contain the information you want, you can **scan** it to select this information.

The passage below is about materials that are made by combining one or more substances.

Scan the passage to find out what each of the following are made from:

- steel
- concrete
- coins
- glass
- polycotton

Write your answers in your notebook.

In the building trade most materials are made by combining two or more substances. For example, glass is made from sand, soda and chalk. Bricks are held together by mortar, a mixture of cement, sand and water. Concrete, made by mixing sand, cement water and gravel, is used in large building work. It can be reinforced with steel. Steel is not a pure substance. It is made from iron with a little carbon added along with tiny amounts of certain other metals like cobalt. There are lots of types of screws. Some are made from brass, which is a combination of copper and zinc. When several different metals are mixed together the product is called an alloy.

The clothes worn on a building site have to be hard wearing. Some fabrics are entirely man-made. For example, waterproof coats might be made of PVC, a type of plastic made from carbon, hydrogen and chlorine. More often the clothes will be made from a combination of natural and man-made fibres. Polycotton is a good example. It is made from cotton and polyester. The coins needed to buy these clothes are made from alloys of copper and nickel.

Skills sheet 40

Revision skills—Making a revision summary 2

One helpful way of learning is to be an active learner. For example, when you revise you could make notes. As you read your work, try to write down the main ideas on paper. Make sure that you understand these ideas. This will make it easier to remember them.

Imagine that you are revising the passage below.

- Skim the passage to find the main ideas.
- Now read the passage more carefully. Revise by making notes as you read.
- Cover up the passage and your own notes. Check how much you remember by writing about Isaac Newton.

> Isaac Newton was one of the greatest geniuses who has ever lived. His great mind tackled many problems. On his mother's farm in Lincolnshire, in 1666, he started his work studying light and colour. He split sunlight into its coloured parts with a prism. These colours, the spectrum, make up the rainbow. He designed a much better sort of telescope that used a mirror instead of lenses, called a reflecting telescope. He did all this before he was twenty-five.
>
> One day, while in the garden, he saw an apple fall. He thought it strange that the apple fell but the Moon did not. He thought that perhaps the rules that govern the Earth also govern the universe. People had thought that the heavens were powered by secret or supernatural forces. Newton explained for the first time how all things are attracted to each other by a force known as gravity. The strength of the force depends on the size of the objects and the distances between them. When we say that something "falls down", we really mean "falls towards the Earth". He realized that it was gravity which held the Moon spinning round the Earth as if on an invisible thread. But for gravity, the Moon would shoot off into space.
>
> From *Famous Names in Science*,
> P. Clark (Wayland 1979)

Skills sheet 41

Writing skills—Using a flow diagram in notes

Some written passages describe the steps in a process or a sequence of events. Making a flow diagram is a good way of organising this information. It makes a good summary and can be easier to remember and learn from than a written passage.

Read the passage below.
Make a flow diagram to show how firm non-tidal land forms from mudflats in **four** stages.

1 → 2 → 3 → 4

So often thought of as bleak, desolate places, estuaries have a magic of their own, from the small rias of southern Devon to the huge intertidal mudflats of Morecambe Bay. Visiting Morcambe Bay in the winter is a birdwatcher's dream, because more than 250,000 birds can be seen, most of them waders, including knot, dunlin, sanderling and oystercatcher.

Estuaries are affected by two daily tides, so there is constant water movement over the intertidal zone. This area is ever changing as suspended silt and debris carried down by the river and by the incoming tide are deposited. Although the erosion and deposition of stones, sand and mud is constant, salt tolerant animals survive, providing a rich source of food for the birds.

Estuaries also offer a region of sheltered water which is why many of Britain's larger estuaries are being considered for harbour and marina developments. Unless these developments are pursued in sympathy with existing wildlife and natural formation of saltmarshes, then those estuaries are doomed.

As the silt builds up, the mudflats are colonised by saltmarsh plants, such as cord grass, which helps to stabilise the habitat. Cord grass has become established in Britain during the last century, and is the most successful pioneer coloniser of mudflats.

Once cord grass is established, further daily deposits of silt build up around the stems and leaves, so that eventually the plants are exposed to air for an increasing amount of time between each tide. Natural reclamation begins, and the mudflat eventually forms a saltmarsh habitat.

With each tidal flooding the saltmarsh is covered with further silt deposits, until it rises to a level which can no longer be reached by the sea. Even though the soil remains heavily impregnated with salt, as the marsh becomes higher it dries out and grasses such as Puccinellia and creeping fescue colonise, providing nest sites for skylarks and meadow pipit. The upper marsh eventually gives way to firm, non-tidal land, which is colonised by rushes, reeds and other plants such as sea wormwood. Here, birds like the moorhen, reed warbler and sedgewarbler can commonly be seen or heard.

From *The Guardian*, 18th August 1989

Skills sheet 42

Reading skills—Reading line graphs 4

A line graph shows the relationship between two variables. There is usually a number scale on each axis of a line graph. The numbers are spaced out at equal intervals. This can be very useful.

The graph below shows the relationship between temperature measured in degrees celsius and in degrees fahrenheit.

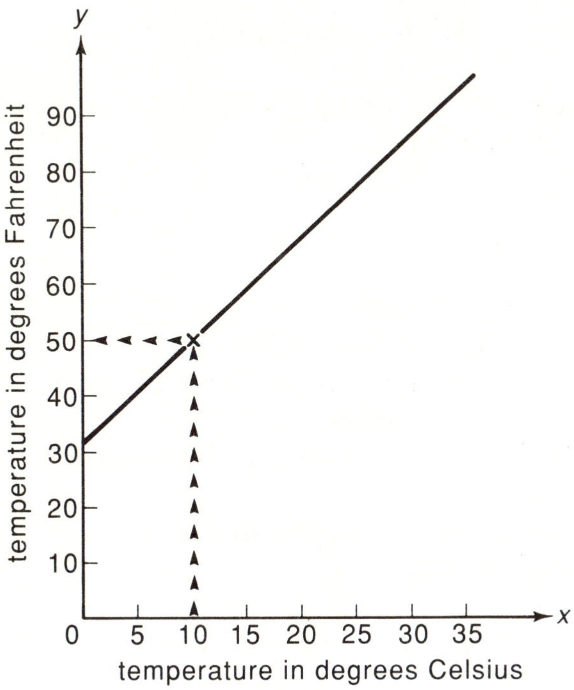

How to find what 10°C is in degrees Fahrenheit

1 Find the number 10 on the X-axis.

2 Run your finger up from this number.

3 Stop when your finger crosses the line on the graph paper.

4 Run your finger from this point across the graph paper. Stop when it crosses the Y-axis.

5 Read the number. It is 50°F.

You can change from degrees fahrenheit to degrees celsius by starting on the y-axis and running your finger across.

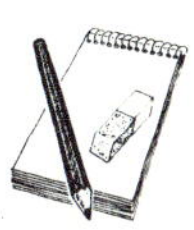

1 Use the graph to change the following Celsius temperatures into Fahrenheit temperatures:

a 20°C

b 30°C

c 35°C

2 Use the graph to change the following Fahrenheit temperatures into Celsius temperatures:

a 77°F

b 59°F

Skills sheet 43

Reading skills—Recognising fact and opinion

A fact is something which another person can check. The other person will agree that the fact is true once he/she has checked it. A fact is true for everybody.

An example of a fact is *Dolphins are mammals.*

An opinion is something which another person might agree or disagree with. It cannot be checked.
An example of an opinion is *Dolphins are cuddly.*

Read the sentences below. Decide whether the writer in each case is giving a fact or an opinion.

a Science is fun.
b Scientists are good looking.
c Chemistry is a science.
d There are moons orbiting the planet Mars.
e The rose is a flower that means love.
f Science fiction is more interesting than historical novels.
g A rugby player with a limp is suffering.
h A tooth is painful when the nerve is affected by tooth decay.
i Bad teeth are horrible.
j Smoking can cause heart disease and stomach ulcers.
k Smoking gives you bad breath.
l Dolphins are not cuddly.
m Water is made from two elements called oxygen and hydrogen.
n A crocodile can grow to 17 metres.
o My watch is fast.
p Your watch looks as if it was made by Donald Duck.

Skills sheet 44

Reading skills—Collating information

You are often asked to use information from several sources to solve a problem, answer a question or complete a project. When you **collate** information you bring it together in an organised way. Then you can use it.

To solve the following problems you will have to collate information from the two tables below. Copy and complete the information boxes for each item.

Problem 1: Which material could each of the following items of clothing be made from?
You are given the washing symbol and ironing symbol.

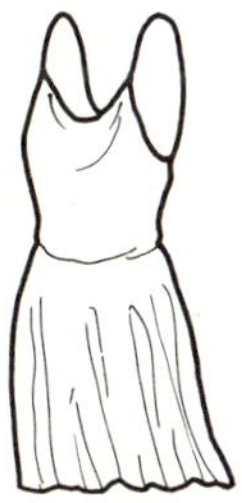

a Information box

Evening dress
Material:

b Information box

Rugby shirt (white)
Material:

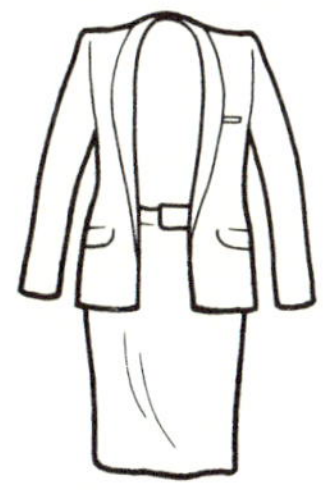

c Information box

Two-piece suit
Material:

Problem 2: What would the washing and ironing symbols be for each of these items of clothing?

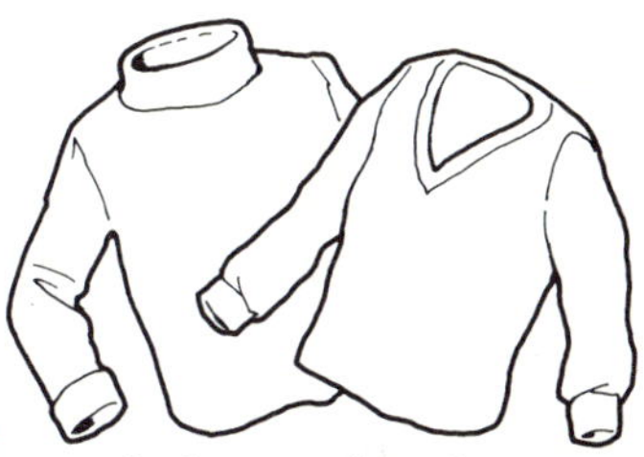

d Information box

Jumpers (not colour fast at 40°C)
Material: 100% acrylic

e Information box

Boiler suit
Material: 100% nylon

f Information box

Shirt (white)
Material: 65% polyester
35% cotton

continued ▶

continued ▶

Washing Symbols

Symbol	Maximum temperatures (machine wash)	Suitable Materials
	very hot (95°C)	**white** cotton and linen
	hot (60°C)	cotton, linen, viscose, colour-fast at 60°C
	hot (60°C)	**white** nylon and polyester/cotton mixtures
	hand hot (50°C)	**coloured** nylon, polyester/cotton, acrylic/cotton
	warm (40°C)	cotton, linen, viscose colour fast at 40°C
	warm (40°C)	acrylics, acrylic/wool, polyester/ wool
	warm (40°C)	wool, wool/cotton, wool/viscose, silk
	cool (30°C)	silk, printed acetate not colour fast at 40°C
	very hot (95°C)	cotton able to be boiled but requiring Drip-Dry
	do not machine wash	materials vary depending on manufacturer

Ironing Symbols

Symbol	Maximum temperatures	Suitable materials
	hot (210°C)	cotton, linen, viscose
	warm (160°C)	polyester mixtures, wool
	cool (120°C)	acrylic, nylon, acetate, triacetate, polyester
	do not iron	only used in cases where ironing might damage the fabric

Skills sheet 45

Revision skills—Making a revision summary 3

One helpful way of learning is to be an active learner. For example, when you revise you could make notes. As you read your work, try to write down the main ideas on paper. Make sure that you understand these ideas. This will make it easier to remember them.

Imagine that you are revising the passage below.

- Skim the passage to find the main ideas.
- Now read the passage more carefully. Revise by making notes as you read.
- Cover up the passage and your own notes.
- Check and see how much you remember by writing about film.

A photographer's choice of film is not only one of size or camera loading. There are also different kinds of emulsion which affect a film's speed and its colour-sensitivity, i.e. its ability to reproduce the natural colours of a scene in black, white and varying tones of grey.

All the popular black and white films are *panchromatic* (pan). This means that the emulsion is more or less equally sensitive to all the component colours of white light and, therefore, records the brightness of different colours fairly accurately in tones of black and white.

Films react to light at different speeds. *Fast* films react quickly and are useful for the low light values of winter, dull days and indoor photography. *Medium fast* films give excellent results for all normal purposes, and *slow* films give extra high quality pictures.

Film speeds are indicated by their ASA numbers, marked on the carton. The greater the ASA number, the faster the film. Of course, film speed must always be taken into account when adjusting the camera's aperture and exposure settings.

Finally we come to the *grain*. This is not very obvious on small prints, but becomes apparent in enlargements as a speckled effect on the print. Generally speaking, fast films have a coarse grain; slow films have a fine, less noticeable grain.

From *How it Works – The Camera*
D. Carey (Ladybird Books 1970)

Resource 2.5

Rusting Picture Quiz

Metal can be protected by

Metal can be protected by

Metal can be protected by

Metal can be protected by

Metal can be protected by

Metal can be protected by